NORTH AMERICAN TRAINS

Steam, Diesel, and Electric Locomotives from Pioneer Days to Modern Times

DAVID ROSS &
BRIAN SOLOMON

BARNES
& NOBLE
BOOKS

NEW YORK

Editorial and design by:
Amber Books Ltd
Bradley's Close
74-77 White Lion Street
London N1 9PF
www.amberbooks.co.uk

Project Editor: Michael Spilling
Design: Jerry Williams

Printed in Dubai

PICTURE CREDITS
Courtesy of David Ross: (Bob Turner) 7b, 9, 14, (A.S. Scott) 17, 21, 27, (Toytrains1)
33, 37, (Campbell McCutcheon) 38, 43, 44, 47, 51, 53, 58, 59, 61, 63, 73, 75 (both),
(Alberta Museum) 79, 85, 99, 107, (Joseph Testagrose Collection) 108 (t), 117, (Timken)
120, (Toytrains1) 121, (Bill Volkmer) 122, (Wickham Leonard) 124, 126, 129, 131,
(P. Haviland) 132, 133, (Toytrains1) 153, (Toytrains1) 154, (General Electric) 175,
(Electromotive) 180, (General Electric) 184, (Electromotive) 194, 221;
Heimburger House: 103 (t);
Joel Jensen: 8, 20, 42, 52, 62, 72, 106, 148, 162;
Millbrook House: 10 (b), 18 (t), 28, 40 (b), 48, 50, 64, 77, 82 (t), 86 (both), 89, 90 (t), 91,
96, 97, 110, 113, 123t, 127, 134 (bl), 138, 139, 140, 143, 144, 145, 152 (b), 155 (t), 157,
159, 161, 167, 169 (b), 171, 173 (b), 176, 182, 183, 187, 190 (both), 195, 197, 202;
Milepost 92½/Cassell:10 (r), 12 (b), 13, 18 (b), 22, 24, 29, 34, 40 (t), 45 (t), 55, 56, 60, 66,
82 (b), 105, 119, 130 (t);
Milepost 92½: 11, 12 (r), 45 (b), 74, 78 (both), 90 (b), 95, 96 (t), 102, 111, 112, 114, 118,
130 (b), 134 (t), 134 (br), 137, 142, 146, 147, 150, 152 (t), 155 (b), 156, 160, 166 (b), 169
(t), 172, 174 (t), 178, 181, 191, 192 (t), 200, 201 (both), 203, 205, 210, 212 (t), 214, 215,
216, 219;
Stephenson Locomotive Society Library: 6, 7 (t), 16, 26, 30, 57, 69, 83, 87, 88, 92, 101,
103b, 108b, 125 (both), 141, 149, 170,
Brian Solomon: 67, 70, 81, 93, 98, 109, 116, 123b, 136, 151 (both), 165, 166t, 173 (t),
174 (b), 177, 179, 185, 186, 188 (both), 189, 192b, 193, 196, 198, 199, 204, 207, 208,
209, 211 (both), 212b, 213, 217, 218, 220 (both);
TRH Pictures: 15, 23, 32, 36, 41, 68, 84, 94, 100, 128, 158, 163, 164.

All maps courtesy of Amber Books Ltd.

ACKNOWLEDGEMENTS
The publishers and author would like to express their gratitude to the following individuals
for help in the location and supply of illustrations for this book: Larry Bohn, A. Pierce
Haviland Jr, Dr S. David Klein, Dr Richard Leonard, Claude Prutton, L. Ruback, Joseph
Testagrose, Robert D. Turner, and Bill Volkmer.
The author would also like to thank: Cynthia Baker of EMD, Bob Bourquin of Timken,
Charles T. Deemer of General Electric, Stephen Jackson of the Musum of the Rockies and
Steven Yakimets of Alberta Railway Museum.

Contents

INTRODUCTION

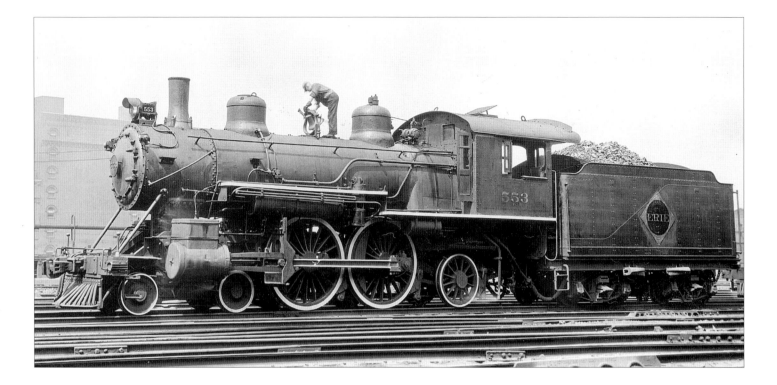

It is a tumultuous history, rich in great events, grandiose gestures, larger-than-life characters, and machines which not only came to give unrivaled performance, but also exerted a powerful hold on the imagination. The coming of the railroads forced the United States and Canada to measure and assess their continental scale, and the railroads then proceeded to conquer that vastness and reduce it to humanly comprehensible terms. The journeys of uncertain months and weeks were transformed into those of timetabled days and hours. Neither mighty river, nor mountain range, nor arid desert could withstand the inexorable advance of the iron road. In the course of eighty years, more than twenty million tons of iron and steel rail were laid over the soil of the United States—230,000 miles (370,000km) of track. The tonnage is greatly understated, as much of the track was double-line, and rails had to be renewed from time to time. The demands of the growing railroad network pushed industrial development forward, while the railroads themselves made it possible for industry and agriculture to spread and grow in scope, output, and wealth.

In their rise from local enterprises to enormous corporations, the railroads exerted profound influence on

The figure of the workman fixing the bell hinge gives scale to the Erie 4-4-2, No. 553. Built in 1903, it was considered a small locomotive for its time. This photograph was taken at Jersey City, in August 1931.

the national economic and political systems, and on national self-perception. Huge fortunes were made by those who seized the moment and had the necessary drive and audacity to keep going. Were they builders or exploiters— or, in some cases, both? Argument still goes on about the contribution of men like Vanderbilt, Gould, Morgan, and Harriman to the American commercial ethos. While the magnates became immensely rich, hundreds of thousands of men and women learned what it was like to be a wage-earning employee of a vast business whose owners and controllers were remote and inaccessible, and whose decisions brooked no question or protest.

Born out of technological inventiveness, and sustained literally and figuratively by the expansiveness of steam power, the dominance of the railroads seemed secure. But even before they knew it was happening, they were wounded giants. They had opened up the frontier of

Train out at sea—a Florida East Coast "Pacific" locomotive runs with a night train on the long chain of viaducts and keys between Key Largo and Key West. For many decades this route has been converted to a motor road.

industrial technology, but it sped away past them, to produce the automobile and the airplane. The car held out individual freedom and choice, and air travel offered convenient speed and took on the glamour of being the fastest. Railroads were left behind, mired in what was suddenly old technology and hindered by the laws and regulations that their own greedy growth had prompted.

A work-stained Canadian Pacific C-liner, No. 4104, stands at the motive power depot in Nelson, British Columbia. Its use here would be as a helper or relief engine on the mountain grades.

Perhaps they had to be humbled, almost broken, before their virtues became apparent. As environmental concerns grew among the general public, the perception of railroads changed. They were seen as energy-efficient and economical of resources. In an age of blocked freeways and crowded airline terminals, their capacity for speed again became an asset. And in great urban regions, their role in providing mass rapid transit was indispensable.

So the railroads survive and continue to serve, at two extremes. Ultra-modern Acela electric expresses routinely reach 150mph (241km/h), and microprocessor-controlled AC diesel-electrics like the Electro-Motive Division's SD70ACe haul multi-thousand ton freights at up to 80mph (128km/h). And the steam locomotive—of all machines ever constructed the one that seems most to speak to us— still exercises its spell on many tourist and heritage lines. Even if the still unproven technology of magnetic levitation turns out to be practically and commercially viable, wheel-on-rail is unlikely to come to an early end.

CHAPTER 1

BEGINNINGS OF THE RAILROAD

A combination of inventors, enthused by the new steam technology, and coal-owners, wanting to move their product in bulk, introduced America's first locomotives. Merchants soon joined, keen to develop trade, and so, at first on isolated lines, a new industry developed that was to help open up North America.

The story of the powered American railroad begins in a garden. The setting is the Hoboken, New Jersey waterfront, and the date is 1825. Owner of the garden is John Cox Stevens, a man of 76 but very far from being elderly in

Above: Vertical-boilered "Grasshopper" locomotives survived far into the nineteenth century on the Baltimore & Ohio Railroad. Left: During the nineteenth century, more than a thousand patents were taken out for the design of smokestacks and their interior spark arrestors. Almost as many lantern designs appeared.

spirit. Once a colonel in the Revolutionary Army, he has long been interested in modern inventions. His belief in the potential of the steam engine goes a long way back and links him to such pioneer inventors as Robert Fulton and Oliver Edwards. In 1803 he had built a screw-driven steamboat, but his enthusiasm has moved from marine power to the locomotive, which he sees, presciently for his time, as something that will make canals redundant and revolutionize transportation on land. Such machines have been running in England since around 1812, at first in very

9

Best Friend of Charleston 0-4-0T

Charleston & Hamburg Railroad: 1830

This working replica of Best Friend of Charleston was built in 1928 and incorporates certain twentieth-century refinements, like a padded seat for the driver.

Vertical boilers were used on the earliest American locomotives, and frame construction was normal as a consequence. The horizontal boiler was adopted on the model of British imports.

The first home-produced steam locomotive in the United States, *Best Friend* was designed by E.L. Miller and built at New York's West Point Foundry. It was the predecessor of all tank locos, with a well tank fitted inside the frame. The boiler was vertical, providing steam for two front-set cylinders driving the coupled wheels. Best Friend was recorded as hauling a five-car passenger train at 20mph (32km/h). Public service on the line began in January 1831, the first American railroad to work a regular steam-powered schedule. On June 17, the boiler exploded and it was rebuilt as *Phoenix*.

Boiler pressure: 50psi (3.5kg/cm²)	**Cylinders:** 6x16in (152x406mm)
Driving wheels: 54in (1371mm)	**Heating surface:** not known
Grate area: 2.2sq ft (0.2m²)	**Tractive effort:** 452lb (206kg)
Total weight: 8820lb (4t)	

small numbers and with many operating problems, but engineers there are tackling the problems and bringing out exciting new designs. Stevens wants to see the same energy applied in the United States, and to show what is possible, he has built his own locomotive, albeit a small-scale one. It runs round his garden, on the guide-rail principle, not on flanged wheels, and as its builder delightedly shows every visitor, it works.

British Inspiration

Stevens's little engine was the first steam locomotive to run in the United States, but it was intended to be a spur to others, not a commercial machine. Other engineers were also interested in what was going on across the Atlantic, and in 1825 the Pennsylvania Society for Internal Improvement sent William Strickland to Britain. He visited several rail sites, including the world's first locomotive factory, Robert Stephenson & Company of Newcastle, and wrote a book, *Report on Canals and Rail Roads*. Another proponent of the new traction was the chief engineer of the Delaware & Hudson Canal Company, John B. Jervis. Despite his canal background, he shared Stevens's view on the future of the steam railroad. The same view was held by one of his associates, Horatio Allen, a confident young man with a gift for self-expression. In 1827 Allen made the Atlantic crossing to England; by his own account, he was doing it for himself, to "go to the only place where a locomotive was in daily operation and could be studied in all its practical details." In fact, he was sent as Jervis's representative, and was authorized to place orders for locomotives on behalf of the Delaware & Hudson company. He ordered four, three of them from the ironfounders Foster Rastrick, of Stourbridge in the English Midlands, and a fourth from Robert Stephenson in Newcastle.

The idea was that the locomotives should be used on feeder lines bringing coal from the pit-heads to the canal wharves, and the first of these lines was laid out to a 4ft 3in (129.5cm) gauge between Carbondale and Honesdale in Pennsylvania. The Stephenson engine, *Pride of Newcastle*, was the first to be delivered, arriving at New York Harbor on January 15, 1829. Amid great public interest, it was exhibited in steaming order, mounted on blocks so that its motion could be seen, as there were no tracks laid. For some reason, possibly excessive weight, it never seems to have been shipped on to Honesdale, and it is assumed it was used as a stationary engine. A cylinder from it is preserved at the Smithsonian Institution. The first of the Stourbridge locomotives was also displayed at New York, and was then transferred by barge to Honesdale. Named the *Stourbridge Lion*, it was the first full-size locomotive to run in the United States. Its operational career was extremely brief, consisting of one demonstration run with Allen at the

John Bull 0-4-0
Camden & Amboy RailRoad
1831

Boiler pressure: 50psi (3.5kg/cm²)	Cylinders: 9x20in (228x508mm)
Driving wheels: 54in (1294mm)	Grate area: 10.07sq ft (0.93cm²)
Heating surface: 296.5sq ft (27.5cm²)	Tractive effort: 1270lb (575kg)
Total weight: 22,045lb (10t)	

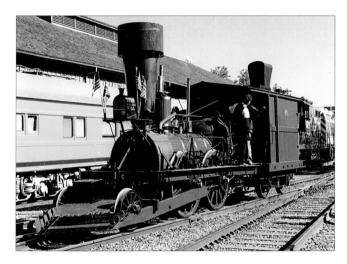

This photograph of a replica *John Bull*, with the added pilot in place, shows how American engineers thought of the front bogie as "rolling out the road," and guiding the locomotive into a curve.

The first locomotives to run in North America, imported from England by the Delaware & Hudson Canal Company in 1829, were relatively primitive colliery types similar to Locomotion No. 1. From 1831 the new railroad companies were able to benefit from the many improvements brought about in Britain. Nevertheless, the British models were often found unsatisfactory for American conditions. The consequent adaptations, and the rapid rise in demand, generated a home-grown locomotive-building industry which by the end of the 1840s was producing around 400 units a year, to distinctively American designs. *John Bull* was shipped in parts from Robert Stephenson & Company to the Camden & Amboy, and assembled at Bordentown, New Jersey. Its cost was almost $4000. On November 12, 1831, it pulled a demonstration train for members of the New Jersey legislature, and went into regular service on partial completion of the line in September 1833, along with three other Stephenson types which had been built at Hoboken. *John Bull* was a four-wheel, inside-cylinder engine, of the "Planet" goods class, built to the 4ft 10in (1472mm) gauge. It had not been running long before modifications were made. By 1832 a leading truck and pilot had been fitted, and later it was equipped with headlight, cab, bell and whistle. By the late 1840s it was being used only on lightweight passenger trains, and in 1849 it was jacked up for use as a boiler-testing plant for new engines. By the 1850s it was already regarded as an antique, and though most old engines went for scrap or drastic rebuild, *John Bull* survived, and in 1876 was shown as "America's first locomotive" at the Centennial Exhibition in Philadelphia. It was partially restored at this time. In 1885 the Pennsylvania Railroad, which had absorbed the Camden & Amboy in 1871, presented the engine to the Smithsonian Museum. It made a run from New York to Chicago in April 1893. Since 1940, it has been a static exhibit. The tender is not the original, which was a four-wheeler adapted from a Camden & Amboy car, but dates from the mid-nineteenth century. Built as an eight-wheeler, it was changed to its present four-wheel form in order to better represent the original. But there is little left that is truly original about *John Bull*, except the boiler.

De Witt Clinton 0-4-0
Mohawk & Hudson Railroad: 1831

Boiler pressure: 50psi (3.5kg/cm2)	**Cylinders:** 5.5x16in (139x406mm)
Driving wheels: not known	**Grate area:** not known
Heating surface: not known	**Tractive effort:** not known
Total weight: 8,818lbs (4t)	

The *De Witt Clinton* was said to be capable of hauling five passenger carriages at a speed of 30mph (48km/h) on level track. It weighed four tons in working order, and had a boiler pressure of 50psi (3.5kg/cm2).

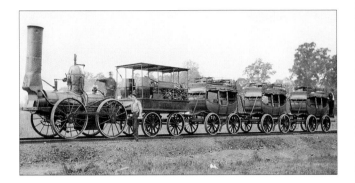

One of the first American-built locomotives with a horizontally set boiler, this was the shape of things to come, though it had inside cylinders on the British model driving the crank axles.

The demands of American operation soon left the 0-4-0 type behind. This loco, designed by John B. Jervis, was not a great success, but incorporated three features unseen before. One was a protective roof for the crew, an early form of the cab; another was an integral tank built into the tender; the third was all-iron wheels—previous locos had had wooden wheel-centers. An early image of *De Witt Clinton* shows it hauling a set of cars closely modeled on the stage-coaches of the time. The dimensions are not known.

controls, on August 8, 1829. Too heavy for the tracks, it was stored away for some years and its boiler was eventually used as a stationary engine. Contrary to what is still sometimes asserted, this engine was not designed by Jervis, but by its English builder, John Urpeth Rastrick.

A false start like this could not halt the development of railroads. Other companies were already being planned or started up. The country's first public railroad, the Baltimore & Ohio, had been incorporated on February 28, 1827. Its tracks were being laid in 1829, though they did not reach the Ohio River for another 24 years. At this time many people seriously doubted the ability of locomotives to haul trains on an uphill grade, and the Baltimore & Ohio proposed to use horse traction. Anxious for their own businesses, the proprietors of stage-coach companies poured scorn on the noisy, clanking, unreliable iron horse. In 1829 the engineer Ross Winans and Scranton iron-works owner Peter Cooper, built a small locomotive, *Tom Thumb*, purely

for demonstration purposes: the prime aim was to show that, contrary to George Stephenson's expressed view, a steam locomotive could pull a train round a curve of less than 900 feet (274.3 meters) radius (150 feet—45.7 meters—to be precise). On August 22, 1830 it pulled a carriage containing 24 influential merchants and businessmen, and a few wagons, on the Baltimore & Ohio line. On its return trip, the stagecoach operators Stockton & Stokes put on their fastest coach and team on the parallel roadway. In the ensuing race, *Tom Thumb* unluckily lost steam, and the horses won.

But the point about curves was proved; and it was a hollow triumph for the horse. The power of steam had been clearly shown at the famous Rainhill test in England, in October 1829, when speeds and load-hauling capacities far beyond what was possible with horses had been demonstrated by the winning locomotive *Rocket*, built by George and Robert Stephenson. Several Americans attended this event, including Winans, and E.L. Miller, who was promoting a railroad to link Charleston and Hamburg in South Carolina, and had recruited Horatio Allen as his engineer. John Stevens and his two sons were the prime backers of another line, the Camden & Amboy in 1830, which linked—at first with a river ferry at each end—Philadelphia and New York.

Competition

Very soon, a number of differences between North American railroads and their British models began to appear. In Britain, a small country, trunk routes linking the major cities and forming the basis of a national network were envisaged from an early stage. In the much vaster United States and Canada, the railroads were seen as a means of opening up the hinterland of individual eastern cities, and also of protecting their trade from encroachment by others. Canada's first railroad, the Champlain and St Lawrence, opened on July 21, 1836, was typical of this approach. In the 1830s and 1840s, the vision of transcontinental linkage by rail had scarcely arisen. Instead of seeking union and ease of long-distance conveyance, the American railroads began in an atmosphere of mutual competition and exclusion. A prime weapon was gauge

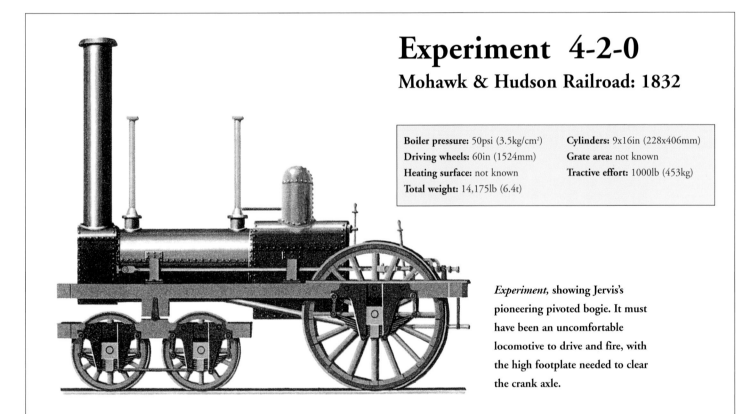

Experiment 4-2-0
Mohawk & Hudson Railroad: 1832

Boiler pressure: 50psi (3.5kg/cm²)	**Cylinders:** 9x16in (228x406mm)
Driving wheels: 60in (1524mm)	**Grate area:** not known
Heating surface: not known	**Tractive effort:** 1000lb (453kg)
Total weight: 14,175lb (6.4t)	

Experiment, **showing Jervis's pioneering pivoted bogie. It must have been an uncomfortable locomotive to drive and fire, with the high footplate needed to clear the crank axle.**

Another John B. Jervis design, built by the West Point Foundry, this engine was the first to incorporate a leading truck, or bogie. The truck had an outside frame and bearings, with suspended springs. The 4-2-0 wheel arrangement was the first distinctively American type, and flourished between 1835 and 1842. In the United States tracks were often lightly laid and twisting, and the swiveling truck kept engines on the road where a rigid wheel arrangement might have derailed. Nobly, Jervis did not patent this contribution to locomotive design. Experiment had other unusual features, including driving wheels in rear of the firebox. Among the fittings was "a good and convenient hand force pump, with copper pipes to connect with the water tank on the tender waggon"—effective injection of feed water into the boiler was an as-yet unsolved problem of locomotive design. The engine had two inside cylinders and link motion modeled on a Stephenson 0-4-0.

The outside frame was of seasoned white oak, strengthened with iron braces and supporting outside bearings for the driving wheels. It was originally built as an anthracite burner, but poor steaming led to the rebuilding of the firebox for wood-burning in 1833. Despite this, it was claimed that *Experiment* ran at 62mph (100km/h) in 1832. Later renamed *Brother Jonathan,* the locomotive was rebuilt in 1846 as a 4-4-0.

width, and a classic example was the Atlantic & St Lawrence line from Portland, Maine, to Montreal, which was laid to a gauge of 5ft 6in specifically to prevent traffic from flowing on to the lines west of Portland. These, linking it to Boston and New York, were laid to the "standard" gauge of 4ft 8.5in (143cm).

The Canadian Grand Trunk and the associated Great Western systems were also built to the 5ft 6in (167cm) gauge. From the 1830s, three systems, each with a different gauge, converged upon New York. Those which would eventually form the New York Central in 1853 were of standard gauge; the New York and Erie was of six foot gauge, as was the Delaware, Lackawanna & Hudson line. Apart from the standard gauge New Jersey Central, most New Jersey lines, like the Camden and Amboy, were built to a gauge of 4ft 10in (147cm), just too wide to give a fit to standard gauge axles. In the words of the railroad historian George Rogers Taylor, such uncoordinated building showed "the limitations of merchant capitalism." State legislatures, also dominated by the merchants, played an important part in both protecting and attempting to control the activities

of railroads within their jurisdictions. It was typical that the Erie Railroad should have its original terminals at Piermont and Dunkirk, within the confines—and the legal protection—of New York State. Though on some lines, a third rail was added to accommodate trains of different gauge, a great deal of expensive alteration work had to be undertaken throughout the entire eastern United States and Canada, between the 1860s and 1890, before 4ft 8.5in (143cm) really did become standard gauge.

Commercial Interest

The early American railroads were largely financed by city merchants, who saw them as a method of developing and concentrating their own commercial interests. From the beginning, there was a demand for speed and cheapness of construction, to get the line operative as quickly as possible. Improvements could follow on, once the railroad was paying its way. Consequently, American gradients were steeper, curves were tighter, and rails usually lighter, than in Britain or Europe. The first lines were laid using the strap-rail—a thin strip of iron nailed down to provide a running

---

Lancaster 4-2-0
Philadelphia & Columbia Railroad: 1834

Boiler pressure: 120psi (8.4kg/cm²)		**Cylinders:** 9x16in (228x406mm)	
Driving wheels: 54in (1370mm)		**Grate area:** not known	
Heating surface: not known		**Tractive effort:** 2448lb (1110kg)	
Total weight: 16,975lb (7.7t)			

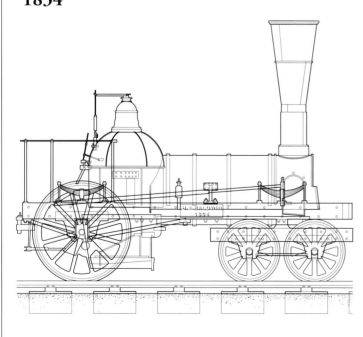

Diagrammatic drawing of a Baldwin 4-2-0 locomotive of the Lancaster type, built for the Philadelphia & Columbia Railroad in 1834.

Matthias W. Baldwin (1795–1866), the son of a carriage builder, was a mechanic who turned locomotive builder in 1832. This was his third engine, one of five built that year in his Philadelphia works, based on Jervis's *Experiment* and sold to the Commonwealth of Pennsylvania for $5500, including the tender. It was a successful design and until 1842 Baldwin built only 4-2-0s, establishing a reputation for sticking to tried-and-true design. A notable feature was the half-crank axle, with the rods driving the wheels directly; but Baldwin dropped this from around 1840.

Lancaster did not have a cab, and was wooden-framed without iron cladding. It did heavy duty until 1850, and was scrapped in 1851.

Traveling on Whistler's Western

In the late 1830s, Englishman George Combe made a detailed diary of his experiences on several railroad journeys in the United States. He had the privilege to ride George Washington Whistler's Western Railroad of Massachusetts shortly after a portion of that line opened for traffic, and his account of this journey was published in *Notes on the United States of North America during a Phrenological Visit in 1838–40.* Combe's writings were reprinted in August Mencken's railroad treatise *The Railroad Passenger Car*: "On October 29 [1839] we left Springfield and started for Worcester by the railroad, which has been opened since we traveled to Springfield a month ago. Yesterday a stray horse had its legs and head cut off on this railroad by the engine, and the night before a carter had left a cart with stones standing on the track, which a train loaded with merchandise had run into in the dark and been smashed to pieces. We hoped to be more fortunate and were so; but although we encountered no danger, our patience was sufficiently tried. About 10 miles [16km] from Springfield we came to a dead stop and the whole train stood motionless for three hours, enlivened only by occasional walks in the sunshine and visits to a cake store, the whole stock of eatables in which was in time consumed, the price of them having risen from hour to hour in proportion to the demand.

"The cause of our detention was the non-arrival of the

train from Worcester, which, from there being a single track of rails, could pass our train here and nowhere else. We heard nothing of its fate and expected it to arrive every minute till four o'clock, when at last an express on horseback came up and announced that it had broken down but that it was now cleared off the rails and that we might advance. Again I admire the patience and good humor of the American passengers which never forsook them in all this tedious detention. "At 6:00 p.m. we arrived at Worcester, but here found ourselves in another fix. The afternoon train from Boston does not arrive until 7:00 p.m. and we could not proceed to the city until it appeared. It was now dark, and for another hour and a half the passengers sat with exemplary patience in the cars. At half past seven we started again and arrived in Boston about 10 o'clock, with pretty good appetites, as we had breakfasted at half past seven in the morning and been allowed no meal since that hour. The car was seated for 56 passengers and contained at least 30. There was no aperture for ventilation and when night came on, the company insisted on shutting every window to keep out the cold. A few who, like us, preferred cool air to suffocation congregated at one end where we opened two windows for our relief."

So ends Combe's account of a most frustrating journey. Thankfully, delays such as those he experienced were largely eliminated by the advent of the telegraph, which aided in the dispatching of trains. The construction of a second track, and eventually the installation of line-side signals, also significantly improved railroad operations.

Above: This 1886 engraving, titled "The Modern Ship of the Plains," attempts to portray the experience of traveling aboard a long-distance train. In reality, early railroad cars were far more cramped than illustrated here.

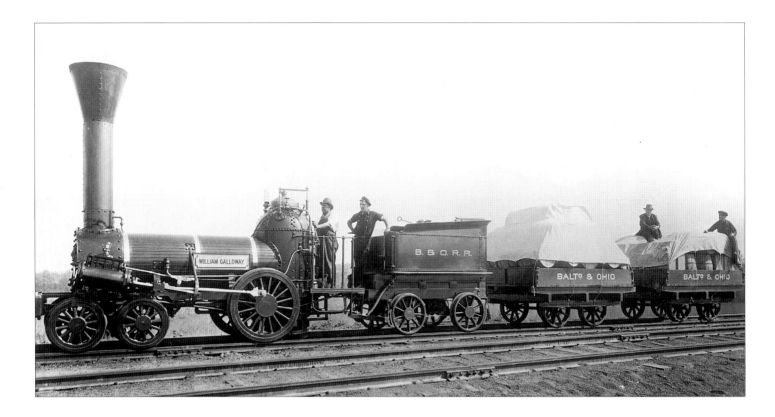

This replica model of the famous 1837 *Lafayette* steam locomotive was built for the Baltimore and Ohio company in 1927. The *Lafayette* is believed to be the first American locomotive to feature a horizontal boiler.

surface on top of longitudinal timbers. The iron straps had a propensity to break and to bend upwards, forming "snakeheads": a serious hazard for the next oncoming locomotive. Bridges and lineside structures were of basic design, normally timber-built, and lacking walls or protective railings. Stone-built viaducts were rarities, and the timber trestle was by far the most common type of bridge. Platforms at depots were nonexistent. Locomotives, cars, and wagons were all lightweight.

When in 1831 the Baltimore and Ohio Railroad held a competition to find a suitable American-built locomotive, it stipulated that entries should not weight more than 3.5 tons. Even for the time, this was a very modest weight: *Rocket* had weighed 5 tons and bigger engines had since been built in England. But the load-bearing capacity of the tracks was the deciding factor. Details of the other entrants are unclear, but the winner of the $4000 prize was a small engine, *York*, built by a clockmaker, Phineas Davis of York, Pennsylvania. A four-wheeler, it had a vertically mounted

boiler, and its upward-jutting rods earned it the nickname of "the Grasshopper." It proved to be a durable design, despite its diminutive size, and several more were built in Baltimore at the Baltimore & Ohio's new Mount Clare workshops, but it was in no way a trend-setter.

The "Best Friend"

Earlier in 1831, the first locomotive to go into regular service on an American railroad had begun work on the Charleston & Hamburg on January 15. Credit for the design is given to E.L. Miller and it was built at the West Point Foundry, in New York State, as an all-American machine, named *The Best Friend of Charleston*. Like Davis's engine, it had a vertically mounted boiler. Unfortunately, this exploded, through the fireman's negligence, on June 17, killing him and causing the first known fatality on an American railroad.

By now, numerous lines, most of them only a few miles long, were under construction. In most cases, their locomotives were imported from England, though often adapted by American engineers on arrival. By 1831, when Jervis designed the four-wheeler *De Witt Clinton* for the Mohawk & Hudson Railroad, the first in New York State, American locomotive design had adopted the horizontal boiler with rear-positioned firebox. This was borrowed from English designs, as was the bar-frame construction that became typical of North American locomotives until the one-piece cast steel frame came into use after World War I. In his second design, *Experiment* (rebuilt in 1846 and renamed *Brother Jonathan*), Jervis incorporated the important new feature of the four-wheel truck, or bogie, in front of the driving wheels, which made a big difference to the stability of the locomotive on the road. At the same time, the old strap-rail was being supplanted by the

Dorchester 0-4-0
Champlain & St Lawrence Railroad
1836

Boiler pressure: 50psi (3.5kg/cm²)		**Cylinders:** 9x14in (228x355mm)	
Driving wheels: 54in (1370mm)		**Grate area:** 8sq ft (0.74m²)	
Heating surface: not known		**Tractive effort:** 910lb (413kg)	
Total weight: 12,560lb (5.7t)			

The Champlain & St Lawrence, opened on July 21, 1836, was Canada's first railroad. *Dorchester*, which pulled the first train, was a lightweight version of the Stephenson "Samson" type, first built for the Liverpool & Manchester Railway in England in 1831. It was basically a "Planet" with wheels of equal size joined by coupling rods, and intended to provide greater traction for the hauling of goods trains. Like the "Planets," it had outside sandwich-type frames

This painting by Adam Sherriff Scott, RCA, recreates the animated scene as Dorchester sets off from La Prairie, Quebec, with Canada's first train on 21 July 1836.

that held the main bearings, and the cylinders and motion were all inside. Although railroad fever came to British North America later than it had south of the border, development was quite rapid.

Norris locomotive 4-2-0
Baltimore & Ohio Railroad (B&O)
1837

Boiler pressure: 60psi (4.2kg/cm²)		**Cylinders:** 10.5x18in (266x457mm)	
Driving wheels: 48in (1220mm)		**Grate area:** 8.6sq ft (0.8m²)	
Heating surface: 394sq ft (36.6m²)		**Tractive effort:** 2162lb (957kg)	
Total weight: 44,090lb (20t)			

The Norris locomotive had an impressive chimney, but dispensed with a dome and had a steam regulator inside the boiler.

The Baltimore & Ohio's Mount Clare works built this replica of Norris's *Lafayette*, B&O No. 13, in 1927. The original was built in 1837. Note the bar linking the rear-wheel tender brakes.

Baldwin's main rival in Philadelphia was William Norris, who set up as a locomotive builder in 1831. In 1837 he was the first American manufacturer to export to Europe (Austria). In the previous year, he had built a 4-2-0 with outside cylinders, *The Washington Country Farmer*, for the Philadelphia & Columbia; and eight on similar lines were ordered by the B&O. They represented a combination of British and American ideas, with Bury bar-frames and circular fireboxes, a front bogie with inside bearings, and outside cylinders. The Norris engines performed well on the B&O gradients. The longer, larger boiler saved them from the lack of power experienced by Bury's 2-2-0s in England. Their reputation as hill climbers was such that 15 were ordered by the Birmingham & Gloucester Railway in England, to work on its 1 in 37 Lickey incline.

upturned-T profile iron rail developed by Robert Stevens, which was safer, far more durable and allowed much greater speeds.

The performance of the first lines was watched with great interest and widely reported on, not merely in terms of speed and general novelty, but in terms of commercial success. In this respect, their effectiveness was not in doubt. Two men with a locomotive could move far more coal or cotton in the course of a day than a much greater number of men and horses. And the cost, per ton-mile, was far less. The same was true of every other bulk commodity. The cost of a new locomotive, at around $5000, could be earned back within a year. Its life expectancy, while not certain, was expected at least to match that of a horse.

By the mid-1830s, the larger towns which did not have a railroad, or plan to have one, were beginning to feel the danger of economic decline. Presidential approval of railroads was bestowed by Andrew Jackson, who made a brief run on the Baltimore & Ohio and visited the Mount Clare shops in June 1833. Almost four thousand miles of railroad track were laid by 1840, on a variety of gauges. The greatest impediment was the big rivers, whose width, speed, and capacity for flooding demanded something more substantial than trestles.

Cost and design difficulties held the companies back for a time, and freight and passengers had to be trans-shipped by means of ferries. Though some notable bridges, like the Erie's great stone Starrucca viaduct, were built in this decade, it was not until the 1850s that the era of great railroad bridges began. By that time, too, more of the railroad promoters were looking beyond their own backyards. The potential of the iron road for long-distance transport was being appreciated.

Two new aspects of economic life helped this by creating new traffic. The growth of industry in the East, most notably in parts of Pennsylvania and Massachusetts, and the accelerating rate of immigration and internal migration toward the Middle West, encouraged the railroad operators to extend their sights. But the distances were great, as were the physical obstacles, and the industry's infrastructure was insufficiently developed as yet—progress was slow. By 1850 the fast-growing city of Chicago had two local railroad lines, but was not yet linked by rail to the industrial east. A decade later, things would look very different. Heavy industry and the railroads were locked in a mutual embrace from the beginning, and the development of each aided the other. Iron and steel works, supplied by rail, sold much of their product to the railroads; and the same reciprocal relationship existed with the coal mines. In the course of the 1830s a new kind of factory appeared—the locomotive works.

The West Point Foundry of New York did not capitalize on its early start, and the first of these was set up in 1831 by William Norris in Philadelphia, with Colonel William H. Long of the US Topographical Corps of Engineers as his first partner. Norris was the first exporter of locomotives, scoring a notable success by selling his 4-2-0 type to England in 1838. Matthias W. Baldwin, who—like Phineas Davis—had begun as a watchmaker before tackling larger machinery, also set up his locomotive shop in Philadelphia in 1831.

Humble beginnings

The Baldwin plant was to become the world's biggest steam locomotive manufacturer. A distinctively North American look was established very early on, marked by a wide-diameter chimney, a leading four-wheel truck, and the pilot (or cow-catcher). This latter was an essential item on a light-weight locomotive running on an unfenced track, or sharing a public highway, where a collision with a cow could easily cause derailment. Although the very first locomotives had burned coke, wood quickly became the staple fuel, being both abundant and cheap, and also producing a smoke less noxious than that of coal.

Other early locomotive works were those of Thomas Rogers in Paterson, New Jersey, from 1835; and James Brook, not to be confused with the later Brooks Locomotive Works of Dunkirk, New York, was building engines in Philadelphia in 1837. By the 1840s, importing of locomotives to the United States had ceased, though Canadian railroads, where British financial and political interests remained strong, supplemented the products of the Canadian Locomotive Company (founded in 1850 at Kingston, Ontario) with imports from British builders.

CHAPTER 2

DEVELOPMENTS
AND THE
CIVIL WAR

As American railroads developed, systems began to replace individual
lines, companies expanded across state boundaries, and the federal
government started to take an interest. Technical development
brought the telegraph, while the Civil War presented a new set of
demands with the railroads enrolled in the war effort on both sides.

In 1836 the 4-2-0 locomotive was proving too light and of
inadequate tractive power for the growing weight of the
trains, and the first 4-4-0 engines appeared. These became
known internationally as the "American type," and their

**Above: An early form of piggy-backing: loading carts on truck-
waggons on the Long Island Railroad in the 1870s.**
**Left: Gilt and glory, from the days when stack, lamp, and dome
dwarfed the boiler—the preserved Eureka & Palisade 4-4-0 built by
Baldwin in 1875.**

greater power and larger tenders helped to open up the
prospects for longer-distance traffic. As the railroads
became more numerous, their vulnerability to external
factors became revealed. The financial crisis known as "the
Panic" of 1837 hit many railroad companies badly, but in
the general process of expansion, it was a temporary hitch.
Nevertheless, it pointed up the fact that the railroads were
businesses, and dependent on a sound national economy
and money supply. They were also dependent on the
abilities and qualities of their own directors—a point of

great importance for the future. Bankruptcies and failures were frequent from an early stage. The growth of a railroad line into a "system" or network could be accomplished by the canny purchase of an ailing rival or neighbor as well as by extending the tracks. City and State governments were often pressed into supporting railroad development, but might also be enlisted to oppose it: the canal and road-teamster companies also had their interests to defend.

Large-scale immigration into the Midwest, where there were no towns or productive farmland, showed up the disadvantages of the merchant-sponsored railroads. By the late 1830s, the situation was approaching crisis-point. Immigrants were arriving in greater numbers each year; there was a vast extent of uncultivated land, but no transport system other than the ox-hauled covered wagon. Part of the answer was supplied by the state government in

the form of land grants, first used in the building of the Illinois Central Railroad, and awarding territory for every new mile of railroad. Thus the railroad was provided with a degree of security and a source of future income by letting the ground, and providing the transport for the settlers. The government set conditions, including the completion of the 700-mile (1125km) road within six years, and the payment of seven percent of the company's gross income. But the Illinois Central went ahead, and Chicago became the focal point of north-south and east-west railroads. Civic as well as state authorities were pressed to back railroad development, if only for fear of losing out.

In 1846 a special committee of the City of Philadelphia's Select and Common Council recommended that the city should invest strongly in the proposed Pennsylvania Railroad, arguing that: "The trade of this city, already

Gowan & Marx 4-4-0
Philadelphia & Reading Railroad (P&RR): 1839

Boiler pressure: 80psi (5.6kg/cm²)	**Cylinders:** 12.6x16in (320x406mm)
Driving wheels: 42in (1066mm)	**Grate area:** 12sq ft (1.1m²)
Heating surface: not known	**Tractive effort:** 5140lb (2331kg)
Total weight: 24,250lb (11t)	

Gowan & Marx was one of the most powerful engines of its time, though developments soon superseded it. A "birdcage" spark arrestor is fitted to the chimney.

The name of this early goods 4-4-0 came from a London banking firm that did business with the P&RR. The builders were Eastwick & Harrison of Philadelphia and the specification was for an engine to haul coal trains at slow speed. Its equalizing lever, linking the coupled axles, was developed by Eastwick & Harrison in 1838. The lever was a vital contributor to its general effectiveness, letting it ride a rough road without derailing. It had the Bury "haycoc'" type of boiler, but with an oblong, not round firebox, giving it a larger grate than other engines, which helped it to develop more power. The boiler pressure is quoted at 80–130psi (5.6–9.1kg/cm2). Its valve gear, patented by Eastwick in 1835, was cumbersome, requiring movement of the valve ports, rather than of a sliding

valve, in order to engage reverse gear, and this was later changed. A 6-ton (6096kg) tender was fitted. On December 5, 1839, it pulled the first train between Reading and Philadelphia, and on February 20, 1840 it hauled a 472-ton (479t) train of 101 cars on this line. Even at little more than walking pace, this was a great achievement. With further modifications, it was traded in to Baldwins against a new locomotive in 1859, having run 144,000 miles (231,739km) for the Reading. Gowan & Marx caused great interest in Europe, and inspired the invitation to its builders to set up their factory in St Petersburg, Russia.

6-2-0 Locomotive
Various Railroads: 1837

Boiler pressure: 60psi (4.2kg/cm²)		**Cylinders:** 10.5x18in (266x547mm)	
Driving wheels: 84in (2133mm)		**Grate area:** 11.4sq ft (1m²)	
Heating surface: Not known		**Tractive effort:** 4660lb (2113kg)	
Total weight: 44,080lb (20t)			

Various American builders tried out a locomotive type pioneered by John B. Jervis with *Experiment,* whose essential feature was a very large pair of single driving wheels set at the rear of the boiler. Most were built around 1837, though it continued to the end of the 1840s. William Norris built several, and one of these, *Lightning,* for the Utica and Schenectady Railroad in 1849, was claimed to have exceeded 60mph (96.5 km/h) with eight loaded cars. But the advent of the 4-4-0 effectively killed off the "single driver" locomotive.

This 1847 locomotive is ascribed to Robert Stevens of the Camden & Amboy. It is really a 4-2-2-0, with two extra and larger carrying wheels in rear of a front truck.

The "STEVENS" TYPE 1847

retarded by improvements on the North and South, will be so curtailed by the Baltimore and Ohio Railroad at Pittsburgh, and the completion of the railroad from New York to Lake Erie, as to drain the public works, and impoverish the city and state."

Legal Hurdles

American railroads placed other demands on government. Lines running over state boundaries, and into federal territory, created a legal precedent that had to be resolved. Interstate commerce became a thorny issue; state governments still tended to favor "their" railroad companies over intruders from elsewhere. As the railroads grew wealthier, they were able to put pressure on "their" representatives to ensure favorable treatment. Issues relating to railroads and the extent of federal and state control were debated constantly both in the newspapers read by the general public and in such new specialized publications as the *Railroad Journal* and *Railroad Advocate*, both established in the early 1830s. And the variability of gauges was

becoming a problem. Even in 1832, articles in these railroad journals pointed out the military disadvantages of a break in gauge: they had an eye on British-ruled Canada, but also on the internal situation.

There was an increasing awareness, in the second and third decades of railroads, that a qualitative change of great importance had occurred in national life. In many serious and thoughtful books and essays on modern life and political economy, the role of the locomotive and the railroad was deeply considered. The June 1846 issue of *Hunt's Merchant's Magazine* had an article by Charles Fraser on "The Moral Influence of Steam", exploring the idea that steam power upset that "great law of the universe, which makes labor the portion of man, and condemns him to earn his bread by the sweat of his brow." This theme echoes through the 1840s and 1850s.

Writers saw steam power as a historical culmination and not, as we now do, as the first accelerative phase of a technological era. Classically educated, they tended to write in terms of the past. Theodore Parker, a prominent

Atlas 0-8-0

Philadelphia & Reading Railroad (PRR): 1846

Boiler pressure: not known	Cylinders: 15.5x20in (393x508mm)
Driving wheels: 46in (1167.5mm)	Grate area: not known
Heating surface: not known	Tractive effort: not known
Total weight: 44,800lb (20.3t)	

The wide bell-mouthed chimneys of American locomotives, seen in so many variations, were filled with any one of a number of patent baffle systems to reduce the emission of sparks, live coals, or burning wood embers.

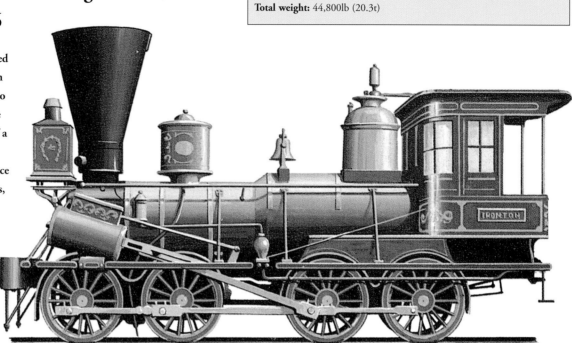

In the 1840s, American locomotive design continued to focus on the problem of reconciling heavier loads with uneven track and sharp curves. Despite his conservative reputation, Matthias Baldwin had come up with an approach in 1837 (perhaps as a means of getting around Campbell's patent for the 4-4-0 type). He rebuilt one of his 4-2-0s as 0-6-0, all wheels of the same diameter, and coupled. The essential point was this: the drive was connected to all wheels, but the front truck wheels could move laterally, independently of each other and of the rear drivers, while all axles remained in parallel. This was the "flexible beam truck", allowing the wheels to be more widely spaced than the normal 0-6-0 arrangement; and though the movement allowable was limited, it was enough to negotiate a curve of 150ft (45m) radius. Baldwin extended the concept to eight-wheel freight engines, with a wide space between the front and back pair of coupled wheels, and continued to build the type until 1866. The development of the 4-6-0, with its superior speed and good tractive effort, effectively killed off the flexible beam truck, which had been efficient only with slow-speed trains. These, incidentally, were Balwin's first engines equipped with sandboxes and roofed-over cabs.

apologist for the new technological world, wrote in the April 1850 issue of *Scientific American*: "At the voice of Genius … Fire and Water embrace at his bidding, and a new servant is born, which will fetch and carry at his command … and run errands up and down the continent with men and women on his back … The Fable of Orpheus is a true story in our times."

By the time that was written, the iron road had also reached the West Coast, with the establishment of the Sacramento Valley Railroad in 1849. Its first locomotive, *Elephant*, had to be shipped round Cape Horn to reach its place of work. But a vast gap still separated this pioneer line from the railroads of the East. American route mileage amounted to 9021 miles (14,517km) in 1850.

During the decade 1840 to 1850, an innovation of great importance was that of the electric telegraph, first used on the London & Birmingham line in England. The ability to "wire" ahead was of course of great benefit to commerce, government, and individuals. Railroad tracks, generally taking the most direct way between centers of population, and with a single owner of the ground, were the obvious routes for the overhead wires to follow, and many were lined with telegraph poles. The rail depots made good telegraph stations. But the telegraph also proved a boon to the railroads themselves. In the first years of operations, trains were dispatched into a sort of limbo. Timetables had to be rigidly adhered to, as once a train was on its way, there were no means of telling where it was until it had arrived.

Even then, its arrival was not known at the dispatch point. Information was always lagging behind events. When there were breakdowns or extra time was taken at stations, lengthy delays were inevitable, especially as most lines operated on single track and there was a natural dread of head-on collision—a "cornfield meet" in railroad slang. Now, with the telegraph, train dispatching and control became much more flexible. The train dispatcher at a central control office could obtain, and send, instant information from and to stations down the line. This enabled him to take delays into account, to issue changed instructions about crossing points on the single track, and generally to keep traffic moving as efficiently as possible. The printing telegraph system, based on the code devised by Samuel Morse, was first used on the Baltimore & Ohio Railroad on May 24, 1843. The Erie Railroad's general superintendent, Charles Minot, joined with Ezra Cornell in forming the New York and Erie Telegraph Company, the forerunner of New York and Western Union Telegraph.

Two processes can be seen at work among the railroad companies in the 1850s. New ones were still being formed in large numbers, as communities joined in the rush to attach themselves to the ever-spreading network. But also, consolidation was taking place. In 1853 the seven separate

WORKING ON THE RAILROAD
Boiler Explosions

Great power must be harnessed with great care to prevent unleashing a terrible destructive force. Inventor James Watt warned against the use of high-pressure steam, yet most steam engines—and consequentially nearly all locomotives—built after 1800 used high-pressure steam. The danger he feared was the risk of a boiler explosion, destroying the engine and possibly killing its crew and anyone unfortunate enough to be standing nearby. Boiler explosions can be triggered in a number of ways, the most common being a low water level in the boiler. If the top of the firebox (known as the crown sheet) is not covered with water, it will overheat and fail, resulting in a sudden catastrophic release of pressure. In the nineteenth century, boiler explosions were an all too common occurrence. One such horrific accident near Boston was reported in *The New York Tribune*, with the article reprinted in the August 28, 1875, issue of *The Railway Gazette*:

"Freight engine No. 1, standing in the Fitchburgh Railroad freight yard at Charlestown, blew up this afternoon with terrific violence. The engineer and fireman were blown to the top of a car in the rear of the tender, but strangely escaped serious injury. A switchman on the engine was, however, horribly scalded . . . The violence of the explosion was so great as to blow a fragment weighing 200lb [91kg] through the wall of the freight house, 20ft [6m] distant. The men inside escaped injury. Rails were torn from the track beside the engine and bent as though made of lead. One rail was carried 15ft [5m] and forced through the wall of the freight depot . . . One piece of the boiler, weighing 32lb [15kg], was blown into the air, and fell nearly a quarter of a mile [400m] from the scene of the explosion, passing through the roof of the St John's Episcopal Church, on the corner of Bow and Richmond streets. The fragment fell into the main aisle, within 3ft [1m] of where a woman was engaged in washing the floor . . ."

The incidence of such explosions was greatly reduced with improvements in locomotive design. Boiler failures also became less common with the introduction of stronger materials and more effective safety devices, along with better training of crews.

concerns that operated the railroad from Albany to Buffalo and Niagara became a single entity, the New York Central, bringing three other roads in as well. Steamboats at first provided its link from Albany downriver to New York City. With the appearance of larger companies, operating over

longer routes, engineering works became more grandiose and the great river barriers were conquered, one by one, by metal bridges. The biggest river of all, the Mississippi, was first bridged at Rock Island in 1854, creating a through route from Chicago into Iowa. Among the most striking,

Elephant 4-4-0
Sacramento Valley Railroad (SVR) 1849

Boiler pressure: not known	**Cylinders:** 15x20in (381x508mm)
Driving wheels: 71in (1802mm)	**Grate area:** 9.63sq ft (0.9m²)
Heating surface: 710sq ft (66m²)	**Tractive effort:** not known
Total weight: 56,000lb (25.4t)	

When it was bought by the SVR in 1855, *Elephant* had already had a varied career. With two inside cylinders, and external valve gear operated through cylindrical-cased valve boxes set at an angle to the frame, it was a product of John Souther's Globe Works in Boston, and built to the 5ft (1524mm) gauge, probably for a Norfolk, Virginia, line. It was shipped to San Francisco in July 1850 and used briefly on the waterfront by a land-clearing contractor before the city authorities banned it. But it was the first steam engine to run in California. The Sacramento Valley, the state's first railroad, bought it in 1850 to supplement two smaller engines, and it was renamed *Garrison* after the line's president. It ran well for 10 years, an 1863 derailment causing little damage. In 1865 it was regauged to the

The locomotive in its final form as *Pioneer*. In outline, it looks a typical 4-4-0 of the 1870s, but the inside cylinders remain an unusual feature. The big tender shows that it was used on main line services.

standard 56.5in (1435mm) when the SVR became the western end of the transcontinental line. In original form, it had handrails fixed on a riveted external bar frame. In 1869 it was rebuilt and modernized, with link motion valve gear, though it retained its inside cylinders. Again renamed, as *Pioneer,* it ran until 1879, when it was taken out of regular service. In 1849 it had been a big engine for the time, but things had moved on. It was use occasionally until 1886 when, despite its historic interest, it was broken up for scrap.

The Erie Railroad's bridge at Old Portage, New York. Over 800ft (243.8m) long, it was 234ft (71.3m) above the river bed. Built 1852, it burned down in 1875, to be replaced by a metal structure.

though far from being the longest, was the New York Central's suspension viaduct over the Niagara River, within sight of the tremendous Falls. It was completed in 1855. In 1859 the St Lawrence was crossed at Montreal by Robert Stephenson's Victoria Bridge, whose surface presented 30 acres (12 hectares) of iron for rustproof painting. There were many heroic tasks for engineers, like John A. Roebling, designer of the Niagara Falls Suspension Bridge, and his son Washington, who worked with his father on the Brooklyn Bridge—and their workforce—but in an industry begun by engineers and visionaries, the appearance of large companies brought to the fore a new kind of dominant personality, the railroad magnate. The architect of the New York Central was Erastus Corning, a manufacturer of nails and other iron articles, president of the Utica & Schenectady Railroad. He was not interested in railroads for their own sake, but because they fitted into an industrial and commercial system in which he was an important player.

Other big players were coming on to the railroad scene, attracted by the growing scale of rail business, the potential for future development, and the possibility of making a very great deal of money. In 1862 Cornelius Vanderbilt, once the youthful owner of a single sail-powered New York ferryboat and by now the "Commodore" of a great river and sea-

Susquehanna 0-8-0
Philadelphia & Reading Railroad: 1854

Boiler pressure: 90psi (6.3kg/cm²)	**Cylinders:** 19x22in (482x558mm)
Driving wheels: 43in (1091mm)	**Grate area:** 23.5sq ft (2.2 m²)
Heating surface: c 1000sq ft (93 m²)	**Tractive effort:** 14,120lb (6970kg)
Total weight: 60,480lb (27.43t) (engine only)	

Ross Winans was a maverick among locomotive suppliers. Around 1840, he established himself at Baltimore, next to the Baltimore & Ohio's workshops. Wanting to develop a good coal-burning firebox (a universal problem at the time), he built the "Camel" type locomotive, with a sloping firebox at the rear and the driving cab perched above the boiler. This was the only type of locomotive that Winans' factory built; the total was around 300. It was the first coal-burning locomotive produced in quantity, and its large and wide grate, placed behind the locomotive's frame and wheels, took up the full width available. The fireman stood on the tender.

The first of the line, "Camel," was supplied in 1848 to the Boston & Maine, but was rejected after road tests; it was then sold to the Reading Railroad. Its performance seems to have been good, but apart from its odd appearance, it had a number of idiosyncrasies unlikely to appeal to a Master Mechanic. Winans persevered with steadily larger fireboxes. He found regular customers in the Baltimore & Ohio and Philadelphia & Reading lines, both of which ran slow-speed, heavy coal trains (the "Camel" was ill-suited to speeds over 15mph [24km/h]) but few others expressed interest. By 1862 demand had ceased, and Winans closed his factory.

Susquehanna was a typical "Camel," looking as if it had carried off a signal cabin from somewhere. The front tube of the apparent double funnel was an ash container, with a door at the base. Firing the huge box was a fireman's nightmare. Winans had incorporated feed-hoppers into his design, to get the coal to the front of the fire,

Baltimore & Ohio No. 65, built by Winans in 1850, shows the type, though it has lost, or did not have, the apparent "double funnel." The fireman could scramble up the steps to take occasional refuge in the cab.

but the firemen objected to the double task of shoveling coal from the floor up to the firing platform of the tender, and then into the hopper. The driver, perched high, had an unusually good view, though partly obscured by the very large dome. The design had significant shortcomings. The main structural problem was the link between the firebox, which tended to sag, and the boiler. The boiler was weakened by the steam dome, which may account for the low pressure employed. The feedwater pump injected cold water at the side of the firebox, reducing the heat of the boiler. The placing of the firebox made the tender-locomotive drawbar link difficult. The drawbar, passing through the ashpan, often became red-hot.

Even in its time, the "Camel" was derided by rival builders. Winans' claim was for simplicity and ruggedness, but the engines were badly finished and lacked boiler lagging, considered essential on most lines. At around $10,000 per locomotive, they were not cheap. Its main influence on later design was the "Camelback" locomotive with Wootten firebox, but that was designed to burn anthracite waste, not coal, and was at least partly supported by wheels. For all their drawbacks, the "Camels" continued almost to the end of the century. The last went for scrap in 1898.

The General 4-4-0
Western & Atlantic Railroad: 1855

Boiler pressure: 140psi (9.8kg/cm²)	Cylinders: 15x22in (381x558mm)
Driving wheels: 60in (1523mm)	Grate area: 12.5sq ft (1.15m²)
Heating surface: 784.4sq ft (72.8m²)	Tractive effort: 6885lb (3123kg)
Total weight: 50,300lb (22.8t)	

The relative lightness of American bar-frame construction is shown in this print of *The General;* there is no running plate alongside the boiler and "the works" are on view (and easily accessible for repair and maintenance).

By 1855 the "American" type 4-4-0 had developed into the brightly painted form, with shiny brass and copper-work, often with balloon spark-arrester smokestack and a big headlamp, familiar from many illustrations and Western movies. *The General*, built at Rogers Locomotive Works, Patterson, New Jersey, was famously hijacked during the US Civil War at Big Shanty, Georgia, where the great engine chase took place. It was typical of many others that led less dramatic lives as the basic work-horse of the rapidly growing American railroad network. Basic features of the design were level-set cylinders, a long-wheelbase truck, a deep, narrow wood-burning firebox, bar frames, big wooden cab, and an eight-wheel tender. Valve gear was much improved, with Stephenson's link motion normally replacing the old gab gear, which had permitted only "backward" or "forward." Designers were very conscious of the esthetic aspect of their engines: William Mason, a Massachusetts builder, wrote in 1853, "We want them, of course, strong workers, but we want them also good lookers… we shall hope to see something soon on the rails that does not look exactly like a 'cooking stove on wheels'." *The General*, much restored and now discreetly oil-fired, is preserved at Chattanooga, Tennessee.

going fleet, disposed of his nautical interests, and applied his acquisitive and expansive energies to railroads. In 1860 there were 30,626 miles (49,286km) of railroad in the United States and 2065 miles (3323km) in Canada.

An era of furious expansion was about to begin. Whereas before, the financing of railroad companies had been managed on a local basis, the increasing size and revenues of the railroad industry was becoming an important factor in the growth of financial institutions, stock exchanges, merchant banks, and dealers in securities. Boston and New York were the first important financial centers. With this development, investors in railroads came to take a wider-ranging view, placing their money not on a basis of local knowledge and in the expectation of seeing their own business benefit, but in the trust of a prospectus for a distant line of which they had no personal knowledge, and in the expectation that their investment would pay a regular dividend. There was a general feeling that railroads were a good and safe thing, the flagships of an expanding economy.

The Civil War

In the critical year of 1861, railroads were part of the fabric of life, at least in the United States east of the Mississippi and in Canada east of the Detroit River. Like other

American institutions, they would undergo severe testing and troubles in the Civil War. Though the northern states had twice the mileage of the south, both sides had substantial railroad networks, concentrated in the eastern states in the case of the Confederacy. There was no sense of a national railroad network yet, and no physical link between the Union and Confederate lines. The southern Mississippi to the west, and the Ohio and Potomac rivers to the north, were not yet bridged. Railroads, for the first time, were pressed into a major war effort. The most crucial zone was, of course, where the two sides abutted, across northern Virginia and Kentucky, and the two companies most severely affected by warfare were the Baltimore & Ohio and

the Louisville & Nashville. War also hit companies in other ways: the Seaboard & Roanoke board split, with the president holding board meetings and declaring dividends in Richmond, and the secretary doing likewise in Philadelphia. In engineering terms, the North had a major advantage since it possessed all the most important locomotive works, which continued to build during the war. On the whole, too, its lines were better laid, with much more double track. Some of the more rural Southern railroads still ran on the original strap-rails. Strategists quickly appreciated the value of the locomotive as an aid in waging war. The armored train, the ammunition train, the howitzer and mortar trains were all devised and put into

250 Class 2-6-0
Erie Railway: 1862

Boiler pressure: 120psi (8.4kg/cm2)	**Cylinders:** 17x22in (431x558mm)
Driving wheels: 54in (1370mm)	**Grate area:** 21sq ft (1.95m2)
Heating surface: 1255sq ft (116.5m2)	**Tractive effort:** 10,596lb (4805kg)
Total weight: 79,520lb (36t) (engine only)	

The American 2-6-0 had made its appearance in 1850. This class of 6-ft gauge anthracite-burning freight haulers built by Danforth, Cooke of Paterson, New Jersey, was the largest yet to appear, and confirmed the virtues of the type. Its firebox, a patent design by James Millholland of the Philadelphia & Reading, had a grate formed of water-holding tubes: this was also used on some other hard-coal burners around this time. The "Mogul" designation for the 2-6-0 type

"Mogul" No. 334 of the Central Vermont, built at Rhode Island in 1884, and seen here at Burlington, Vermont, thirty years later, shows the typical "wagon-top" boiler of the nineteenth century.

did not come in until 1872, by which time it had been overtaken by larger main-line freight locomotives, but it retained its usefulness as a typical short-haul engine for light trains and side roads.

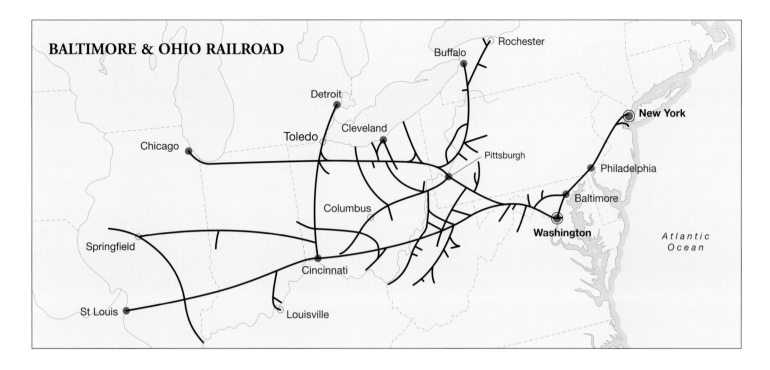

BALTIMORE & OHIO RAILROAD

The Baltimore & Ohio connected the port of Baltimore with the interior of the country. The line originally reached as far as Wheeling, Virginia (now West Virginia), and was later extended to St Louis, Chicago, and numerous other cities.

action in the course of the struggle. So, of course, were the hospital trains. Military railroads were built to bring guns to bear on crucial targets, and the Union army began its long involvement with locomotives. But the prime contribution of the railroad was to do for both sides what it had always done best; what indeed it was created to do. That was to move goods and people, in large amounts and large numbers, speedily from place to place.

Conflicting Interests

There were many headaches for those whose job it was to organize and manage these movements. Changing trains, enforced by break of gauge and the lack of end-on connections between lines serving individual cities, had often irritated passengers before, but now they were sometimes a serious impediment to rapid troop deployment, particularly in the Confederate States. Most of the tracks west of the Mississippi were of 5ft 6in (167cm) gauge; to the east there was a mixture of standard gauge, 4ft 10in (147cm) gauge, and 5ft (152cm) gauge. Montgomery, Alabama, was typical of many cities in having two railroads

of different gauge with terminal stations in different parts of the city center.

The experience, however, was radically different for those lines which crossed the battle zone and those which lay behind it, especially those of the North. A great increase in traffic and in government contract business meant full employment and prosperity for lines like the Pennsylvania and the New York Central. Profits rose dramatically. Within the greater conflict, a struggle between the military strategists and local business interests was soon apparent. Richmond, an important railroad center, had three railroads entering it from the north and another three from the south, all of them standard gauge except for one, the Raleigh and Danville. None of these lines were connected with one another, something which suited their owners and the merchants of Richmond, but which presented the military men with a serious difficulty. In the end, when military demands prevailed over mercantile objections, it was with the understanding that they could be used for military purposes only.

Similar objections arose in Philadelphia, where goods and passengers between New York and Washington had always had to change trains and stations, to the advantage of local freight companies and workers. By 1863, under intense pressure from government, and from New York business interests, connecting lines were built to enable trains to take

No. 1 4-4-0
Great Northern Railroad (GNR): 1862

Boiler pressure: 120psi (8.4kg/cm2)		**Cylinders:** 12x22in (304x558mm)	
Driving wheels: 63in (1599mm)		**Grate area:** not known	
Heating surface: not known		**Tractive effort:** 5000lb (2267kg)	
Total weight: 102,000lb (46t)			

Railroads were spreading fast in the American Midwest. The first train to run in Minnesota was pulled by this engine on the St Paul & Pacific Railroad, a constituent line of the Great Northern, which ultimately became a sector in the transcontinental railroad. No 1, bearing the name *William Crooks*, is preserved, but in a much-restored form. It was built in 1861, by Smith & Jackson, of Paterson, New Jersey, and taken by barge up the Mississippi to St Paul from the

An almost exact contemporary of the Great Northern No.1, this 4-4-0 of 1863 was built in Taunton, Massachusetts, by William Mason for the US Military Railroads. It is named *General Haupt*, after the Union forces' chief railway engineer.

railhead at La Crosse, though the line was not yet open and it did not enter service until 1862. 4-4-0s were the typical motive power of the St Paul & Pacific. The railroad did not reach the Pacific until 1893.

a through, if somewhat indirect route, without the necessity to change. Especially in the Southern cities, it was often stipulated that such connections should be removed after the end of hostilities, but this would rarely happen.

A degree of self-interest was also apparent in the northern companies. When Cornelius Vanderbilt complained in December 1863 about the government's requisitioning of locomotives, he was answered in straight terms by a telegraph from Secretary of War Edwin Stanton: "The engines referred to were seized by order of this Dept. from an absolute and paramount necessity for the supply of the armies on the Cumberland … they are absolutely essential

for the safety of those armies and the order cannot be revoked … whatever damage your Company may sustain the Govt. is responsible for but the military operations and the supply of the arms at Chattanooga in the judgment of this Dept. and no doubt also in your judgment are superior to every other consideration … I hope that you will not only throw no obstacle in the way of a speedy forwarding of these Engines to Louisville but that you will use your well known energy in aid of the government to hurry them forward."

Some remarkable troop movements were carried out, and caused new chapters to be urgently added to military textbooks. The 30,000-strong Army of Tennessee, under General Braxton Bragg, was moved in the summer of 1862 from Tupelo, Mississippi, to Chattanooga inside a week: a journey of 770 miles (1239km) that would once have taken at least five times as long. In the fall of 1863, the Union moved 25,000 soldiers of the Army of the Potomac from Virginia to Chattanooga, in a series of trains, in just over eleven days. In the course of such exercises—and these were two of the largest among very many others—railroad men,

both civil and military, found themselves tackling a multitude of fresh organizational problems: how to keep track of far-flung locomotives and crews; how to ensure fuel supplies; how to provide enough cars to carry troops; how to feed the troops; how—if possible—to provide sanitation for such numbers. Inevitably, they found themselves discussing such matters as cross-country routes, inter-company collaboration, and how desirable it would be to have a nationwide standard gauge.

Thatcher Perkins 4-6-0
Baltimore & Ohio Railroad: 1863

Boiler pressure: 75psi (5.25kg/cm²)	**Cylinders:** 19x26in (482x660mm)
Driving wheels: 58in (1472mm)	**Grate area:** 19.4sq ft (1.8m²)
Heating surface: 1114sq ft (103.4m²)	**Tractive effort:** 10,300lb (4670kg)
Total weight: not known	

Thatcher Perkins's 4-6-0, No. 117, as restored, at the Baltimore & Ohio Railroad Museum. Note the absence of locomotive brakes. These did not become standard until well into the 1880s.

The origins of the 4-6-0 go back to the late 1840s. In March 1847, the Norris Works of Philadelphia constructed a ten-wheeler, *Chesapeake*, for the Philadelphia & Reading Railroad. Its design is generally credited to Septimus Norris, who later attempted to place a patent on the 4-6-0 wheel arrangement. Despite good reports of performance, the design was slow to catch on. Baldwin was still wedded to the 4-2-0 at this time, and did not offer a 4-6-0 design in his catalog—widely circulated among railroad companies—until after 1852. Many engineers felt that the four-wheel front truck bore too little weight and was liable to jump the rails, and that the design offered no real advantage over the 4-4-0. The leading coupled wheels, and sometimes the second set also, were invariably unflanged on the early 4-6-0s. The earliest 4-6-0s were designed as freight engines, but by the mid-1850s, this model was established on several lines as a useful mixed-traffic type, which was able to haul both fast passenger and goods trains.

Thatcher Perkins had been designing locomotives from the 1840s. Large ones were his specialty, including an 0-8-0 for the Baltimore &

Ohio in 1848, of which line he was Master Mechanic. In 1851, he became a partner in the Smith, Perkins loco works of Alexandria, Virginia. They built a ten-wheeler, *Wilmore*, for the Pennsylvania Railroad in 1856. In 1863 the Baltimore &Ohio commissioned a 4-6-0 design from Thatcher Perkins for its Allegheny Mountain section between Piedmont and Grafton, in present-day West Virgina. Built at the Baltimore & Ohio Mount Clare shops, they were intended for passenger service. Their weight was such that they could not be introduced until track and bridges had been strengthened. No 117 of this class operated until 1890, when it was taken out of service. Shown at various exhibitions, it was steamed and ran at the railrosad's centennial celebration in 1927. Though heavily restored, it has survived and remains preserved at the Baltimore & Ohio's Baltimore Museum. Although neither a mechanical or stylistic trend-setter, nor a specially distinguished performer, it well represents the handsome style of its period. The boiler pressure, at 75psi (5.25kg/cm2), was curiously low and there must have been some difficulties feeding the cylinders. Perkins designed other 4-6-0s, including a 5ft (1524mm) gauge engine for the Louisville & Nashville Railroad, of which he became Master Mechanic in 1868; quite different to No 117, it was on a long wheelbase (25ft/7614mm) with 59in (1497mm) wheels; this was the 4-6-0 as freight hauler.

Though many US 4-6-0s were built, it remained overshadowed by the 4-4-0 in the nineteenth century and by the "Pacific" and eight or ten-coupled locomotive after 1910.

Consolidation 2-8-0
Lehigh & Mahanoy Railroad:1866

Boiler pressure: 120psi (8.4 kg/m²)*		**Cylinders:** 20x24in (507x609mm)	
Driving wheels: 48in (1218mm)		**Grate area:** 25sq ft (2.3m²)	
Heating surface: not known		**Tractive effort:** 20,400lb (10,070kg)*	
Total weight: 85,720lb (38.88t)			

A later D&RG 2-8-0. The
drive is on the second coupled
axle, as became most common
with two-cylinder, simple-
expansion "Consolidation"
locomotives.

The Lehigh & Mahanoy was a new coal-carrying line with severe gradients, and its Master Mechanic Alexander Mitchell designed for it a "super freight" locomotive in 1865, with eight coupled wheels and a front Bissell pony truck, with solid wheels. Some trouble was found in getting a builder, but eventually Baldwins took on the job, in April 1866. By August the engine was in service. During construction, the line merged with the Lehigh Valley Railroad, and the name of the new locomotive was chosen to celebrate the event. The newest developments were incorporated, including steel tires from Krupps in Germany, who had pioneered this improvement, and a steam injector. The engine cost $19,000 to build, plus $950 war tax, but the railroad was eminently satisfied with its investment. James I. Blakslee, the Superintendent, wrote to Baldwins: "She is a perfect success . . . I am satisfied she can out pull any machine ever built of her weight."

The real success of Consolidation was not in tractive power, which could be matched by an 0-8-0; but in its ability to operate with a heavy load on a sharply curving track at higher speeds than any railroad had dared to attempt before, and with a maximum axle load of 8.4 tons (8.5t). Nevertheless, in all respects this was a locomotive at the leading edge of design. Its truck was not a Bissell one but a new patent one by William Hudson, superintendent of the Rogers Locomotive Works, with a heavy equalizing lever linking the truck frame to the leading coupled wheel spring hangers. The long boiler, 15ft (4568mm) from firebox to smoke box, could make plenty of

steam, and its big cylinders delivered the power to the wheels, with a long rod driving the third coupled wheels. Its single injector was supplemented by feedwater pumps on both sides, worked off return cranks on the last coupled wheels. It burned high-quality anthracite coal. The eight-wheel tender, mounted on two trucks, had a high canopy roof over the coal compartment.

Further engines of the class were ordered and considerable interest was aroused in other companies. But they were cautious about purchasing, partly because of its unusual length and greater cost, which left little change out of $20,000. But steadily the 2-8-0 won its reputation as a heavy freight hauler. It was found to be as advantageous on narrow gauge as it was on standard gauge. In 1873, Baldwins built a 3ft (913mm) gauge "Consolidation" for the Garland extension of the Denver & Rio Grande Railroad, which, as the Superintendent reported, "moved up the 211-feet [65-m] grades and around the 30-degree curves seemingly with as much ease as our passenger engines on 75-feet [23-m] grades with three coaches and baggage cars". From 1876, when it became the Pennsylvania Railroad's standard freight locomotive, the type grew very rapidly in popularity. Its greater capital cost was soon offset by the work it did. On the Erie Railroad, the managers calculated in 1878 that 55 2-8-0s did the work of 100 4-4-0s. The success of the "Consolidation" launched the American trend toward ever-larger and more powerful locomotives.

TRAVELERS' TALES
Youthful Enterprise

On April 8, 1862, the day after the Battle of Shiloh, a 15 year-old newsboy who worked the trains on the Grand Trunk Railroad, ran into the office of *The Detroit Free Press* and asked if he could have a thousand copies of the latest edition to sell. He was very young, and poorly dressed, and the man in charge "regarded me as if perhaps I might be crazy," but the persuasive lad got his papers, on trust, and had them packed into the baggage car of the north-bound train. He had made a plan. "All along the line I had made friends of the station-agents, who were also the telegraphers, by giving them candy and other things in which a train-boy dealt in these days … I wired ahead to them, through the courtesy of the Detroit agent, who was also my friend, asking them to post notices that when the train arrived, I would have newspapers with details of the great battle.

"When I got to the first station on the run, I found that the device had worked beyond my expectations. The platform literally was crowded with men and women anxious to buy newspapers. After one look at that crowd I raised the price from five cents to ten and sold as many newspapers as the crowd could absorb. The advertising worked as well at all the other stations. By the time the train reached Port Huron I had advanced the price of the Detroit Free Press for that day to thirty-five cents per copy and everybody took one."

The boy netted enough cash from that exploit to take a course in telegraphy himself. He did not stop there— his name was Thomas Alva Edison.

Sabotage

Acts of war multiplied the operational problems from the beginning. Railroad tracks, running across open country, were vulnerable to sabotage. Trestle bridges could be set on fire and reduced to heaps of ashes. Locomotives could be rendered unusable by smashing the valve gear with sledgehammers. Various ways were found of tearing up and ruining the tracks: a single horse could bend a rail that had been loosened from the ties at one end; rails were bent around tree trunks, or piled above a bonfire of ties and lumber and, when heated, twisted into fantastic shapes. The smarter generals, who soon cottoned on to the value of railroads in support of an army, were equally aware of their value to the opposing forces. Stonewall Jackson held off an attack on the Baltimore & Ohio's Martinsburg yard until it was full of engines, then stormed it, removed some for military use, cut off the track access, and tried to destroy the rest. The line lost 67 locomotives in the course of the war. Intense pressure was placed on the engineers to restore lines and equipment in the minimum possible time. The Union general William Tecumseh Sherman was reputed to have threatened to place his chief engineer in the front line of troops unless the timetable for rebuilding the still burning trestle over the Oostanaula River was reduced from four days to two (in the end it took three). In territory often stripped of trees, miracles of improvisation took place. In the latter stages of the war, Southern troops destroyed their own railroad installations to prevent their use by the Union army. Both sides reduced the yards and depot at Atlanta to a devastation of rubble and broken metal. At the end of the war, with buildings, turntables, and passenger and freight cars left in a shattered state through Kentucky, Virginia and Georgia, the Southern railroad companies were in a parlous condition. Even in April 1863, a Joint Committee Report to the Georgia General Assembly stated bluntly that: "The supply of the rolling stock and machinery of our several Rail Roads, and the condition of their road beds, is such that, unless measures are taken to meet their necessities, the days of transportation by rail in the Confederacy are numbered." Emergency action included the lifting of less strategic lines for use in areas where transport was vital, but companies and communities did not give up their services willingly.

CHAPTER 3

THE GREAT EXPANSION WEST

By mid-century, the railroads were a dominant feature in the
American economy, sustaining the ever-greater growth of industry.
To the general public, the most dramatic change wrought by the
railroads is the opening up of the West, with the first
transcontinental lines.

Yale President Arthur T. Hadley, surveying the business aspect in *The American Railway*, published in 1889, noted some effects of the Civil War on the railroads: "Hard as it is to understand," he wrote, looking back only thirty years, but

Above: They also serve who only sit and wait … A crossing flagman sits by his booth, his signal flag by his side.
Left: The celebrated scene at Promontory, Utah, where the first transcontinental line was completed on May 10, 1869. Union Pacific and Central Pacific exchange greetings from west and east.

into a very different country, "there seems to have been a positive jealousy of interstate traffic. The war did much to remove this by making the different sections of the country feel their common interest and their mutual dependence. It also had more direct effects. It produced special legislature for the Pacific railroads as a measure of military necessity; and this was but the beginning of a renewal of the land-grant policy, no longer through the medium of the States, but in the Territories, and by the direct action of Congress." Thus military, political, and commercial reasons combined to generate energy and resources for the great push westward. The essential first step was made by Congress with the passing of the Pacific Railroad Act, signed by President Lincoln on July 1, 1862, in the middle of the Civil War.

Though federal interest was vital, and eastern financial interests equally necessary to get such a massive undertaking on its way, the prime movers were in California, whose growers and merchants felt awkwardly cut off from the rest of the country. The Sacramento Valley line assumed a new significance as the terminal leg of the proposed transcontinental railroad. Five men were behind the Central Pacific, formed to build the line eastward from Sacramento: four were businessmen, Collis P. Huntington, Mark

Hopkins, Charles Crocker, and Leland Stanford; the fifth was an engineer, Theodore Judah, the most ardent apostle of the line. Typically, the four businessmen would become multi-millionaires; the engineer, disenchanted with their methods, would drop out. He died in 1863.

Physically it was a heroic task, worthy, as the railroad historian Oliver Jensen suggests, of an epic poem. From the east, beginning at Omaha, Nebraska—in anticipation of a not-yet built link across Iowa to Council Bluffs, and a Missouri bridge—the Union Pacific company began construction across the plains and toward the eastern ramparts of the Rockies. In the west, Charles Crocker had marshaled an army composed largely of Chinese immigrant

4-2-2
Philadelphia & Reading Railroad: 1880

Boiler pressure: 135psi (9.5kg/cm²)		**Cylinders:** 18x24in (457x609mm)	
Driving wheels: 78in (1980mm)		**Grate area:** not known	
Heating surface: 1400sq ft (130m²)		**Tractive effort:** 11,439lb (5187kg)	
Total weight: 63, 949lb (21t)			

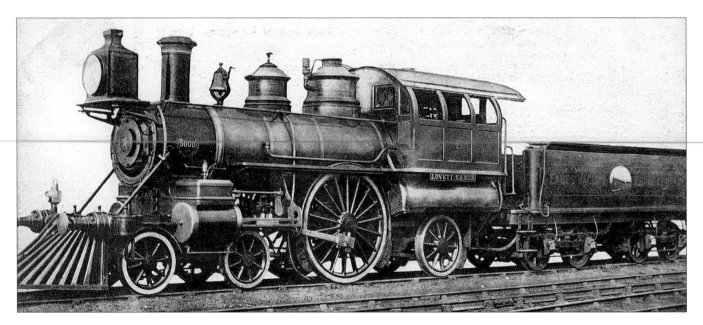

A single set of driving wheels was used in this engine, the 5000th locomotive built at the Baldwin works in Philadelphia. It was intended for lightweight passenger trains to be run at the then high speed of 60mph (96.5km/h) on the Bound Brook line between Philadelphia and New York. A special feature was an auxiliary steam cylinder just in front of the firebox, which bore down on the fulcrum of an equalizing lever joining the driving and trailing axles. The aim was to transfer weight to the drivers when starting, then

Baldwin's 5000th—by 1880 the "single-driver" type was a rarity on North American rails, though still common in Great Britain. The cab is built over the firebox, access steps are on the tender.

redistribute it. The locomotive was later sold on, and is best known as sharing the name of its new owner, Lovett Eames, inventor of a vacuum brake, who sent the engine to England to demonstrate his system. It was broken up at Wood Green, London, in 1883.

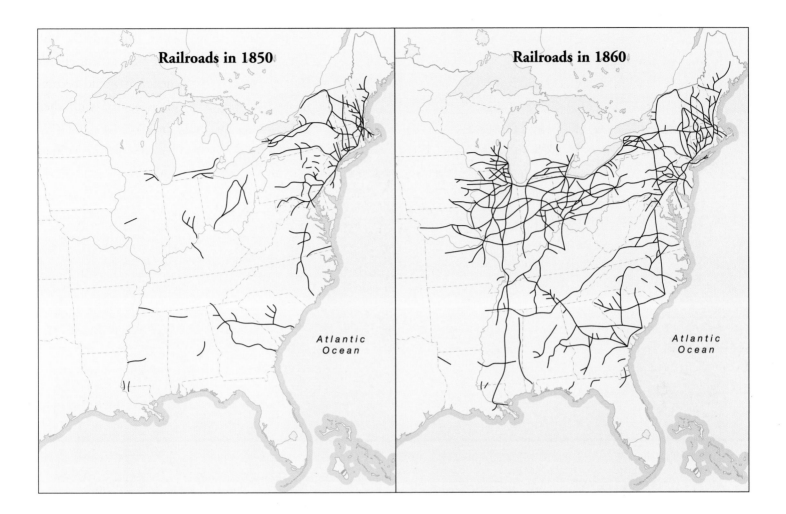

Railroads in 1850

Railroads in 1860

Atlantic
Ocean

Atlantic
Ocean

The maps above show the enormous growth of American railway networks in just one decade, from 1850 to 1860. United States railroad building stressed east-west routes and effectively altered the flow of traffic from a more traditional north-south pattern.

laborers to build the Central Pacific section through the Sierra and into Nevada. The gauge, originally set by Abraham Lincoln at 5 ft/1.52m (the Californian norm), was altered by pressure from the eastern and midwest roads to standard by an Act of Congress in January 1863. No meeting point was set, and the surveyors of both sides, riding and measuring through Utah, far ahead of the construction gangs, ignored one another to plan out hundreds of miles of parallel line. There was an excellent commercial reason for this apparent foolishness. Construction costs were guaranteed by Washington at a handsome rate.

Finally, the first coast-to-coast link was completed on May 10, 1869, at Promontory Summit, Utah, when the engines *Jupiter* of the Central Pacific Railroad and No 119 of the Union Pacific, came gently to a halt on the single track, with

the golden spike between them. Bottles were passed around and toasts were drunk. Photographs were taken, and sometimes subsequently altered to make the occasion more stately and to include one or two ladies. The moment was also commemorated in typical manner by Bret Harte in his "Locomotive Dialogue":

> *What was it the engines said,*
> *Pilots touching, head to head,*
> *Facing on the single track,*
> *Half a world behind each back?*
> *—and ending:*
> *Said the Union: "Don't reflect or*
> *I'll run over some director!"*
> *Said the Central: "I'm pacific,*
> *But when riled I'm quite terrific.*
> *Yet this day we shall not quarrel;*
> *Just to show these folks this moral:*
> *How two engines, in their vision,*
> *Once have met without collision.*

Shay type
1880

A three-truck Shay, from the cylinder side, showing the flexible drive. This is the same model as the preserved engine shown below.

Boiler pressure: 200psi (14kg/cm2)	**Cylinders:** 13x15in (330x381mm)
Driving wheels: 36in (914mm)	**Grate area:** 27.75sq ft (2.6m2)
Heating surface: 905sq ft (84m2)	**Superheater:** 189sq ft (17.5m2)
Tractive effort: 38,200lb (17,324kg)	**Total weight:** 188,000lb (85.28t)

Below: A well-preserved three-cylinder, three-truck Shay photographed in Maryland, in September 2000.

Ephraim Shay designed the first really effective geared locomotive. He sold his first one in 1880 and took out a patent in June 1881. He wanted to make an engine that could draw lumber cars on temporary hillside tracks, applying maximum haulage power to low-speed operation. His solution was to transmit the power from vertically mounted cylinders by means of a piston-driven crankshaft, which in turn operated drive shafts via universal joints, turning the axles of four-wheel trucks on which the engine rode. The first Shay ran on two trucks; the last, built for the Western Maryland Railroad's Chaffee branch in 1945, had three; the biggest, Class D, weighing 150 tons (152.4t), had four. All axles were powered and a Shay could take its load up a 1-in-10 grade relying on its own adhesion. Apart from the drive system, the most distinctive feature was the off-center boiler barrel, placed to left of center to balance the cylinders, both or all three of which were placed on the right-hand side.

In 1882, Shay assigned manufacturing rights to what was to become the great Lima Locomotive Company, and Lima included standard models of two, three, or four trucks in its catalog. Though Shay locomotives went all over the world, the great majority were bought by logging companies in North America, and of the several different types of geared locomotives for forestry work, the Shay was by far the most frequently used.

The specification here is for a three-truck superheated Shay of the 1930s.

The expansive era was often reflected in locomotive decoration. Sparkling UP 4-4-0 No. 23 sports a set of elk horns fixed to the lantern, in this shot at Promontory, Utah, from May 1869.

As the telegraphers passed on the news, there were celebrations across the country. At Sacramento, "thirty Iron Horses gaily bedecked and drawn up into line screeched out a concert of joy." The two engines, standard 4-4-0 types, were modest forerunners of the giants which would wheel huge trains across the mountain and prairie in years to come. Traffic on the newly opened line was at first less than expected, but still, that single track was to form the spinal cord of the world's largest economic and industrial region, and in a figurative sense also served, as a more dramatic symbol than any other to make that wide region a nation and to show its capacity for success in vast enterprises.

Costs and Corruption

However, the great achievement coincided with a fall from grace. The fault lay with the managers of both companies. Access to the supposedly unlimited funds of the federal government might have been a temptation to more saintly persons than Collis P. Huntington of the Central Pacific and Thomas C. Durant of the Union Pacific. Huntington's methods were more subtle, as befitted one who became an expert on Washington lobbying. He was the architect of the

successful campaign to get the railroads' original land grant doubled in extent, in 1863. Durant, George F. Train, Oliver Ames, and the other Union Pacific promoters, whose style of running the company resembled ferrets fighting in a sack, were more blatant money men. They set up a business modeled loosely on the French *Crédit Mobilier*, and with the same name. It was supposed to be the construction company for the railroad. In fact, the Credit Mobilier of America subcontracted the vast bulk of the building work to others, at the lowest possible rates. Its true function was to charge the highest possible rates to the Washington and exploit all other sources of income from its land grants.

The owners of the Credit Mobilier became vastly rich, and almost openly used their funds as bribes and sweeteners to those officials and congressmen who might have asked awkward questions or made difficulties in other ways. A culture of money-grubbing and deceit came to cloud the whole business of railroad construction. In fairness to the

Journey on the Pacific Railroad

In 1884 *The Pacific Tourist*, an illustrated guidebook for westward travelers, described the compelling ride on the Pacific Railroad (the common name for the Union Pacific, Central Pacific, and connecting lines in those times). The publication's evocative account no doubt enticed many new travelers onto this highly scenic route:

"On the second day out from Omaha the traveler is fast ascending the high plains and the summits of the Rocky Mountains. The little villages of prairie dogs interest and amuse everyone. Then come in sight the distant summits of Long's Peak and the Colorado Mountains. Without scarcely asking the cause, the tourist is full of glow and enthusiasm . . . Ah! It is this keen, beautiful, refreshing, oxygenated, invigorating, toning, beautiful, enlivening mountain air which is giving him the glow of nature, and quickening him into greater appreciation of this grand impressive country. The plains themselves are a sight . . . the vastness of wide-extending, uninhabited, lifeless, uplifted solitude. If ever one feels belittled, 'tis on the plains, when each individual seems but a little mite, amid this majesty of loneliness. But the traveler finds with the Pullman car life—amid his enjoyments of reading, playing, conversation, making agreeable acquaintances, and with constant glances from the car window—enough to give him full and happy use of his time . . .

"You soon ascend the Rocky Mountains at Sherman, and view there the vast mountain range, the 'Backbone of the Continent,' and again descend, and thunder amid the cliffs of Echo and Weber Canons [*sic*] . . . It is impossible to tell of the pleasure and joys of the palace [car] ride you will have – five days . . . It will make you so well accustomed to car life, you feel, when you drop upon the wharf of San Francisco, that you had left genuine comfort behind, and even the hotel, with its cosy parlor and cheerful fire, has not its full recompense.

"Palace car life has every day its fresh and novel sights. No railroad has greater variety and contrasts of scenery than the Pacific Railroad. The great plains of Nebraska and Wyoming are no less impressive than the great Humboldt Desert. The rock majesties of Echo and Weber are no more wonderful than the curiosities of the Great Salt Lake and the City Desert. And where could one drop down and finish this tour more grandly and beautifully than from the vast ice-towering summits of the Sierra into the golden grain fields of California, its gardens, groves, and cottage blossoms?"

The completion of the first transcontinental route spurred an intense railroad building boom in the West. This Nevada Northern locomotive is pictured against the spectacular, and challenging, terrain that typifies the westernmost United States.

railroad promoters, it should be noted that their cupidity was not unique. When the Act of Congress authorizing the transcontinental line stipulated that US-made rails must be used, the rail manufacturers promptly raised their prices by 80 percent.

Some honest men, like the Union Pacific's first engineer Peter Dey, from whom the chicanery could not be hidden, simply got out. Others remained and got on with the job. General Grenville Dodge, a long-time advocate of a Pacific railroad, was seconded from the US Army as engineer to replace Dey, and completed the task with military efficiency. An era was opening of unparalleled economic and industrial expansion, with the population rising dramatically through immigration and a soaring birth rate, and with a sense of unlimited opportunity for those

The curved steel truss viaduct at Georgetown, Colorado. Here the Union Pacific loops back to cross over its own track, seen at lower left, as it gains height for the climb through the mountains.

prepared to seize the initiative. New schemes and financial devices could be introduced and peddled to a public which was both gullible and excitable, and which was being taught to be greedy. Regulation, at federal and state level, ran far behind the pace of innovation. Corruption was rife. No wonder the confidence man came to be regarded as both a typical figure and the arch-villain of the time. Almost everybody else's loss might still be somebody's gain. Railroads were bought up cheap by speculators such as Jay Gould, Cornelius Vanderbilt, and Jim Fisk. Such men, though they became "railroad kings," were not railroad men in the sense of seeking to run a first-class enterprise or providing communities with a worthy service. To them the railroad companies they owned were of significance merely as generators of cash, even if they reveled in their wealth and status and rode the lines in their private, sumptuously decorated "palace-cars." Gould openly boasted that he did not build railroads, but bought them. Some railroads—the Pennsylvania under Thomas Alexander Scott was a prime

New problems need new solutions: three storeys high, the dormitory and supply cars of the transcontinental line's work-force could be moved on behind the ever-advancing head of steel.

example—were well run by men who understood the nature of the railroad business. They were to be the exceptions. Vanderbilt began the railroad era of his career by buying cheap stock in the New York & Harlem Railroad, which had a connection to Albany; it was unprofitable but as soon as he was in charge, he made it pay its way. Before long, he controlled the whole of what was to be the New York Central system and was involved in constant rivalry and financial skirmishing with his even less scrupulous rivals Daniel Drew, Fisk, and Gould, who controlled the Erie Railroad. Vanderbilt did his utmost to buy the Erie, but the "Erie Ring," resorting to openly criminal tactics, absorbed his millions and printed yet more stock certificates. Each side "owned" judges on its payroll. Fisk and Gould, aware that there is no honor among thieves, betrayed Drew and left him penniless. Gould's empire extended across the country, taking in at various times the Wabash & Missouri around Chicago and the Union Pacific, as well as the Western Union Telegraph Company. His ambitions and Fisk's went beyond railroads. In September 1869 they attempted to corner the American gold market but succeeded only in bringing on a national financial crisis. Fisk was shot dead by a rival for his actress lover in January

1872; Gould was finally pushed out of the Erie in that year, only to team up with the like-minded Russell Sage who was at the head of the Union Pacific. He died, a millionaire many times over, in 1892, by which time he seemed a relic of a bygone age. Gould's great rival Vanderbilt, who died in 1877, was more successful in retaining control of his many companies and in creating a dynasty. His son William was an efficient and less ruthless extender of the family's already colossal fortunes. A further major scandal broke in 1872 with the exposure of the Credit Mobilier's doings. On all sides, respectable figures ran for cover. But the railroads had lost their reputation as a good thing and were rewarded with public mistrust, which look several decades to dissipate.

A further blow hit the reputation of railroad developers with the collapse of the Jay Cooke and Company in 1873. Cooke had taken over the promotion and construction of the Northern Pacific Railroad, selling stock and bonds in the United States and Europe. When war broke out between France and Germany in 1870, his European finances were disrupted, and the ever-growing building costs far exceeded what was raised in bonds. The firm went bankrupt; the Northern Pacific's dreams of reaching Oregon were stalled at Bismarck on the Missouri River. A financial panic ensued, which drained the value of all railroad stocks and caused the worst business and money crisis the country had yet experienced.

Shares and Bonds

Shareholders, theoretically the ultimate owners of the companies, hardly ever had their interests put first. The typical procedure of railroad management was to first issue shares, and then to issue bonds. These were sometimes mortgage bonds, against the value of property, buildings, and rolling stock, or simply loan bonds sold at a specific rate of interest. Whatever kind they were, the interest on bonds

Forney Tank Locomotive 0-4-4T

Manhattan Railway: 1885

Boiler pressure: 120psi (8.4kg/cm²)		**Cylinders:** 12x18in (304.5x456.8mm)	
Driving wheels: 51in (1294mm)		**Grate area:** 9sq ft (97m2)	
Heating surface: 565.2sq ft (52.5m²)		**Tractive effort:** 5180lb (2350kg)	
Total weight: 41,440lb (18.8t)			

A "Manhattan Forney," with its slim chimney, closed-in cab, Belpaire firebox, and small bunker, typical of the first "elevated" engines. Bells and cow-catchers were not needed.

Matthias Forney, who was both a technical journalist and a practicing mechanic, was one of the few American advocates of the tank engine. In 1866 he took out a patent on a tank locomotive, arguing that the concentration of weight would improve traction. But while tank engines were widely used elsewhere, they found little favor on American railroads, chiefly because of their heavy axle-load and restricted water capacity. Few customers appeared for the Forney type until, in 1878, the New York Elevated Railroad took it up. The "El" had opened in 1868 as one of the first inner-city rapid-transit lines, going overhead while London went underground. The iron-framed trestles could not support heavy locomotives, and the line's first tiny engines lacked power to pull long trains. The Forney type served the system well until electrification was completed in 1903, by which time the New York system had over 300 of them. Many were sold on to other lines.

The first elevated Forney weighed just under 15 tons (15.25t), and this gradually crept up to around 24 tons (24.4t) in later engines. Carried on four axles, this did not overstress the track

Built by Vulcan in 1913 for the 2ft (609mm) gauge Monson Railroad, this Forney was photographed at the Edaville Family Fun Park Railroad in Massachusetts.

supports. Built for stop-start work, and painted bright red, these were among the first American engines to have brakes, using the Lovett Eames vacuum system. They were also, in John H. White's words, "put in diapers" in order to minimize ash, oil, and water falling through the trackwork; for a similar reason, they burned only the best hard steam coal.

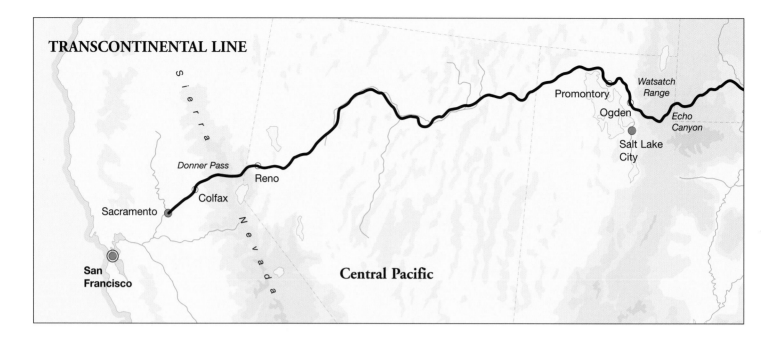

TRANSCONTINENTAL LINE

The first transcontinental line was a joint effort by two great railroads. The Central Pacific started in Sacramento, California, and worked eastward over the Sierras, while the Union Pacific began in Omaha, Nebraska, and built west across the plains.

had to be paid before the company could declare a dividend. After operating expenses, payments to the directors, and payment of interest to bondholders—these usually included the directors, who had issued bonds to themselves at extremely favorable prices—the companies very often paid no dividend at all. Shares in a railroad bought up by the Fisk or Gould interests were very soon effectively worthless. In addition, though the bonds were supposedly issued to add to the company's capital reserves, or to pay for equipment, much of the income received from their sale simply vanished into the private fortunes of the directors. Control of the company was ensured by the process of issuing "watered stock"—stock certificates sold at a price below their face value. The effect of this was to further reduce the value of individual shares and to turn certain favored persons into majority shareholders.

Fast Freight

Another typical development was that of the "fast freight" companies from the mid-1850s. Taking advantage of the expanding rail network linking the midwest agricultural producing areas to the eastern consuming areas, these companies built their own box-cars and offered a through rate of carriage from loading point to destination, without

the expensive and time-consuming trans-shipping from company to company which was still the rule. The fast freight companies also offered highly advantageous rates. This was possible not merely through cost-saving but because railroad directors and officials were involved with these companies, and ensured that the fast freighters in turn got excellent prices from the actual load-hauling railroads. Many railroads lived on the verge of bankruptcy, or were operated by receivers. The little man at the bottom of the financial heap saw the dividend of his railroad shares drop or disappear; the big investor with funds in fast freight saw his profits rise.

But fast freight helped to show the potential of bulk shipping across several railroad systems as the way forward. This resulted in cooperative arrangements between the railroad companies, pioneered by the "Red Line" scheme of 1866, in which a Chicago merchant could consign a load through to Boston or New York without trans-shipping. By

Opposite: At West Sixty-Fifth Street, New York, the harbor-side freight yards of the New York Central & Hudson River Railroad stretch into the distance. On the right are a water tower and locomotive roundhouse. The buildings have a transient air; nothing was static here for very long.

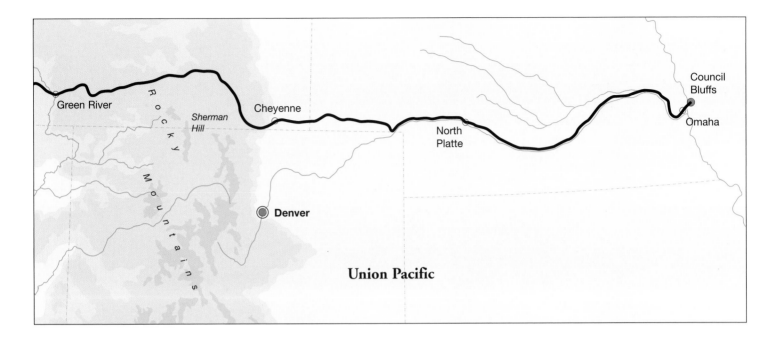

the end of the 1870s, there were Blue, Green, and White Lines, among others, and fast freight systems of one kind or another were responsible for almost all long-range freight traffic. This traffic had grown to an enormous extent, partly because the railroads gradually took over almost all the internal waterborne trade, partly through the hyper-expansion of the economy. Construction of new freight lines and linking lines went on apace. In 1891 Boston was the focus of 31 fast freight services, all battling for a share of the grain trade to the port. In Illinois, Missouri, and Iowa fast freight agents, wheeling and dealing, sought to offer the

best rates while consignors shopped around. Despite the great volume of traffic, the effect again was to harm the profitability of the railroads.

Looking back at these extraordinary events and procedures, it is possible to say that at least the job got done. Thousands of miles of railroad were laid during the 1860s and '70s. But it was an age of world railroad expansion, achieved in most countries without the excesses of the United States. America was unlike any other country, however: not an imperial dictatorship like Russia, not a strongly centralized republic like France. Britain, another country where government largely stood back from railroad development, was far smaller in size and exercised more control on joint stock companies. America's patchwork of independent minded states, new territories, and Indian lands, recently embroiled in a bitter Civil War, was still at a formative stage. At the basis of it, however, there was the Constitution and the rule of law—a law that would ultimately be asserted. Among modern historians of the railroads there is a tendency to play down the importance of the "robber barons," whose personalities may have artificially inflated their contributions, in favor of looking at the work of their underlings—engineers, surveyors,

Heisler Geared Locomotive
1889

Boiler pressure: 160psi (72.5kg/cm²)	**Cylinders:** 9.5x10in (24x25cm)
Driving wheels: 30in (76mm)	**Grate area:** not known
Heating surface: not known	**Tractive effort:** 7200lb (3265kg)
Total weight: 36,000lb (16.33t)	

The Heisler locomotive shared the same general purpose as the Shay type, that of operating lumber trains over steep, twisting, and lightly laid tracks. It too delivered a drive to four-wheel trucks via a crankshaft. But the boiler was centrally mounted in conventional fashion, and the cylinders set in a V formation on each side, balancing each other, and driving the centrally mounted crankshaft. One axle of each truck was driven, the other was linked by an outside connecting rod. Charles Heisler's first locomotive was built in 1891, by the Dunkirk Engineering Company of New York. The design was patented the following year. Regular production was from 1894 at the Stearns Locomotive Company, of Erie, Pennsylvania. This company was liquidated in 1904, and in 1907

Its works code-name "Arctic," the two-truck Heisler could pull 787 tons (800t) on level track. Built for the W.H. Eccles Lumber Company, this is one of numerous preserved examples.

became the Heisler Locomotive Works. They built engines until 1941, when lack of demand forced the closure of the works.

Though speed was hardly a requisite, Heislers were reckoned to be the fastest of the geared locomotives. They were used mostly by American logging and mining companies, and approximately 625 were built. Specifications are for the two-truck smallest model, code-name "Arctic," from the 1908 catalog, which could pull 787 tons (800t) on the level, or 15 tons (15.5t) up a 1-in-10 grade.

administrators, who were instrumental in doing the real work of the railroads. Many real achievements and Herculean tasks were obscured by the antics of the few great exploiters. Even so, in 1889 Arthur T. Hadley had to admit, in *The American Railway*, that undesirable things could still happen: "A

railroad may be built as a blackmailing job. If a company is sound and prosperous, speculators may be tempted to build a parallel road, not with the idea of making it pay, but because they can so damage the business of the old road as to force it to buy them out. They build the road to sell."

At a momentous meeting in Atlanta on February 2, 1886, it was decided by the broad-gauge companies of the south to synchronize a date for a change to standard gauge on all their lines. Work and preparation for this had long been in hand on most of them, for the chosen date was very close, May 31 to June 1 of that same year. In most cases the difference was only a matter of three inches, but a vast coordinated program of stock conversion or replacement was necessary. The actual job of shifting the outer rails was easy enough on straight track, but more difficult on curves and switches.

The successful conversion demonstrated that the Southern companies had completed the slow recovery from the damage and demoralization of the war and post-bellum years. Here as elsewhere, however, financial manipulation and secret share deals bled out much of the companies' cash resources. Indeed, the dominant Richmond & West Point Terminal Railway and Warehouse Company would be so shaky by 1901 that a reluctant J.P. Morgan had to take it in hand and create the Southern Railroad system from its moribund parts.

However, a valuable contribution to the national system was made when, over two days, some 13,000 miles (20,920km) of track were added to the standard gauge network. In this case, "standard" was 4ft 9in (144cm), the gauge of the Pennsylvania Railroad, which had been the principal interchange line with the South. This perhaps gave some ground for the Pennsy's claim to be "the Standard Railroad of the World," though it also had substantial investment in some of the Southern roads. The half-inch difference remained a source of minor inconvenience, though most cars could run on both the "true" standard of 4ft 8.5in (143cm) and the 4ft 9in (144cm) one.

Gauge Standardization

Progress toward gauge standardization had been steady for some years in both the United States and Canada. Public opinion played a strong part after the "Angola Horror" of 1867. This disaster was caused by the use of a "compromise car," so called because its five-inch tire treads were supposed to run on both the 4ft 9in (144cm) gauge of the Cleveland & Toledo, which owned it, and the 4ft 10in (147cm) of the

---

TRAVELERS' TALES
No Time Like Train Time

One of the railroads' contributions to modern life was the introduction of standard time zones. Before time zones were established in North America, every community had their own "solar time," which was not ideal for the practical operation of railroads. To minimize confusion among employees, railroads set a common company time, usually based on the solar time at a principal city or at the company headquarters. This was then used as a standard in the dispatching and scheduling of trains.

August Mencken, in his book *The Railroad Passenger Car*, relates an episode from T.S. Hudson's *A Scamper through America*, describing a trip on the Baltimore & Ohio after the railroad had agreed upon its own official timekeeping, but before the introduction of standard national time zones:

"We left Washington for the West in the forenoon, taking parlor-car tickets for Cumberland and sleeper tickets thence to Cincinnati for night traveling. A great source of inconvenience in traveling is what appears to be the foolish arrangement of clocks. An attempt is made by every large place to use solar time, hence trains are made to run as nearly as possible to the time of the sun. In the 40 hours' ride now commenced, we had three times—Washington, Vincennes, and St Louis. It became indispensable to carry with our watches a reconciliation card with little dials showing the hour at a dozen different places when noon at New York."

Lake Shore Railroad. The compromise car, on a Lake Shore express bound for New York, derailed and fell fifty feet from the bridge over Big Sister's Creek, New York. In the ensuing fire from its overturned heating stove, 41 lives were lost. Ironically, the derailment was caused by a "frog," a safety device intended to guide derailed wheels back on the track.

Compromise cars continued in freight haulage use until well into the 1870s, despite being frowned upon by the more cautious railroad managers. In the north, the six-foot (182cm) gauge Erie Railroad was finding its exceptional width an embarrassment by 1863, though its financial travails prevented any action. It was 1878 before the

No 999 4-4-0
New York Central & Hudson River Railroad (NYC&HRR): 1893

Boiler pressure: 190psi (12.6kg/cm²)	**Cylinders:** 19x24in (483x610mm)
Driving wheels: 86in (2184mm)	**Grate area:** 30.7sq ft (2.8m²)
Heating surface: 1927sq ft (179m²)	**Tractive effort:** 16,270lb (7378kg)
Total weight: 204,000lb (92.53t)	

Designed to be a racer, this one-off locomotive ran the eastern leg of the "Empire State Express" between New York and Chicago. Built at the line's own West Albany works, it was a typical American 4-4-0 with bar frames and two simple expansion outside cylinders, except for its unusually large coupled wheels.

These wheels carried it to a claimed world speed record of 112 mph (180km/h) on 10 May 1893, running with a four-car train down a 1-in-350 gradient. On the previous day it had also been timed at a sustained maximum of 103mph (166km/h), but both speeds, timed by the train's conductor, remain unverified. Speed records must be confirmed by an experienced recorder or

With a handsome wood-bodied vestibule car attached, No. 999 of the New York Central &Hudson River Railroad poses for the camera. The "Empire State Express" was an early and trend-setting exercise in combined locomotive-and-train styling.

dynamometer car equipment. It was wonderful publicity for the train and the line, however, and there is no doubt that No. 999 was a very fast locomotive. Its performance in 1893 laid the basis for the celebrated "Twentieth Century Limited" express. No. 999, with some modifications, including standard 78in (1981mm) coupled wheels, is preserved at Chicago.

Railroad installations took up wide expanses of ground. As the network became more heavily used, signaling systems had to be improved, interlocked with switches to guard against human error.

railroad completed laying a third rail, enabling standard-gauge stock to be hauled over its system. In Canada, the broad-gauge Great Western laid a third rail from Windsor, Ontario, to Niagara Falls in 1867, and claimed it could run broad and standard gauge cars in the same train. The Canadian Grand Trunk system finally changed over to standard gauge in 1874.

Time's a Changing

It was at least 1900 before "standard" truly became standard everywhere in North America, except for those lines, usually in mountain and hilly districts, which were built for operational reasons to a narrower gauge and sought no connection to the wider network.

As a by-product of long distance railroads, Americans received a new demarcation of time. Up until then, each community set its own time by the position of the sun. Solar time, as it was known, naturally varied from city to city. In the planning of a railroad journey, this gave the traveler a serious problem. Confusion was inevitable when three different clocks in one station, as at Buffalo, showed three different times. In each state, up to 40 different times might be kept. In theory, and sometimes in practice, it was quite possible for a train to arrive at the next depot at a time earlier than it had left the first. The essential source of timetable and other information for travelers, Appleton's regularly issued *Railway and Steam Navigation Guide*, provided a list of variant times from the New York and Washington standards, to help in journey plans.

One of its editors, William Frederick Allen, came up with the solution of dividing the country into four time zones, within each of which the railroad companies, at least, would work to a common time. This eminently sensible and practical proposal was put into action on November 18, 1883. Since then the United States, generally without knowing it, has lived, worked, and slept by railroad time.

CHAPTER 4

SIZE AND SAFETY

As trains became heavier and travel faster, the issue of safety became more important. But safety was expensive, and railroad managements were often disinclined to invest where there was no lucrative return. Passengers and railroad workers paid the price until government reforms were forced on the railroad companies.

The 1870s and 1880s were years of intensive railroad building, of frenzied speculation, share-dealing, takeovers, reverse takeovers, amalgamations, and alliances among the steadily growing number of railroad companies. Much of this activity was related to financial juggling; railroad

Above: Two engineers pose at the aftermath of a boiler explosion in 1889; the iron casing has been blown to pieces.
Left: A locomotive passes through a woods on a snowy evening— vigilance from the crew was essential in poor weather conditions.

finance remained the most promising route to instant wealth. In the real business of rail transportation, however, solid progress was being made in various ways.

An important development had been made at quite an early stage. Ross Winans, something of a maverick among locomotive engineers, has been credited with building the first bogie passenger car, for the Baltimore & Ohio in the mid-1830s; though the Philadelphia & Columbia was also an early user. The earliest cars had been four-wheel versions of the old stagecoach, adapted to run on rails. Winans's car established the pattern for the future: a long open vehicle with end platforms on to which the doors opened. Articulated four-wheel trucks at each end rode the curved and undulating tracks well and gave a more stable ride than the pitching, yawing progress of the original cars. Bogie cars were standard by 1837, when the ticket agent for the Lancaster & Harrisburg Railroad was advertising "large and splendid eight-wheel cars," though many refinements were still to be made, including heating. At Bordentown, New Jersey, on the Camden & Amboy, enterprising boys sold hot bricks to passengers in wintertime. Soon stoves were introduced, and vegetable oil lamps or candle lanterns gave the cars a dim light from the last years of the 1830s. The Cumberland Valley Railroad was first to introduce cars with

---

TRAVELERS' TALES

A Novice Passenger's Ticket Troubles

Early American railroads were a potpourri of different companies, each operating their own trains. This made things confusing for the novice traveler, especially since some trains used a number of different lines. "Coupon tickets" valid for travel over several different railroads were introduced to simplify passengers' paperwork and save them the inconvenience of having to purchase individual tickets for each line traveled on. However, not everyone was clear on this system, as illustrated by a humorous tale relayed by Horace Porter, Vice-President of the Pullman Palace-Car Company, in an essay published in the late 1880s:

"A United States Senator-elect had come by sea from the Pacific Coast who had never seen a railroad till he reached the Atlantic seaboard. With a curiosity to test the workings of the new means of transportation of which he had heard so much, he bought a coupon ticket and set out for a railway journey. He entered a car, took a seat next to the door, and was just beginning to get the 'hang of the school house' when the conductor (who was then not uniformed) came in, cried: 'Tickets!' and reached out his hand toward the Senator. 'What do you want of me?' said the latter. 'I want your ticket,' answered the conductor. Now it occurred to the Senator that this might be a very neat job on the part of an Eastern ticket-sharp, but it was a little too thin to fool a Pacific Coaster, and he said: 'Don't you think I've got sense enough to know that if I parted with my ticket right at the start I wouldn't have anything to show for my money during the rest of the way? No sir, I'm going to hold on to this till I get to the end of the trip.' The conductor, whose impatience was now rising to fever heat, said: 'I don't want to take your ticket, I only want to look at it.'

"The Senator thought, after some reflection, that he would risk letting the man have a peep at it, anyhow, and held it up before him, keeping it, however, at a safe distance. The conductor, with the customary abruptness, jerked it out of his hand, tore off the first coupon, and was about to return the ticket, when the Pacific Coaster sprang up, threw himself upon his muscle, and delivered a well-directed blow of his fist upon the conductor's right eye, which landed him sprawling on one of the opposite seats. The other passengers were at once on their feet, and rushed up to know the cause of the disturbance. The Senator, still standing with his arms in a pugnacious attitude, said: 'Maybe I've never ridden on a railroad before, but I'm not going to let any sharper get away with me like that.'

"'What's he done?' cried the passengers.

"'Why,' said the Senator, 'I paid 17 dollars and a half for a ticket to take me through to Cincinnati, and before we're five miles out, that fellow slips up and says he wants to see it, and when I get it out, he grabs hold of it and goes to tearing it up right before my eyes.'

"Ample explanations were soon made, and the new passenger was duly initiated into the mysteries of the coupon system."

"Atlantic" No 153

Atlantic Coast Line: 1895

Boiler pressure: 170psi (12kg/cm²)		**Cylinders:** 19x24in (482x609mm)	
Driving wheels: 72in (1827mm)		**Grate area:** 26.25sq ft (2.4m²)	
Heating surface: 2047.2sq ft (190m²)		**Tractive effort:** not known	
Total weight: not known			

In this first "Atlantic," the firebox was about 12in (350mm) deeper than would have been possible without the pony wheels. The effulgence of the boiler barrel was achieved by using highly polished "Russia iron" for the lagging plates.

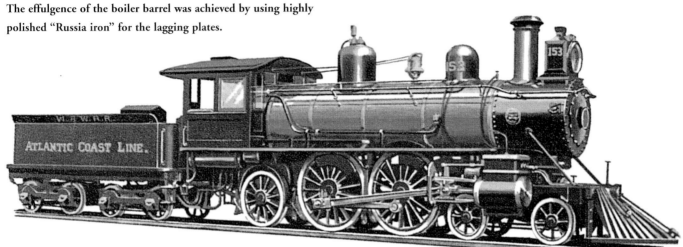

Baldwins built this first "Atlantic," and the 4-4-2 soon became widely used, not only in the United States but in Britain and France, as it answered a general need for more power. The essence of the design was outside cylinders and a large firebox supported on the trailing wheels. This enabled the firebox to be some 12in (304mm) deeper and also wider, though the first "Atlantic" took little advantage of this. Baldwin's historian also noted that the type provided greater comfort and safety for the crew, with the cab behind, instead of on top of, the driving wheels. No 153 was a substantial locomotive, with a boiler of 60in (1523mm) in diameter, of parallel rather than the common wagon-top type. The smokebox was extended forward and provided space for a headlamp mounting in front of the chimney. The cylinders drove the rear pair of coupled wheels, and were operated by slide valves positioned on top. The valve gear was inside, operating the valves by means of rocker shafts.

It was an effective engine, and a similar type was built for the Concord & Montreal Railway in the following year, still with a narrow firebox. Very soon, however, the advantages of the type were being better deployed (see the "Camelback" of 1897).

sleeping bunks in 1836. By 1865 passenger accommodation was considerably improved. Kerosene lamps were becoming standard, fitted in the clerestory or deck-light: the raised central portion of the roof, whose sidelights also allowed for better light and ventilation in daytime. On longer distance trains, cars also had a tiny toilet compartment, waterless, that vented straight onto the track. Wooden bodies were still the norm.

Pullman to the Fore

Though they were comfortable enough, especially in first class, the long distances between cities made overnight travel necessary, and this became a real possibility as company systems extended. George Mortimer Pullman, a cabinet-maker by trade, saw the possibility of the specially fitted sleeper car as early as 1858, when he converted two cars of the Chicago & Alton Railroad, but the Civil War delayed further action. It was in 1864 that his first car, *Pioneer*, appeared. Its upper berths could be folded away, so that, as *The Daily Illinois State Register* noted, "When the car is not used for sleeping purposes … every appearance of a berth or bed is concealed, and in their stead appear the most comfortable of seats." A patent heating and air circulation device replaced the old stoves.

The Pullman car was an immediate success, soon found on all long-distance routes, while the builder's name became

"Camelback" 4-4-2
Philadelphia & Reading Railroad: 1897

Boiler pressure: not known		**Cylinders:** 19x24in (482x609mm)	
Driving wheels: 72in (1827mm)		**Grate area:** 26.25sq ft (2.4m²)	
Heating surface: 2047.2sq ft (190m²)		**Tractive effort:** not known	
Total weight: not known			

The Pennsylvania Railroad was America's leading operator of "Atlantics." Most were rear-cab, but three "Camelbacks" were built, with a grate area of 68 sq ft (6.3m2)—vast for the time.

The wide Wootten firebox, patented by John H. Wootten in 1877 and intended for burning culm (waste anthracite coal from colliery dumps), was ideal for the "Atlantic" type. Culm was much cheaper than normal coal, though it required some care in use, with a "thin fire and a light draft" recommended to prevent the engine from blowing it all out of the stack before it was half-burned. This firebox left no room for the normal front look-out windows of a cab, and consequently the cab was moved, first on top of the firebox, then later further along the boiler. Though this helped the driver's look-out, it was a happy consequence rather than a prime reason.

Baldwins built a 4-4-2 for the Atlantic City Railroad of New Jersey in 1896, just before it was taken over by the Philadelphia & Reading Railroad. It was provided with a massive Wootten firebox, and the driver's cab was placed astride the boiler in the fashion known as "Mother Hubbard" or "Camelback," which was very popular in 1890s America, and used on many different locomotive types from express engines to yard switchers.

The term should not be confused with Ross Winans' "Camel" engines of an earlier generation. A very modern touch on this loco was that the driver and fireman communicated with each other by telephone. In the summer of 1897, this class was put on the "Atlantic City Flyer," then the fastest scheduled service in the world: 56 miles (90km) from Camden to Atlantic City in 50 minutes.

The despatcher's times, proudly shown in Baldwins' official history, show that the engines consistently beat this timing, the best average speed being 71mph (114.5km/h) with six cars behind the tender. The load varied between five and six cars, with around 420 passengers. On the New York Central in 1901, a class of Alco-built "Atlantics" easily beat a three-and-a-half-hour schedule between Albany and Syracuse (147.8 miles/237.8km) with sleeping-car trains loading up to 980 tons (996t).

The Philadelphia & Reading Railroad's "Camelback" was a Vauclain compound, using a system patented by Samuel M. Vauclain, formerly Baldwins' works superintendent, now a partner in the business. He would later become the railroads' Chairman and one of American's great railroad men. Vauclain's sustem had four cylinders, all outside, with the high-pressure cylinders set above the low-pressure ones, and formed in a single casting with the steam chests and half of the smoke box saddle.

Both piston rods drove a single crosshead and connecting road on each side; and a single piston valve actuated both cylinders on each side. It thus obviated the need for internal drive (American engineers had detested crank axles from the very first). A bypass valve allowed live steam to enter the low pressure cylinders on starting.

The tender was mounted on two four-wheel trucks, with a capacity of 9 tons (9.14t) of coal and 5954 gallons (22,538l) of water. Despite the success of the "Atlantics", the compounding system did have its problems, partly caused by the heavy reciprocating masses required to counteract the piston thrust, and partly by difficulty in balancing the work of the high and low pressure cylinders.

Vauclain would continue to develop his ideas on compounding. He was an inventive engineer, with many patents to his name, including those for a flexible locomotive boiler, which was fitted, though not for long, to six locomotives of the Santa Fe in 1910 and 1911.

synonymous with luxury travel. In 1867 the Pullman Palace Car Company was incorporated. It began producing "hotel cars" as well, the first of these appearing on the Great Western Railway (later Grand Trunk) of Canada. Travel, at least for the wealthier, was becoming gracious rather than gruesome. On June 20, 1865, *The Chicago Tribune* observed that one no longer need think of: "… changes of cars by night, and rushes for seats of your party by day, of seats foul with the scrapings of dirty boots, of floors flowing with saliva, of coarse faces and coarse conversation, of seats you cannot recline in, of the ordinary discomforts of a long journey by rail." No wonder Mr Pullman became an extremely rich man.

The worst aspect of all mid-century cars was their vulnerability in collisions and derailments. Wooden-bodied, loose-coupled, built on lightweight frames, usually with coke stoves and oil lamps, they tended to "telescope" in the event of a collision, and could become firetraps. Many dreadful accidents of this type happened, and the news and fear of such events also encouraged a more critical and sometimes hostile public attitude towards the railroads.

Freight

The earliest freight cars were also quite lightweight, with a loading capacity of five tons at most. They were not owned by the railroad, for as an engineer of those times, George Cobaugh, later recalled: "All cars were owned by individual parties. All the companies had nothing but locomotives and would pull any car for anyone that paid a certain amount for each wheel per mile, which was called wheel toll. They would charge more wheel toll for a loaded car than for an empty one." This system did not survive the early years, except that many bulk shippers continued to use their own freight cars. The demands of traffic managers prompted the steady enlargement of freight cars, and on these too the

Four locomotives on snow patrol put power behind the plow in a scene once familiar in midwestern winters. Compacted snow was very hard to shift; the technique was to back away, then charge the drifts at speed.

A breakdown on the line. While the engineer and his mate tackle the problem, passengers offer their advice, or pass the time in their own way. There is no telegraph, and the conductor will have posted flags to warn oncoming trains.

bogie arrangement became standard. Twenty-ton carloads were normal by mid-century.

Boxcars were the typical freight vehicle, their roofs and sliding doors providing security both against weather and theft. Open cars were chiefly used for coal and mineral transport. More specialized freight cars made an early appearance, with ventilated cattle cars, flatbed timber cars, and tank cars. In cities, freight depots occupied wide stretches of land, and the need for interchange of traffic between companies caused the building of multi-tracked switching yards where trains could be broken up and re-assembled. Omaha, Louisville, Cincinnati, and a host of other cities became railroad centers on a vast scale. At terminal points, freight-handling facilities grew with the ever-expanding traffic. As much as possible of the work was mechanized, using cranes, elevators, and other mechanical equipment for loading and unloading.

North American railroads, in their main centers at least, led the world in terms of mechanization and efficient materials handling. The prime reason for this was the sheer bulk of traffic; to shift this constant volume, the most up-to-date methods had to be used. Secondarily, railroad operators knew from the start that mechanization was a good investment: one man operating a grain hopper or coal chute was far cheaper, over a few years, than hundreds of men with shovels, and achieved a vastly greater throughput of work. Strapped for cash as they most usually were, the railroads did not neglect these important ancillary aspects. They were helped in this respect by the fact that, with few

Sleep-Walking Engines

Some steam locomotives were known by depot staff as "night-walkers" because of a habit of moving off by themselves while stabled at night after a day's running. The cause was a buildup of pressure in the cylinders, which, if the reverse gear were not placed fully in neutral position, set the pistons in motion and moved the engine. Locomotives rolled one way into the turntable pit, or the other way and broke through the roundhouse wall. Some were actually chained up to avoid this. The problem occurred most on oil-burning engines with long boilers, and throttles mounted in the dome. It was eventually traced to the uneven contraction, as the boiler cooled, of the throttle linkage, the dry steam pipe, and the boiler shell. The linkage rod and dry pipe shrank more quickly, and had the effect of lifting the throttle valve off its seat, even though the throttle had been shut off in the cab. Pressure then slowly mounted in the cylinders until it was enough to move the locomotive. The problem largely disappeared after 1925, when the throttle mechanism was mounted outside the boiler shell, normally at the front end of the boiler.

exceptions, they did not feel the need to make large investments in plant for building locomotives or cars. Engines and rolling stock were ordered as required, from outside contractors, at keenly negotiated prices.

Safety First?

Early locomotives had no brakes, other than on the tender wheels, whose screw-down brake was merely intended to keep the engine stationary. Early cars had wooden shoe brakes operated by a lever. With the bogie car came cast-iron brake shoes worked by a wheel-and-chain mechanism. This arrangement remained standard for a long time, though it required the employment of numerous brakemen, who operated the brake wheels in response to the "Down brakes!" whistle from the locomotive engineer, or the conductor's orders, or their own knowledge of the route. Their base was the rearmost vehicle, the caboose, but much of their time was spent on the roofs of freight cars, an airy

A twelve-wheeled bogie Pullman sleeping car, with vestibule and skylight roof—the ultimate in traveling luxury in the 1870s. The pipe of the heating stove can be seen at the end of the car.

and unprotected perching place, which was safe enough because the speed of freight trains was usually very slow. As trains became heavier, and began to travel faster, the hand-operated brake grew less effective. Steam brakes were in use on a very few locomotives from the 1850s. Various efforts were made to introduce a continuous braking system throughout passenger trains, without much success. In the 1850s, a number of serious accidents occurred, whose cause was less the speed of the train or trains involved, than their inability to come to a rapid stop.

A contributing factor to some of these accidents was the lack of proper train control. Although the telegraph offered a reliable method of locating and arranging train positions along the line, few companies used it in this way at first. For regular services, a rough timetable was pasted in the locomotive cab, including details of where trains should pass on single-track lines. But long delays often meant that engineers and conductors had to make on-the-spot decisions about carrying on when the anticipated meet did not happen. This could lead to the dreaded "cornfield meet" when two trains collided head-on.

A young engineer, George Westinghouse, developed the

"Santa Fe" Class 900 2-10-2
Atchison Topeka & Santa Fe Railroad: 1903

"Santa Fe" became the type-name for the 2-10-2 locomotive, at least in America. At this time, the tenders of American locomotives had not yet developed into huge vehicles.

In 1902 Baldwins built their 20,000 locomotive, and also their heaviest yet, a 2-10-0 freight class for the Santa Fe. It was the first tandem compound to have the four cylinders mounted outside in pairs, low pressure behind high pressure, each pair sharing a common piston rod. The enlarged 2-10-2 version—the first of its kind—followed in 1903. The drive was to the middle coupled wheel, which was flangeless. This compound system, another brainchild of Samuel Vauclain, proved popular for a time, being used on locomotives in Russia and other countries as well as on other American locomotives. But it was not a lasting solution; like his vertically mounted paired cylinders, any inequalities of steam distribution set up stresses, which affected the riding of the locomotive as well as reducing its efficiency. The powerful double thrust on the connecting rods provided a strong tractive effort, but had its own problems of stress. Seventy-six of the class were built

between 1903 and 1904, all for freight service; the first 40 were coal burners, the rest were oil-fueled. All were later converted to two-cylinder, simple expansion types. With large cylinders, 28x32in (718x820mm), their nominal tractive effort was raised to 74,800lbs (33,922kg). After this time, compounding became rarer on American railroads, except on articulated locomotives. A big boiler and efficient simple-expansion cylinders could develop the necessary tractive power, with fewer operational and maintenance problems.

Boiler pressure: 225psi (15.75kg/cm²)		
Cylinders: hp 19x32in (482x812mm); lp 32x32in (812x812mm)		
Driving wheels: 57in (1461mm)	**Grate area:** 58.5sq ft (5.43m²)	
Heating surface: 4796sq ft (445.4m²)	**Tractive effort:** 62,800lb (28,480kg)	
Total weight: 287,240l (130.2t) (engine only)		

Lamp signals were vital in switching yards. On the right, swung vertically in a short circle across the track, it instructs the engineer to "Move back"; on the left, swung vertically at arm's length, it means, "The train has parted!"

"straight air" brake in 1869. An air reservoir on the engine fed a pipe that ran the length of the train, with flexible connections between the cars. The pipe was linked to air cylinders in each car, and a valve in the cab allowed air under pressure to enter the pipe and cylinders, and apply the brakes. Release of the valve expelled the air and released the brakes.

By 1872, the system was improved to allow for automatic brake application: air pressure kept the brakes in the off position, and any reduction—as when a coupling parted—instantly applied the brakes. A pump on the locomotive supplied the necessary air pressure for the system. Westinghouse's system, first demonstrated on the Pennsylvania Railroad, unquestionably worked, but it was not cheap to install. The railroad companies did not want to know about it. It was

More lamp signals. Swung across the track in the lower arc of a semicircle, it instructs the engineer to stop. Raising and lowering the lamp vertically indicates to the engineer, "All clear to move ahead."

an extra piece of equipment, it drew steam away from its proper purpose of driving the rods, and it required the payment of a royalty to the Westinghouse Company. They were shamefully slow in implementing it, and it was not until Congress passed the Railroad Safety Appliance Act of 1893 that its use was generally accepted. By 1905 virtually all locomotives were fitted with the air brake system.

The same act also provided for the compulsory use of automatic coupling equipment. This too had been available for a long time before its use became general. The link-and-pin couplers in general use caused a steady toll of death and serious injury among switchmen in the railroad yards. They had to dodge between moving cars to hitch or unhitch them. "Carelessness" was often the company reaction to such accidents. Compensation need not be paid if a man had only himself to blame. An automatic coupler was devised by Eli H. Janney in the years after the Civil War. It joined cars firmly and safely, and could be decoupled from the side of the track. Despite its effectiveness, it was rarely used, but it was essentially Janney's device that was finally put into general use by the Master Car Builders' association from 1895. Among its other advantages were that it speeded up yard switching dramatically and required the use of fewer switchmen.

CHAPTER 5

RAILROADS, GOVERNMENT, AND PEOPLE

Who owned the American railroads? What were they for? In the later nineteenth century these simple questions were far from easy to answer. The interests of shareholders, users, and staff often came second to the ambitions of the great railroad tycoons, while the government showed little desire to intervene.

Trackage was being extended at a great rate. In the 1850s, American route mileage rose from 9021 to 30,635 miles (14,517km to 49,300km); in the decade of the Civil War it rose more slowly to 52,914 miles (85,154km); by 1880 it reached 93,296 miles (150,141km); by 1890 it was 163,597

Above: This innovative pedal car enabled track inspection to be carried out at speeds well above walking pace.
Left: The locomotive seems like a denizen of the woods as it ambles through with its train of vintage cars.

miles (263,276km), and by the end of the nineteenth century it stood at 193,346 (311,151km). In 1910, with a total of more than 230,000 miles of track, two-fifths of the world's railroad mileage was in the United States.

The decade between 1880 and 1890 stands out as the peak era of line construction, and in fact the extraordinary scale of railroad building at this time, with its concentration of capital and the spread of competition, was a main cause of the economic depression of 1893-98. Railroads dominated the economy. Writing in 1910, Emory R.

Bo-Bo

Baltimore & Ohio (B&O), Mount Royal Electrics: 1896

In the mid-1890s, Baltimore & Ohio pioneered mainline electrification to pacify opposition to its proposed Baltimore Belt Line, an improved route that involved a long tunnel underneath residential areas. The electrification section was very short and used an unusual form of rigid overhead. The initial electric locomotives were short articulated machines built by General Electric and used gearless motors. These were used to tow steam-powered trains through the tunnels (locomotive and all). After the turn of the twentieth century, the overhead system was scrapped in favor of an electric third rail. By 1912 the original locomotives had been supplanted by more modern ones. Although only a few miles long, railroad's electrification demonstrated the practicality of electrifying heavy railroad operations.

Baltimore & Ohio was the first mainline steam railroad to embrace electrification when, in 1896, it electrified its new Baltimore Belt Line.

Type: Bo-Bo, electric
Power: Not known
Tractive effort: 45,000lbf (200kN)
Max. operating speed: 60mph (96km/h)
Weight: 192,000lb (87t)
Overall length: 27ft 2in (8.268m)
Max. axle load: 48,488lb (22t)
Gauge: 4ft 8.5in (1435mm)

Johnson noted that four years earlier, the par value of the capital stocks and bonds comprising the capitalization, or "securities," of the railroads amounted to $14,570,000,000, more than ten times the capital stock and surplus of all the banks in the country.

Era of the Tycoons

The later nineteenth and early twentieth centuries saw the appearance of a new generation of railroad tycoons. The dominant figure was J.P. Morgan, a banker who gravitated to railroads simply because they were the biggest businesses and so the best means of making a huge fortune even greater. As the nation's super-financier, Morgan was frequently called in to prevent catastrophe after lesser figures had run their companies (if not their own bank balances) hopelessly into the red. Needless to say, he worked his miracles at a price. Banks, steel, and railroads all nourished his fabulous wealth. His first great railroad coup was to organize the secret sale in England of much of William H. Vanderbilt's railroad stock. Vanderbilt remained a big shareholder and company president, but from then on Morgan was the power behind the New York Central. A man of reason more than a builder, Morgan nevertheless spent when necessary to maintain the efficiency and, sometimes, the prestige of his lines. In the slump between

1893 and 1898, when almost two-thirds of American railroad mileage was in the hands of receivers, Morgan lines continued to pay dividends and meet their obligations (as did some others, including the Pennsylvania Railroad). Other prominent figures were more closely identified with individual lines or the hands-on running of companies. Henry Villard schemed and struggled to complete the Northern Pacific to Portland, and hold it under his own control, though he lost it in the dreadful year of 1893, when J.P. Morgan & Company took over.

Another single-minded rail magnate was James J. Hill, who built up the Great Northern Railroad into an important trunk line linking the mid-west with Portland. Without benefit of land grants or subsidies, he showed it

Railroads with substantial routes westward in the 1890s included the Central Pacific (CP), Union Pacific (UP), Southern Pacific (SP), Atchison, Topeka, and Santa Fe (ATSF), Northern Pacific (NP), Great Northern (GN), Denver & Rio Grande (RG), Denver Pacific (DP), Chicago & North Western (C&NW), Chicago, Burlington & Quincy (CB&Q), Kansas Pacific (KP), Texas & Pacific (T&P), and Oregon Railways Navigation Company (OR&N).

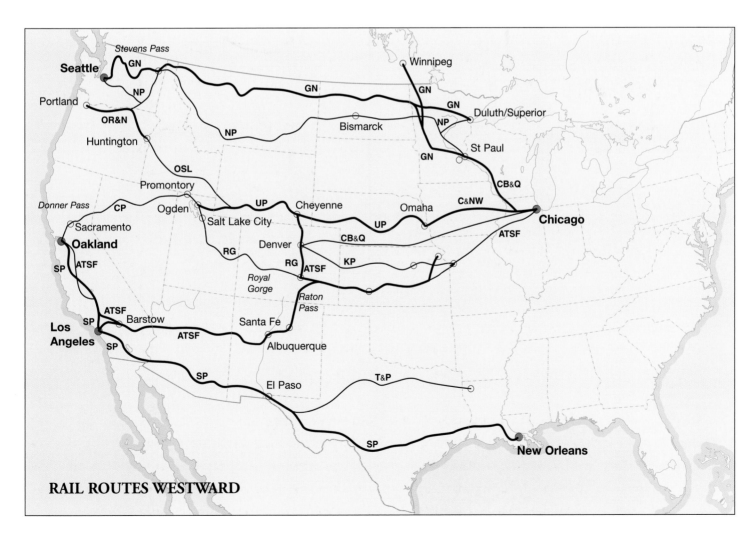

RAIL ROUTES WESTWARD

was possible to build a profitable route across the great spaces of the northwest, if costs were kept under close control.

Of similar mold was his rival Edward H. Harriman, originally involved with the Illinois Central, who from 1893 took the Union Pacific into respectability and profit. He was one of the proponents of "community of interest," the buying of shares in one railroad company by another, not as a financial ramp or to gain complete control (this was by now forbidden by law), but to promote cooperation between neighboring lines. But Harriman had the instincts of an empire-builder, and the Union Pacific's acquisition of a stake in such lines as the Southern Pacific, the Baltimore & Ohio, and the New York Central, had everything to do

with his ambition to create a single and dominant transcontinental system. He achieved this, for a time, between 1906 and his death in 1909, by gaining control of the Baltimore & Ohio. In 1913 the Union Pacific sold its Baltimore & Ohio interests.

New Laws

"Community of interest" was not necessarily a good thing for railroad customers. It enabled companies to agree on fixed rates and non-competing services. In the mid-west, the new farming communities became hostile to the railroads that had brought them into existence. There were good reasons for this: they were a captive market, utterly dependent on the railroads for supplies and the transport of

"Prairie" type 2-6-2
Lake Shore & Michigan Southern Railroad: 1903

Boiler pressure: 200psi (14kg/cm²)	**Cylinders:** 20.5x28in (525.6x718mm)
Driving wheels: 81in (2076mm)	**Grate area:** not known
Heating surface: not known	**Tractive effort:** 25,000lb (11,337kg)
Total weight: 320,000lb (145t)	

With smaller front and larger rear carrying wheels, the "Prairie" combined six-wheel traction with the big firebox of the "Atlantic."

In 1901 Baldwins sold the first "Prairie." This was meant to offer greater power than the 2-6-0, but many lines preferred the 4-4-2 "Atlantic" for passenger trains. The front four-wheel bogie, as opposed to a two-wheel truck, was more secure at high speed, and with its large-diameter driving wheels, it was intended for tightly timed passenger trains of light weight.

But the "Prairie" was versatile and other lines used it for freight. This model was built by Alco for the Lake Shore, and is one of the

most elegant American locomotives of its time. Between 1906 and 1907, the Northern Pacific acquired 150 2-6-2s from the Brooks Works, with 64in (1615mm) drivers. These were lighter than the Lake Shore engines, but their tractive effort was 50 percent greater. Many survived as yard switchers into the 1950s. The "Prairie" also spread to Europe, especially Italy and Eastern Europe. Some were built in "Camelback" versions, including one for the Leigh Valley in 1902.

TRAVELERS' TALES

Miss Woods and the Southern Pacific

In the golden age of American railroading, railroaders who took it upon themselves to get the job done were greatly admired. This was an age of rugged individualism and self-determination. Such is the tale of a woman telegrapher on the Southern Pacific route over Donner Pass, related by Southern Pacific chroniclers Neill C. Wilson and Frank J. Taylor in their popular history *Southern Pacific, the Roaring Story of a Fighting Railroad.*

About 1900, the Southern Pacific's Miss Woods— whose first name seems to have been forgotten—was a telegrapher at the depot in Truckee, California, at the base of the steepest part of the ascent over Donner Summit. This is a place

known for exceptionally heavy snowfall—the stuff of which legends are made. Miss Woods was a tall, healthy, good-looking woman in her early 30s—proud of her job and resourceful. During the winter storms that often plague operations in the High Sierra, the Southern Pacific's Miss Woods all too often found herself cut off from the rest of the railroad. Snow would tear her telegraph lines down, and, during the height of a blizzard, it was impossible to find anyone with the wherewithal to get the lines back up again. This did not

stop Miss Woods from getting the trains over the road.

Donner was the Southern Pacific's link between California and the East, and, in those days, the only practical way east from northern California. Therefore, it was crucial that trains made it over the mountains with minimal delay. Without the aid of Southern Pacific dispatchers, the intrepid Miss Woods would direct the trains as she saw fit. She might hold a heavy westbound freight for the Overland and make an eastbound take the siding for a loaded train of perishable fruit. Back then, the Southern Pacific's Donner had just one mainline track, and Miss Woods knew as well as anyone how to make the most of that single track. Legend has it that, during the height of a storm, she would be out in the snow, wrapped tightly with a shawl around her ears, mittens on her hands, with a bright lantern in her hand, keeping the railroad moving.

Above: The telegraph console at a railroad station was crucial to daily operations. The telegrapher, working from a desk such as this preserved example shows, decoded messages from the dispatcher and passed them to the crews.

their produce. There was nothing to stop the railroads from pushing rates to the maximum, and in a famous phrase, they proceeded to charge "what the traffic will bear." Rates were never published, but the farmers knew full well that they paid far more than the big shipping companies. The farming communities responded by forming cooperatives, known as "granges," which lobbied strongly in the state

legislatures. The "Granger States" enacted legislation to fix freight rates, and backed new lines to open up more territory. "Communism!" shrieked Collis P. Huntington. The railroad companies fought back hard through their own newspapers and political nominees, but in the post-1873 climate, their position was not a strong one. They took their case to the Supreme Court, which ruled against

them. In fact, they might have saved their vocal energy and their fighting funds. Independent economic analysts soon showed that the railroads lost nothing through the Granger laws; and perhaps even did slightly better where rates were controlled. The companies were reacting blindly to what they saw as a threat because it was outside their control. It was not very clever. Unsurprisingly, perhaps, by the 1860s there were business operators who could outsmart the railroad managers. The most notable were Henry Flagler,

Workers lay track in this 1898 railhead scene on the Prescott & Eastern Railroad, Arizona. Across relatively firm and level country, as much as 10 miles (16km) of track could be laid in a day.

who later would himself become the railroad king of Florida, and John D. Rockefeller, of the Southern Improvement Company, later to become Standard Oil. The railroads were charging 35 cents a barrel to ship oil east from Ohio. Flagler negotiated a special rate of 10 cents for

---

TRAVELERS' TALES
Attention: Stolen Station

Many railroad stations in the early years were substantial structures of above-average durability. Others were more diminutive in stature and strength.

In its April 14, 1906 issue, *The Railway and Engineering Review* reported a most unusual story. One assumes that the station in question was a fairly minimal structure, probably little more than a light shelter:

"According to the New York Herald, two station buildings have been stolen from the Central Railroad of New Jersey, at Bayway, N.J. About a year ago, the wooden station building at that place disappeared mysteriously, and no trace of it has ever been found. The company then erected another, but one night a pack of thieves fell upon it and carried it off."

Talk about temporary facilities!

Mallet 0-6-6-0

Baltimore & Ohio Railroad (B&O): 1904

Boiler pressure: 235lb (16.45kg/cm)
Cylinders: hp 20x32in (513x820mm); lp 32x32in (820x820mm)
Driving wheels: 56in (1436mm)   **Grate area:** 72.2sq ft (6.7m²)
Heating surface: 5586sq ft (518.8m²)   **Tractive effort:** 71,500lb (32,426kg)
Total weight: 334,500lb (151.7t) (engine only)

Affectionately known as "Old Maud," and the world's largest in its day, the first American Mallet-type loco portended even mightier things to come. Built by Alco, it served on freight trains in the Western Pennsylvania mountains. A compound type, with low pressure cylinders driving the first, articulated set of wheels, and high pressure cylinders driving the rear, fixed wheels, it satisfied the American railroads' desire to get maximum adhesive grip in banking heavy trains on the long, curving mountain grades. About 80 of this type were built, of which some were converted to

Baltimore & Ohio No. 2400, "Old Maud"—in the early twentieth century, Alco were the specialists in big Mallet locomotives. The type originated in Europe, but soon Alco were exporting "Mallets" to France and other countries.

2-6-6-0. Early American Mallet users generally preferred the 2-6-6-2 configuration, allowing the use of a wide, deep firebox. They were very slow, but at this time sheer slogging power was most important, to move the heaviest possible trains.

his own company, and then imposed what he called the "drawback": the railroads paid Southern Improvement the 25 cents per barrel which they earned on transporting other companies' oil. It was to deal with such practices that in 1887 the Interstate Commerce Commission was established, the initiative coming from Senator Shelby B. Cullom of Illinois.

Again the railroads protested noisily, but as it turned out, the Commission, with limited powers of investigation and enforcement, was easily circumvented. Only from 1903 and even more from 1906, when its powers were increased, was it able to wield some enforcement powers and to fix rates. In classic evasion style, the railroads adopted techniques, including blatant lying, to get round the Commission's efforts to pin them down. If rates were fixed, the railroads

paid "rebates" to favored large customers. Despite solemn denials, rebates continued to be paid up to 1918. In the early years of the twentieth century, politicians, economists, and industrialists were obsessed by the question of how far state control should be extended over the railroads. Arguments over "the Railroad Problem" raged, but a satisfactory compromise was never achieved. Harriman may have considered himself a cut above the likes of Jay Gould or even Vanderbilt, but the painstaking investigations of the Interstate Commerce Commission showed him to be an adept in their black arts. In 1898 he and his associates bought the profitable and well-run Chicago & Alton Railroad for $39,042,200. The capital indebtedness of the company was then $33,951,407. By 1906, through bond issues, this had been increased to $114,610,937. Of that

S-Motor

New York Central: 1904

New York Central was considering the electrification of its exceptionally heavily traveled Park Avenue line in Manhattan, New York City, when a disastrous collision between two packed passenger trains in January 1902 forced the issue. The disaster was caused as a result of a train overrunning a stop signal obscured by dense locomotive smoke in the Park Avenue tunnel and ramming the train ahead of it. Excessive locomotive smoke was the problem and New York passed laws prohibiting the use of steam locomotives in New York City. New York Central responded by pioneering heavy electric railroad traction, a project undertaken in conjunction with the construction of an all-new and greatly expanded terminal, the world famous Grand Central Terminal. To develop practical electrification, New York Central assembled a team of some of the foremost engineers. A prototype electric locomotive was built in 1904 by General Electric at Schenectady, New York. In its original configuration, this locomotive employed a 1-Do-1 wheel arrangement and was known as T-Motor. It drew 660V DC from a third rail. A fleet of similar electric locomotives was built following

New York Central S-2 electric at Mott Haven Yard in the Bronx, New York, in 1961. Later these pioneering electrics were used in switching service.

Type: 1-Do-1 (later modified to 2-Do-2) third-rail passenger electric	
Power: 660V DC at 2200hp (1640kW)	
Tractive effort: 32,000lbf1 (45kN)	
Max. operating speed: 80mph (128km/h)	
Weight: 200,500lb (90.9t)	
Overall length: 37ft (11,278mm)	
Max. axle load: 35,500lb (16t)	
Gauge: 4ft 8.5in (1435mm)	

the success of the prototype. After a derailment in 1907 that killed many passengers, the locomotives were rebuilt with a 2-Do-2 wheel arrangement and reclassed as S-motors. In later years, the S-motors were largely relegated to switching duties. A few served until the early 1980s, and several have been preserved, including the pioneering S-1 electric.

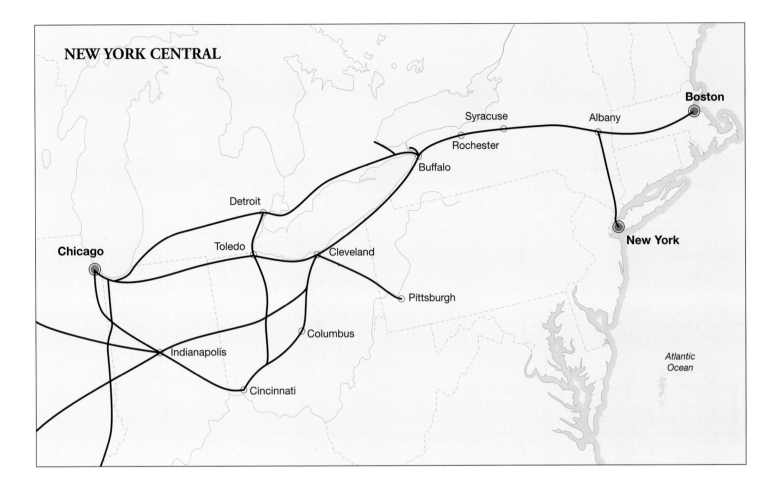

NEW YORK CENTRAL

The New York Central was one of the most important railroad systems on the continent, serving the most populated and industrialized region of America. Affiliated lines included the Boston & Albany, Pittsburgh & Lake Erie, and Michigan Central.

huge sum, around $18,000,000 was spent on improvements and additions to the company's property. The rest, some $62,660,000, simply disappeared.

No wonder the railroads disliked interference of any kind from any quarter. Their view of freedom was the unfettered right to act as they pleased. Efforts on the part of their own employees to form unions were fiercely resisted. In 1877 "community of interest" among the New York Central, Baltimore & Ohio, Pennsylvania, and Erie systems brought about an agreement to raise freight rates, and to cut pay rates to their workers by 10 percent.

Riots and Strikes

Other lines followed the example. As historian Oliver Jensen points out, there was no economic crisis; the companies were paying 10 percent dividends, and it was the year in which William H. Vanderbilt inherited $100,000,000 from his father Cornelius. The workers went on strike, with Pittsburgh the focal point. Riots and battles between striking railroad men and armed militia resulted in 24 deaths and heavy destruction of property. More than 100 locomotives and over 2000 cars were destroyed. With all the power of state and federal governments behind them, the corporations were victorious. The men went back to work, but steadily their "brotherhoods," which were originally mutual aid insurance societies, evolved toward unions, and in 1893 Eugene Debs formed the American Railway Union.

In the stormy year of 1894, the Pullman Company cut its employees' wages by 19 percent, but did not reduce the rental on their company houses. Debs organized a boycott on handling Pullman cars by his members. Strikes erupted on the Chicago railroads, and again troops were sent in. The strikes were broken and Debs was sent to jail. Companies kept and exchanged blacklists of workers considered to be subversive. The railroad unions would in due course become powerful, but their day was yet to come.

CHAPTER 6

THE NORTH AMERICAN LOCOMOTIVE

From the 1850s, a succession of locomotives were built in North America, each of which was styled "the world's biggest." Some were one-offs or failures, but the advent of the "Consolidation" type won over the traditionalists and showed the way forward for powerful freight engines.

More steam locomotives were ordered in 1905 than in any other year in American history: 6300 of them. The locomotive had changed greatly and in many ways from the small machines of the 1840s, when a 4-4-0, with a front

Above: The driving axle of the Pennsylvania Railroad's 149-ton electric locomotive works by a system of rods, cranks, and axles. Left: Ely on the Nevada Northern: once a typical scene throughout North American country railroad depots. Here, a 2-8-0 is ready to leave the yard as the 1910-vintage ten-wheeler clanks by.

four-wheel truck and four coupled driving wheels, was the largest example of its kind. Wood was the basic fuel up to the mid-1860s, and the supply of cordwood for locomotive users was a substantial rural industry in itself: around half a million tons were consumed in fireboxes in 1860.

Though wood was cheap, its calorific value was not as high as that of coke. But coke was very expensive. Engineers were being pushed to develop bigger engines that could pull heavier trainloads. Their progress toward a satisfactory big engine was slow, however. As early as 1838 Isaac Dripps, later Master Mechanic of the Pennsylvania Railroad, had built something called *The Monster* for the Camden & Amboy Railroad.

It had eight wheels, driven by a lever system of extreme complexity, but worked well enough for four larger versions to be built between 1852 and 1854. Ross Winans's "Camels," though powerful in their day, had a number of disadvantages, not least of which was their very slow speed. A few other one-off big engines were built, including an 0-8-0 for the Baltimore & Ohio in 1848, but the problem of efficient heavy load haulage had not yet been resolved.

Fuel Efficiency

In the late 1850s, work was progressing on how to make coal burn better in locomotives and produce less smoke. America had large reserves of coal, both bituminous and anthracite: a ready source of more efficient fuel if the combustion problem could be solved. The solution in the

end turned out to be relatively straightforward, though much patient experiment was needed to establish it. An arch of flame-resistant firebricks was built across the upper area of the firebox, and a deflector plate was attached to the firedoor. These deflected and lengthened the flames from the fire, increased the heat of combustion, improved steam generation, and reduced the production of smoke.

George S. Griggs, Master Mechanic of the Boston & Providence Railroad, patented a brick arch in December 1857, though the idea seems to have been first put into practice by Matthew Baird, a partner in the Baldwin Locomotive Works, on some engines in 1854. Griggs's design did not include a deflector plate, an idea imported from England's Midland Railway, which had been working on the same problem. From 1860 onward, the firebrick arch and deflector plate were incorporated into all fireboxes, and coal became the standard fuel on most lines. Other work on fireboxes was also going on. The wide North American

Gas Electric Motor Cars
Various Railroads
1906

Type: Gas-electric	Power and output: Various
Tractive effort: Various	Max. operating speed: Various
Weight: Various	Overall length: Various
Gauge: Various	

Pennsylvania's East Broad Top was a 3ft (91cm) gauge railway. Its sole gas-electric, M-1, was built in 1926 at the company shops from a kit from the J.G. Brill company. M-1 is preserved on the line, which now operates as a seasonal tourist railway.

Beginning about 1906, American railroads started to acquire self-propelled gas-electric railcars for use on light branch lines and secondary passenger services where steam-powered trains were not cost effective. These gas-electrics, which were commonly known as "Doodlebugs," were built to many different plans by dozens of different manufacturers. In the early days, General Electric was one of the largest producers of gas-electric cars. In the 1920s, the Electro-Motive Corporation established its reputation as the producer of gas-electric cars and ultimately became one of America's foremost diesel-electric builders. Some gas-electrics were powerful enough to pull a trailer or a few freight cars, and were used in mixed train services. By the 1960s, the era of the gas-electric had passed. Some gas-electrics were converted to Sperry rail-defect detection cars.

Above: A Canadian veteran, this 4-4-0, named *Countess of Dufferin* after the Governor General's wife, was shipped up the Red River to Winnipeg in 1876, to become the first locomotive to run in Western Canada.

Below: In the pre-bridge era, the train ferry Solano carries the locomotive and train of the *Overland Limited* across the narrows between Point Costa and Benicia, California, on the route between Sacramento and Oakland.

loading gauge was exploited in a novel design by Ross Winans. Around 1840 he established a factory at Baltimore, next door to the Baltimore & Ohio's Mount Clare workshops. He shared the general preoccupation with developing a coal-burning firebox; in his case, one that could also cope with relatively low grade coal. In 1848 he built the aforementioned Camel, an oddly shaped locomotive with a very wide, backward-sloping firebox at the rear, taking up the full width available. The fireman stood on the tender, the special car carrying fuel, and plied his shovel. The driving cab had to be displaced to a position over and around the boiler.

It was the only type of locomotive that Winans's factory would build. It was also the first coal-burning locomotive to

WORKING ON THE RAILROAD
The Whyte Classification System

North American steam locomotives are identified by the arrangement and number of their wheels, using a system devised by Fredrick M. Whyte and adopted around 1900. Wheels are denoted by their location: leading wheels at the front, followed by driving wheels, and trailing wheels at the rear. Each type of wheel is separated by a dash, and the absence of wheels in a category is indicated by a zero. Each numerical wheel arrangement usually has a common name as well. For example, a Mogul type is a 2-6-0, with two leading wheels, six driving wheels, and no trailing wheels. A Pacific type, or 4-6-2, has four leading wheels, six driving wheels, and two trailing wheels. A few common wheel arrangements, such as the 4-8-4, were assigned more than one name. Normally the 4-8-4 is known as a Northern type, after the Northern Pacific, which was the first to use it. However, some railroads devised their own names; for example, the New York Central called this type the Niagara.

For more complicated types such as tank locomotives, articulateds, and Duplexes, having more than one set of driving wheels and running gear, each set of drivers is counted separately, but the first and last categories are still reserved for leading wheels and trailing wheels respectively. The common Mallet type has two sets of six driving wheels, but no leading or trailing wheels, and thus is designated as an 0-6-6-0. Forney-type tanks, with a rigid frame incorporating both locomotive and tender, are denoted by the letter "T" following the wheel

WHEEL ARRANGEMENT	CLASSIFICATION	WHYTE NAME
<ooOO	4-4-0	American
<oOOo	2-4-2	Columbia
<ooOOo	4-4-2	Atlantic
<oOOO	2-6-0	Mogul
<oOOOo	2-6-2	Prairie
<ooOOO	4-6-0	Ten Wheeler
<ooOOOo	4-6-2	Pacific
<ooOOOoo	4-6-4	Hudson
<oOOOO	2-8-0	Consolidation
<oOOOOo	2-8-2	Mikado
<oOOOOoo	2-8-4	Berkshire
<ooOOOO	4-8-0	Mastodon or Twelve Wheeler
<ooOOOOo	4-8-2	Mountain
<ooOOOOoo	4-8-4	Northern
<oOOOOO	2-10-0	Decapod
<oOOOOOo	2-10-2	Santa Fe
<oOOOOOoo	2-10-4	Texas
<ooOOOOOo	4-10-2	Southern Pacific
<ooOOOOOOo	4-12-2	Union Pacific
<OOO OOO	0-6-6-0	Mallet
<oOOO OOOo	2-6-6-2	Mallet
<oOOO OOOooo	2-6-6-6	Allegheny
<oOOOO OOOOoo	2-8-8-4	Yellowstone
<ooOO OOoo	4-4-4-4	Duplex
<ooOOO OOOoo	4-6-6-4	Challenger
<ooOOOO OOOOoo	4-8-8-4	Big Boy

counts, as in the 2-4-4T. In the side views below, the < represents the front of the locomotive, an "o" represents an axle carrying two nonpowered wheels (used at the front for guiding, or at the back for supporting the firebox), and an "O" is a pair of driving wheels.

be produced in quantity, with a final total of around 300. The original Camel was supplied to the Boston & Maine. After road tests, the railroad turned it down and it was sold to the Philadelphia and Reading Railroad. Its performance, incidentally, appears to have been good, but apart from its appearance, it incorporated a number of idiosyncrasies and novelties unlikely to appeal to a Master Mechanic. Winans found regular customers in the Baltimore & Ohio (in which he was a large shareholder) and Philadelphia & Reading lines, both of which ran slow-speed, heavy coal trains.

The Camel was ill suited to speeds over 15mph (24km/h). In service, the design had its merits. John H.

White, Jr quotes a run recorded around 1859, when the Philadelphia & Reading's 0-8-0 *Susquehanna* took a train of 110 four-wheel coal cars from Pottsville, Pennsylvania to Philadelphia, 95 miles (152km), at 8 mph (12.8km). It used 4.5 tons of coal, costing $2.50 per ton.

The fuel cost, at fewer than 12 cents a mile, compared very well against those of a wood burner, which could run to 25 cents a mile. But by 1862 demand had ceased, and Winans closed his factory. His Camels labored on for a long time; the last of the breed, on the Baltimore & Ohio, went for scrap at the Mount Clare shops in 1898.

Winans's designs were rarely appreciated by locomotive crews: another freight type of his was known as the "Mud-digger." But his Camels could claim to be the ancestors of the most successful wide firebox design of all, John H. Wootten's patent of 1877. He was General Manager (and former Master Mechanic) of the Philadelphia & Reading Railroad. It operated among anthracite mines, where

Class E6 4-4-2
Pennsylvania Railroad (PRR): 1910

Boiler pressure: 205psi (14.4kg/m²) **Cylinders:** 22x26in (558x660mm)
Driving wheels: 80in (2030mm) **Grate area:** 62sq ft (5.8m²)
Heating surface: 2867sq ft (266.3m²) **Tractive effort:** 31,275lb (14,186kg)
Total weight: 231,500lb (105t) (engine only)

The "Atlantic" type was already going into decline in the United States when this class appeared, but the Pennsylvania retained 4-4-2s rather than building a lightweight "Pacific." Eighty-two of class E6 were built between 1910 and 1914, at the Pennsylvania Railroad's Juniata Iron Works, the wide Belpaire firebox making the most of the space above the pony wheels. The prototype had no superheater, but

A Pennsylvania Atlantic in action: a preserved class E7, No. 8063, piloting a D16sb 4-4-0, at Middletown, Pennsylvania, on August 23, 1985. This class antedated the E6 by eight years.

superheaters were fitted to the others. They had a long career in passenger service, the last engine being withdrawn in 1953.

DD1

Pennsylvania Railroad (PRR): 1910

The New York Central S-2 electric at Mott Haven Yard in the Bronx, New York, in 1961. These pioneering electrics were later used in switching service.

Type: 2-Bo-Bo-2, passenger electric	Power: 600V DC from third rail
Output: 2130hp (1587kW)	Tractive effort: 49,400lbf (220kW)
Max. operating speed: 80mph (128km/h)	
Weight: 313,000lb (144t)	Overall length: 64ft 11in (19.787m)
Max. axle load: 50,750lb (23t)	Gauge: 4ft 8.5in (1435mm)

Certainly one of the Pennsylvania Railroad's greatest undertakings was the construction of its New York Pennsylvania Station and tunnels beneath the Hudson and East rivers. To operate its trains underground through these long tunnels, Pennsylvania Railroad chose a 600V DC electrification system and designed a fleet of powerful siderod electrics.

These machines were a semipermanently coupled pair of locomotives based on the 4-4-0 steam locomotive arrangement. In Pennsylvania Railroad parlance, a 4-4-0 was designated as Class D, so these "double D" electrics were designated DD1s and used a 2-Bo-Bo-2 (or, in steam terms, a 4-4-0+0-4-4) wheel arrangement.

Using Westinghouse electrical equipment, Pennsylvania Railroad built 33 DD1 pairs at its famous Juniata Shops in Altoona, Pennsylvania in 1910 and 1911. In later years, a few DD1s were retained for wire train service.

Until the Pennsylvania Railroad had completed its overhead electrification from New York to Washington DC in the 1930s, it used DD1 siderod electrics to haul trains from Pennsylvania Station under the Hudson River to Manhattan Transfer in the New Jersey Meadows, where they were exchanged for steam power.

Wootten observed that there were vast heaps of anthracite waste, known as culm. His wide firebox was designed to burn culm, which it did most effectively, and established the wide, shallow firebox as the best for low grade fuel. His first wide box engines had rear cabs, but the cabs were moved forward to where there was marginally more space. The engines built in this fashion were known as "Camelbacks" or "Mother Hubbards."

They could go very fast, and several thousand were produced up to 1918, mostly as 4-4-2 and 4-6-0 types. The design, like that of the Camels, was confined almost entirely to America, and was not copied anywhere else. The United States was already a large exporter of locomotives, but few other countries had such a generous loading gauge, and the "Mother Hubbard" became the most uniquely American type.

Class H-6-g 4-6-0
Canada Northern Railway
1912

Boiler pressure: 180psi (12.6kg/cm²)	**Cylinders:** 22x26in (558x660mm)
Driving wheels: 63in (1599mm)	**Grate area:** not known
Heating surface: not known	**Superheater:** n/a
Tractive effort: 30,500lb (13,860kg)	**Total weight:** 193,760lb (87.9t)

Unusually for a North American line, the Canada Northern went in for 4-6-0s in a big way, with over 330 in several different classes. The H-6-g numbered 66, all built by the Montreal Locomotive Works during 1912 and 1913 for the opening of the transcontinental through route to Vancouver. The Canada Northern was absorbed into the Canadian National system soon after World War I.

Withdrawal of this class began in 1954, but they survived to the end of the steam era, working on the Canadian National with the

Preserved H-6-g No. 1392, in steam with vintage rolling stock at the Alberta Railway Museum. This would have been a typical scene on Canadian railroads for many years during the steam era.

last one going out of service in 1961. Class H-6-g No 1932 of the Canada Northern, built 1913, is preserved at the Alberta Railway Museum in Edmonton, though with a tender of later date, and is still capable of being steamed.

TRAVELERS' TALES
A Railroad Through the House

The October 30, 1884 issue of *Railway Age* reported the following incident:"At St Louis a few nights ago, a special train on the Missouri Pacific, running between St Louis and Kirkwood, encountered an obstruction in the shape of a house on the track, which it completely demolished, besides damaging the engine . . . It appears that an ingenious house mover, having a contract to move a building [across the Missouri Pacific], consulted the timetables and chose an hour late at night, when he was certain there would be no regular trains to interfere with his work, to cross the railroad tracks. To guard against any possible danger, however, he employed a flagman to stay on guard and flag any train that might happen along. Having done this, he told the occupants of the house to go quietly to bed and he proceeded with his moving. At about 11:20 p.m., when he had just fairly gotten the building on the track, the special came along, and [with] the flagman having deserted his post [the train] dashed into the building with the result above stated. Strange to say, none of the occupants were injured, although the house was a complete wreck."

Although such a bizarre enterprise is certainly not to be encouraged, here is something to remember: when around a railroad line, one should always expect a train in either direction on any track. Had the unfortunate house mover heeded this rule, he may have taken the precaution of contacting the railroad before making his ill-fated decision.

Rapid Growth

The "ten-wheeler," as the 4-6-0 was originally known, did not play a part in the growth process. Although later it would become very numerous, it was little used until late in the century, by which time larger types had already emerged. The first 4-6-0 has been credited to Septimus Norris, whose family works built a ten-wheeler, *Chesapeake*, for the Philadelphia & Reading Railroad in March 1847. Norris tried unsuccessfully to patent this wheel arrangement, but few railroads wanted the type, which was felt to offer little advantage over the 4-4-0. In the United States the locomotive always seemed either too big or too small, though in Canada it later became the standard type of the Canadian Northern Railway, which used several 4-6-0 classes in large numbers.

In 1862 the Erie Railroad catered for its freight engine needs with the new Class 250 2-6-0. At this time the Erie wanted to increase the power on its coal trains, previously pulled by 4-4-0s, and selected the 2-6-0 type as a standard freight locomotive to work on its 6ft (1828mm) gauge line.

The change to an additional coupled axle was prompted by the invention by Levi Bissell of his "safety truck" in 1857. In this, the single front carrying axle was set in a frame which pivoted behind the axle, giving it more freedom to "find the road" and lead the locomotive into tight curves, while the extra coupled axle increased the locomotive's tractive power. Ten were ordered from Danforth, Cooke and Company in 1862. It proved very successful and further orders followed. An anthracite burner, it had a novel grate, formed of iron tubes linking the water spaces at the front and rear of the firebox, an invention of James Millholland of the Philadelphia & Reading Railroad. The 2-6-0 type with swiveling "pony truck" acquired the by-name of "Mogul." It was the success of the Mogul that introduced the first really successful "big" engine.

Opposite, right: The 2-8-2 Mikado type was the most common type of steam locomotive used in North America in the twentieth century. Seen here is the Duluth & Northern Minnesota Railway No. 14, built by Baldwin in 1913.

Consolidation

In 1866 the Lehigh & Mahanoy was a new coal-carrying line with severe gradients, on which even its largest engines, 4-4-0s and 2-6-0s, could only cope with lightweight trains. In 1865 its Master Mechanic, Alexander Mitchell, designed what he called a "super" freight locomotive, with eight coupled wheels, of 4ft (1.2m) diameter, and a front pony truck. Some trouble was found in getting a builder; Matthew Baird of the Baldwin Locomotive Works at first refused. That company much preferred to supply its own designs than to tinker about with someone else's plans. But Mitchell was convinced of the potential of his design, and Baldwin took on the job in April 1866. For months later, the engine was in service. During construction the line

P1 Triplex locomotive 2-8-8-8-2

Erie Railroad: 1914

Boiler pressure: 210psi (14.7kg/cm²)	Cylinders: 36x32in (923x820mm)
Driving wheels: 63in (1615mm)	Grate area: 90sq ft (8.3m²)
Heating surface: 6886sq ft (639.5m²)	Superheater: 1584sq ft (147m²)
Tractive effort: 160,000lb (72,562kg)	Total weight: 864,400lb (392t)

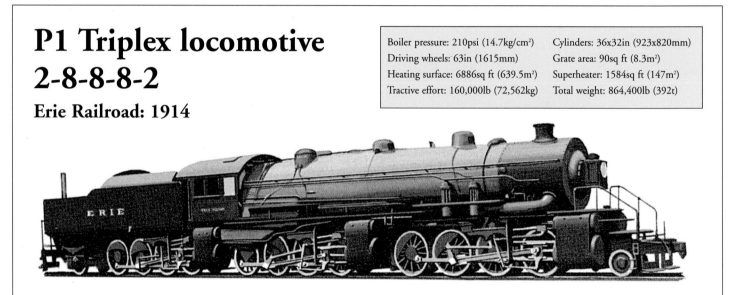

Four of these engines were built by Baldwins, three for the Erie and one for the Virginian Railroad. The latter differed from the Erie engines in having smaller driving wheels and a four-wheel truck supporting the tender. The order was placed in 1913, and designed according to patents granted to George R. Henderson, Consulting Engineer to Baldwins. His aim was to maximize the adhesive weight, and hence the pulling power, of a big road engine. The six cylinders were of identical size and cast from the same pattern. Steam went direct from the boiler to the middle pair, which acted as high-pressure cylinders; they exhausted into the front and rear, low-pressure, cylinders. The front cylinders then exhausted into the stack in order to create a draught for the fire; exhaust from the others passed through a feedwater heater and out through a pipe behind

The theory behind the "triplex" design was sound, but supplying steam from a single boiler to three sets of cylinders was impractical in working conditions.

the tank. Total length was 105ft (32,005mm). The first Erie engine was named Matt H. Shay, in honor of its oldest living engineman. In a test, it hauled a train of 250 loaded cars, weighing 17,912 tons (18,203t) and 1.6 miles (2.5km) long. The Triplexes were intended as pushers on the Gulf Summit grades. Unfortunately, the steam distribution system was inadequate and performance was below expectations. They were dismantled between 1929 and 1933, and the Virginian engine was converted to a 2-8-8-0.

The cab of the "Triplex" was noisy and hot, with a set of cylinders on either side of it. The exhaust vent at the rear of the tender can be also be seen in this photograph.

Originally No. 3 of the Central Pacific Railroad, delivered via Cape Horn on a sailing ship in 1864, this 4-2-2 locomotive was built by Danforth, Cook and Company, of Paterson, New Jersey. Named after one of the Central Pacific's founders, it was renumbered in the 1890s as No. 1 of the Southern Pacific and is still preserved on static display at Sacramento.

merged with the Lehigh Valley Railroad, and the name of the new locomotive, *Consolidation*, was chosen to celebrate the event. The engine cost $19,000 to build, plus $950 war tax, but the railroad was very satisfied with its investment.

The real success of *Consolidation* was in its ability to operate with a heavy load on a sharply curving track at higher speeds than any railroad had dared to attempt before—and could do so with a maximum axle load of up to than 8.4 tons. In all respects this was a locomotive at the leading edge of design. It had greatly improved suspension compared to the early Moguls. The long boiler could make plenty of steam, at a maximum pressure of 120 per square

inch, and its big cylinders delivered the power to the wheels. Further engines of the class were duly ordered. Other companies were at first cautious about purchasing, partly because of its great length and greater cost. But steadily the 2-8-0 won its reputation as a heavy freight hauler. In 1876 it was adopted as the Pennsylvania Railroad's standard freight locomotive, and from then the type grew very rapidly in popularity. Its greater capital cost was soon offset by the work it did.

The Erie Railroad supplemented its Moguls with 2-8-0s, and its managers calculated in 1878 that 55 2-8-0s did the work of a hundred 4-4-0s. The 2-8-0 became the most widely built freight engine in the United States and came to dominate long distance freight services into the twentieth century. However, large as it seemed in 1866, *Consolidation* soon began to look quite small. Its success launched the trend toward ever larger and more powerful steam locomotives, though the real breakthrough here would not come until the next century.

CHAPTER 7

THE CANADIAN
TRANSCONTINENTAL

A combination of commercial, military, and political interests drove
Canadian railway development, in a manner quite different to that
of the United States, though the construction methods and
locomotive design of both countries were closely related, and
cross-border services were established from an early stage.

The St Lawrence & Atlantic Railroad, noted earlier, was Canada's first long-haul route when completed in 1853, running southward to Portland, Maine, to reach a harbor unaffected by the winter freeze-up of the St Lawrence River.

Above: A track gang carries out the daunting task of extending the Grand Trunk Pacific Railway through the Canadian wilderness. Left: In the coastal forests of Vancouver Island a Canadian Pacific diesel-electric crosses a girder truss bridge with a mail and passenger train on the Esquimalt & Nanaimo Railway.

Before it was completed, the Grand Trunk Railway was begun, linking Montreal to Toronto by 1856 and providing a through route to Chicago by 1860. As in the United States, government played a part in railroad development; but in Canada that role was a more strategic one, as well as financial. The development of a rail network in the United States, especially with the completion of the transcontinental route, was watched with some concern by politicians and industrialists to the north. There were fears of Canada's trade passing into American hands, even of

Class T1 "Selkirk" type 2-10-4
Canadian Pacific Railway (CPR): 1929

The origins of the 2-10-4 are with the Texas & Pacific Railway, which had 10 locomotives of this configuration built by the Lima Locomotive Works in 1925. Known as the "Texas" type, it proved an excellent heavy freight engine, and the Texas & Pacific had acquired another 60 by 1929. Like the "Berkshir" type, also built by Lima, it was a "super-power" locomotive. Henry Blaine Bowen, head of motive power at the Canadian Pacific Railway, also opted for 2-10-4s, and offered a $20 prize to staff for the best class name: "Selkirk" was chosen after the range in the Rocky Mountains through which it would operate. Nos. 5900–5919 were built by the Montreal Locomotive Works in 1929; 5920–5929 in 1938; and the final batch, 5930–5935, in 1949: the last steam locomotives built for the railroad. These semi-streamlined two-cylinder simple-expansion engines operated both passenger and freight services through the Rockies between Calgary and Revelstoke, BC. On the long and spectacular climb from Banff, Alberta to Beavermouth, BC, through the twin spiral tunnels of Kicking Horse Pass, they took up to 14-car trains on the transcontinental *Dominio*, of around 1000 tons (1016t), unaided. All services were turned over to diesel haulage by 1954. The last two "Selkirks" built have been preserved.

The Canadian Transcontinental—a "Selkirk" 2-10-4, having negotiated the spiral tunnels, the steep grades, and the bends, emerges into the open air and onto level track.

Boiler pressure: 285psi (20kg/cm²)	**Cylinders:** 25x32in (634x812mm)
Driving wheels: 63in (1599mm)	**Grate area:** 93.5sq ft (8.7m²)
Heating surface: 4886sq ft (453.8m²)	**Superheater:** 2112sq ft (196.1m²)
Tractive effort: 76,905lb (34,877kg)	**Total weight:** 447,000lb (202.7t) (engine only)

CP No. 5935 poses when new in 1949. This locomotive is preserved at the Canadian Railway Museum near Montreal.

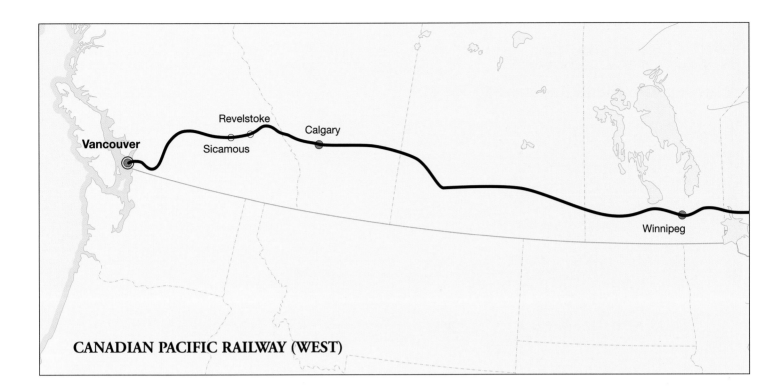

CANADIAN PACIFIC RAILWAY (WEST)

The strategic nature of Canada's first transcontinental line is plain from the closeness to the American border. As in the United States, the effect was to promote the settlement of the prairies and, more gradually, to stimulate east-west trade.

American annexation of British Columbia. These concerns were heightened with the establishment of Confederation in 1867, and a sense of national unity also developed. Four years later, British Columbia agreed to join the Confederation so long as a railroad was built to link the Pacific Coast with the eastern provinces and the national capital at Ottawa.

Scandal

Completion of the line took another 17 years, though 10 of those years were spent in delays and arguments about funding and the best route. In 1873 the Pacific Scandal broke. The accusation that a syndicate run by Sir Hugh Allan had received the contract to build the railroad because of campaign contributions was enough to topple the federal government. Few people believed in the commercial potential of the line, and the early, lean years of the Union Pacific-Central Pacific were not reassuring to

Canadian observers. However, the use of the partly built railroad in conveying troops to put down the North-West Rebellion in early 1885 helped to establish its strategic value. Financed by land grants and government subsidies, the Canadian Pacific Railway was completed in 1885, traversing difficult country north of the Great Lakes,

Leaving a long plume of steam in the frosty air, Canadian National 4-8-4 No. 6104 races down from the uplands with the Vancouver–Montreal "Continental Limited."

CANADIAN NATIONAL R'Y
"CONTINENTAL LIMITED."

No. 9000 2-Do-1
Canadian National Railway (CNR): 1929

In 1928, the newly formed Canadian National Railway made a bold experiment with emerging diesel-electric technology that many consider to be the first successful road diesel. The two-unit machine was the brainchild of Henry W. Thornton and by the Canadian Locomotive Company with Canadian-Westinghouse electrical

Massive in aspect, Canadian National's new twin-unit No. 9000 poses at the Canadian Locomotive Company's works in 1929. Regarded as a test machine, to establish the effectiveness of diesel-electric power, it did not form the basis of a production run.

Type: 2-Do-1, diesel-electric
Power and output: Beardmore diesel producing 1330hp (992kW)
Tractive effort: 50,000lbf (222kN)
Max. operating speed: 75mph (120km/h)
Weight: 374,080lb (170t)
Overall Length: 47ft 1in (1434mm)
Gauge: 4ft 8.5in (1435mm)

components. The two units initially carried the number 9000 and worked together as a single 2-Do-1+1-Do-2 locomotive, producing 2660hp (1984kW). Each unit used a William Beardmore V-12 diesel engine working at 800rpm. The locomotive was designed for freight and passenger service. Later, the two units were split up and one numbered 9001. This later machine survived until 1947. The 9000 was never duplicated, but did prove the capabilities of diesel-electric power.

and passing through Winnipeg, Regina, and Calgary. As with the Central Pacific, Chinese labor was largely responsible for the arduous mountain sections, and it was estimated that nearly one in ten of the 7000 Chinese workers was killed during the work. The last spike was driven by Lord Strathcona, who as Donald A. Smith had joined his fellow Scots-Canadian Jim J. Hill in buying the

bankrupt St Paul & Pacific in 1873. A dynamic American, Sir William Cornelius Van Horne, was in charge of completion and management of the new railroad. In 1889 an eastern arm was extended to St John, New Brunswick, passing through American territory in northern Maine.

With the existence of the transcontinental line, Canada lay open to immigration on a large scale, and development of the Prairie Provinces into a huge grain-growing region, each stimulating the building of branches from the main line to serve growing cities like Edmonton and Saskatoon. The Canadian Pacific's freight rates and levels of service

were already causing protest from customers before the end of the nineteenth century, and its monopoly position did not last long. By 1915 two further trans-Canadian routes had been established. The Grand Trunk Pacific opened up

Class F-2a 4-4-4
Canadian Pacific Railway (CPR)
1936

Boiler pressure: 300psi (21kg/cm²)		**Cylinders:** 17x28in (438x711mm)	
Driving wheels: 80in (2032mm)		**Grate area:** 55.6sq ft (5.2m²)	
Heating surface: 2833sq ft (263m²)		**Superheater:** 1100sq ft (102m²)	
Tractive effort: 26,500lb (12,000kg)		**Total weight:** 461,000lb (209t)	

By the mid-1930s, as road transport grew ever more popular, many railroads developed "super-trains" of one kind or another to protect their traffic. The CPR was well to the fore in this, and introduced four inter-city services in 1936 on its more vulnerable routes. These were Toronto–Detroit, Edmonton–Calgary, and two services between Montreal and Quebec City.

The 4-car trains weighed about 200 tons (203t), lightweight in North American terms, and a "lightweight" locomotive was designed to help run them. 4-4-4 was an unusual wheel formation, for a tender engine at least, though the Philadelphia & Reading in the United States had briefly had some in 1915.

They were built at Montreal Locomotive Works, and had the kind of features normally associated with much larger engines. The two

The Royal York Hotel, a Toronto landmark, rises behind the CPR 4-4-4 No. 2928 of class F-1a standing in the city's Union Station.

simple-expansion cylinders drove the leading coupled axle. The firebox, larger than that of most European large "Pacifics," was fed by a mechanical stoker. All axles ran on roller bearings. To celebrate 50 years of Canadian Pacific transcontinental service, the class was referred to in line publicity as the "Jubilees."

The F-2a probably brought more weight and power to its task than was really needed, and a second batch, classed F-1a, were slightly smaller, with cylinders that drove on the rear coupled axle. Twenty-eight of those were built in 1938; one is preserved. The rest of both classes were scrapped in 1957 and 1958.

Class H1 "Royal Hudson" 4-6-4
Canadian Pacific Railway (CPR): 1937

There was certainly something lionlike about the Canadian Pacific "Hudsons," caused by the styling of the big chimney, whose housing curved manelike back into the boiler top. Its "Royal" tag came not from the king of the beasts, but from No. 2850's having headed the royal train during the visit of King George VI and Queen Elizabeth in 1939. The 4-8-4s were introduced to provide motive power of greater stamina on the long transcontinental run. They were built by the Montreal Locomotive Works to Canadian Pacific's specifications. Combustion chambers were incorporated, extending the firebox at the expense of some boiler length, and mechanical stoking was fitted. The boiler was round-topped, with no dome, but a safety-valve housing set just in front of the firebox.

Sixty-five were built in all, between 1937 and 1945, and a number of modifications produced sub-classes of H1. These included power reversers. Twenty engines had boosters fitted, driving the rear set of trailing wheels, which were larger than the front pair. The last five, built to operate in British Columbia, were oil-fired; and a number of others based in the prairie provinces were later converted to oil burning. The "Royal Hudsons" worked on express duties into the mid-1950s, when the class began to be scrapped. By 1965 all had left the scene, but five have been preserved, of which two remain in operating condition.

In mountain country, preserved "Royal Hudson" No. 2860 takes the "Columbia" train up-grade. Each summer a "Hudson" runs excursions between North Vancouver and Squamish, BC.

Boiler pressure: 275psi (19.3kg/cm²)	**Cylinders:** 22x30in (559x762mm)
Driving wheels: 75in (1905mm)	**Grate area:** 81sq ft (7.5m²)
Heating surface: 3791sq ft (352m²)	**Superheater:** 1542sq ft (143m²)
Tractive effort: 45,300lb (20,548kg)	**Total weight:** 659,000lb (299t)

"Royal Hudson" No. 2858 on static display at the Canadian Railway Museum outside Montreal.

the north of British Columbia, with a terminal at Prince Rupert; and the Canadian Northern provided a second route to the port of Vancouver, and hence access to the trade of the Pacific rim.

Three lines in competition were more than the traffic could sustain, however. In 1918 the Canadian National Railway was formed when the federal government took over the Canadian Northern. The Grand Trunk followed into national ownership in 1923.

Federal Dominance

From 1923 there were two major networks, the privately owned Canadian Pacific and the publicly owned Canadian National, with only a handful of smaller independent lines. It was a very different position to the multiplicity of railroads in the United States, but the two countries were comparable only in physical size and natural resources. Canada's population and economy were much smaller, and the co-existence of public and private rail networks was

Class U1-f 4-8-2
Canadian National Railways (CNR)
1944

Boiler pressure: 260psi (18.3kg/cm²)	**Cylinders:** 24x30in (610x762mm)
Driving wheels: 73in (1854mm)	**Grate area:** 70.2sq ft (6.6m²)
Heating surface: 3584sq ft (333m²)	**Superheater:** 1570sq ft (146m²)
Tractive effort: 52,500lb (23,814kg)	**Total weight:** 638,000lb (290t)

U1 was the Canadian National Railway's designation for "Mountain" 4-8-2s, a design it had used since 1923. The "f" was the ultimate model, 20 in number, built at the Montreal Locomotive Works. They had one-piece cast steel frames, Boxpok-type balanced coupled wheels, and a combined injector and feed water heater of novel design mounted under the running plate. All were given Vanderbilt tenders, mounted on two six-wheel bogies. They perated

Maintained by the Rocky Mountain Railway Society as a static exhibition piece, and with the the Rockies as a background, Canadian National's "Mountain" class U1-F No. 6015 stands fenced off from the tracks at Stettler, Alberta.

fast passenger trains between Toronto and Montreal, a route which competed with the Canadian Pacific line. Six are preserved.

A Canadian National "Pacific" No. 5281 wheels the New York-Montreal *Ambassador* day express over the Central of Vermont's viaduct at West Hartford, Vermont, on July 22, 1956.

politically acceptable. The situation lasted until the privatization of the Canadian National Railway in 1995; and the two companies still remain. Both have substantial involvement in the United States. The pioneer Delaware & Hudson has been part of the Canadian Pacific empire since its bankruptcy in 1991. A number of smaller lines have been sold off, including the pioneer St Lawrence &

Atlantic, acquired from the Canadian National Railway by Emons Transportation Group in 1989.

The growth of the network led to the American Locomotive Company setting up a Canadian subsidiary, Montreal Locomotive Works, in 1904, which overtook the Canadian Locomotive Company to become the country's biggest builder. In that year Canadian Pacific also set up its own Angus workshops, where locomotives were built as well as repaired. Locomotive design and construction in Canada was very much on standard North American patterns, as similar operating conditions obtained.

The Canadian Northern and Canadian National made much greater use of the 4-6-0 type than American lines;

TRAVELERS' TALES

The Thrill of the Sleeper

The Grand Truck Railway inaugurated service between Montreal and Toronto in October of 1856. The following spring it debuted an overnight sleeper service between the two cities. Although such trains would become commonplace in the next century, sleeping cars were state-of-the-art at the time and something of a novelty. *The Montreal Leader* wrote glowingly: "Perhaps in no respect had science achieved results conferring more comfort on the traveler than are to be found on the night cars of the Grand Trunk Railway. Literally we are embodying the dreams of youth, when we read of the travels of Sinbad and of the Flying Horse. Who 20 years ago could have thought it possible that a party of Gentlemen would enter a comfortable saloon and after an hour's chat and a well-served supper each would take a rest upon a lounge and find himself next morning before breakfast time 300 or 400 miles from whence he started, with untired energy and fit for exertion?"

The enthusiasm for this new mode of travel was positively contagious. Never before had Canadians been treated to such speed and luxury.

indeed, off the transcontinental and heavy mineral haulage routes, this was the most typical Canadian steam locomotive. In the later 1920s, both the Canadian Pacific and Canadian National joined the trend toward larger engines. The Canadian Pacific had its "Selkirk" 2-10-4 of 1929, intended to haul both freight and passenger trains over the mountain sections, and the famous "Hudson" 4-6-4 of 1937.

Between these, in 1936, came the class F 4-4-4 locomotives, built to haul fast 200-ton (203t) trains on the Toronto-Detroit, Edmonton-Calgary, and Montreal-Quebec City routes. Canadian Pacific also experimented

EMD GP7/GP9
Various American and Canadian Railroads: 1949

By the time the Electro-Motive Division introduced a proper road switcher model in 1949, all the other major diesel locomotive builders were offering the type. Until introduction of the GP7 (GP standing for "General Purpose"), the Division had focused primarily on the building of small switch engines, F-units for road freight and passenger duties, and its E-units for passenger service.

Prior to the GP7, EMD had dabbled in the road switcher with its

Type: Bo-Bo, diesel-electric
Power and output (based on GP9): EMD 16-567C producing 1750hp (1306kW)
Tractive effort: 44,000lbf (196kN) at 12mph (19.3km/h)
Max. operating speed: 65mph (104km/h)
Weight (based on Burlington Northern GP9): 254,000lb (115t)
Overall length: 56ft 2in (1712mm)
Gauge: 4ft 8.5in (1435mm)

This photograph shows a well-restored EMD GP9 standing on a bridge in Illinois. Although a basic locomotive, the GP9 was so widely used it became a ubiquitous symbol of the American railroad in the 1950s, outselling all of its rivals.

BL2 "Branch Line" locomotive without a great deal of success, and it had also constructed a few hybrid switcher types such as the NW3 and NW5. In 1954 EMD upgraded its locomotive line, introducing a host of small improvements that resulted in substantially better performance and reliability.

Its improved road switcher model was the GP9, which used the 16-567C engine rated at 1750hp (1306kW). This basic locomotive became a ubiquitous symbol of modern American railroading and one of EMD's bestselling locomotive models. More than 4000 were sold to railroads in the United States and Canada.

briefly with a high-pressure boiler 2-10-4. Canadian National's steam locomotive policy centered on large studs of 4-8-2 and 4-8-4 types. In 1929 it pioneered the first effective diesel-electric road engine, the 2-Do-1 No 9000, built by the Canadian Locomotive Company, with the Canadian Westinghouse Company and Beardmore and Company. On both systems, steam survived for a few years longer than on most American railroads, but by 1960 it was gone. Among the last steam powered lines was the Canadian Pacific Chipman-Norton branch in New Brunswick, where two 4-4-0s of 1887 vintage ran over the lightweight tracks and bridges until closure. It might be

WORKING ON THE RAILROAD

Prairie Town

The rapid settlement of the Canadian prairie captured the imagination of F. A. Talbot, who wrote *The Making of a Great Canadian Railway*, chronicling the construction of the Grand Trunk Pacific and published three years before that line reached its western terminus in 1915. He describes in a colorful, almost comical, narrative the rapid coalescence of a town along the railway line: "The growth of a prairie town is a spectacle that cannot be paralleled in any other country. The location of the town is decided definitely, and in a few days the site has been split up by surveyors. Before they have settled down thoroughly to their work, one or two stray pioneers arrive and cast about, possibly assisting the surveyors in menial work … As the surveyors' work approaches completion, other stragglers appear on the scene, and before one can realize the fact, squatters appropriate attractive plots and run up their tents. In a few days a livery stable appears, which within easy distance a frontier hotel springs into existence.

"Two days later the place is overrun by investors and speculators … Within another two days, many a visitor has exchanged his cash for a piece of Canadian freehold, and before the week is out, a store, lumber yard, a variety of timber frame buildings serving as stores, a restaurant, barber's shop, possibly a newspaper, and private dwellings line the main thoroughfare. The complete change from barren, undulating vacant wilderness to a small village of 30 or 50 people has often been wrought in a week …

"If the town happens to be a divisional point, its progress is much more marked, for by the time the railway settles down to do business, the inhabitants may look forward confidently to the company spending something like $30,000 or £6,000 a month in wages among its employees stationed at that point. The elevator appears like magic beside the railway track, and the farmers around the town breathe freely, for here are the facilities for the disposal of their produce on the spot."

In this period postcard view of a cabin in the isolated mountain town of Fraser Lake, British Columbia, a group poses, with surveying equipment visible in the foreground. As the railroads continued to expand in the west, it brought settlement to previously virgin territory.

MLW RS-18

Various Railroads: 1956

On January 11, 1993, a Canadian Pacific RS-18 works at St Martins Junction, north of Montreal. Originally the RS-18 featured a high short-hood.

Alco's Montreal Locomotive Works affiliate produced the RS-18 from 1956 to 1968. In most respects, this model was the same as Alco's RS-11 (specification No. 701), but featured a slightly higher hood style. Rated at 1800hp (1341kW), the RS-18 was comparable to EMD's GP9 road switcher type and used in a variety of services. Canadian Pacific and Canadian National were the primary users of the RS-18 type and they were common on lines in eastern Canada. Canadian Pacific chopped the nose off most of its RS-18s to

improve visibility, and the RS-18 was among the last types of MLW power in service on the railroad, with some locomotives surviving in regular service until the late 1990s.

Type: Bo-Bo, diesel-electric
Power and output: Alco 12-cylinder 251B engine producing 1800hp (1341kW)
Tractive Effort: not known
Max. operating speed: 75mph (120 km/h)
Weight: N/A
Overall length: not known
Gauge: 4ft 8.5in (1435mm)

thought surprising that, with abundant hydroelectric energy available, the Canadian railroads did not embrace electric rather than diesel-electric traction in their modernization programs. The answer lay partly in the great capital cost of installing an electric system. But also, the diesel locomotive, as a self-powered unit, could operate on tracks and sidings, and these would be uneconomic to electrify.

Via Rail Established

During the 1970s, road and air competition were making rail passenger services increasingly uneconomic to maintain. In 1978 the federal government established VIA Rail as a

public corporation to run passenger train services when it became plain that some form of rescue package was essential if they were to continue. Less controversial in the Canadian context than Amtrak in the United States, VIA Rail has provided a heavily subsidized service, but has seen passenger numbers grow significantly.

Transcontinental passenger trains still operate, although most passenger travel by rail is on rapid transit systems in and around the larger cities. In October 2003, the federal transport minister announced the Renaissance II program, a second phase of major investment in passenger transportation, costing $692,500,000 (Cdn) over five years. Since Renaissance I began in 2000, the number of passenger

MLW M-630
Canadian Pacific Railroad (CPR): 1969

Canadian National regional spin-off, Cape Breton & Central Nova Scotia, was among the last lines to operate the M-630s in heavy main-line service. Three MLW M-630s and an RS-18 lead an eastbound freight in 1997.

Type: Co-Co, diesel-electric
Power: Alco 16-cylinder 251E diesel producing 3000hp (2238kW) for traction
Tractive effort: 74,000lbf (329kN) continuous TE
Max. operating speed: 75mph (120km/h)
Weight: 390,000 lbs (177t)
Overall length: 69ft 6in (2118mm)
Gauge: 4ft 8.5in (1435mm)

Alco's Canadian affiliate, Montreal Locomotive Works, continued to build locomotives based largely on its Century-series for several years after Alco ceased American locomotive production. MLW's primary six-motor designs were the M-630 and M-636, models that closely resembled the C-630 and C-636, respectively.

The M-630 was a 3000hp (2238kW) locomotive that used a 16-cylinder Alco 251 diesel. It employed a different style of bogie from that of the C-630 and also had a slightly different hood configuration. Canadian Pacific was the largest buyer of the M-630 type. Fewer than 70 were built for service in North America in the

The size and powerful looks of the M-630 are displayed by No. 724 of the British Columbia Railway, seen here on the fueling road at North Vancouver Depot, on May 29, 1983.

three-year production run that began in 1969. Some of the M-630s were to remain in service on CPR into the late 1990s.

cars, including sleeping cars, has increased by a third, and 21 GE Genesis locomotives were acquired for inter-city trains in late 2001.

Freight, however, overwhelmingly dominates the Canadian railroads today. Three-quarters of all long distance freight is still sent by rail, and Canada is the world leader in the number of rail ton-miles per capita (the United States is a distant second). One of the reasons for this is that new rail lines have been built since the 1950s to facilitate mineral extraction from remote mining areas in the province of Quebec.

In 1998 the railroads' freight revenue amounted to a massive $6,786,685,000 (Cdn); the passenger revenue only acheived to $207,557,000 (Cdn).

GMD GP40-2L
Canadian National Railway (CNR): 1973

The GP40-2L, a model sometimes designated GP40W, was built new for both Canadian National and GO Transit. GO Transit 710 is seen at Eglinton Station in Toronto.

Type: Bo-Bo, diesel-electric
Power: EMD 16-643E3 producing 3000hp (2235kW)
Tractive effort: N/A
Max. operating speed: N/A
Weight: N/A
Overall length: 65ft 8in (2001mm)
Gauge: 4ft 8.5in (1435mm)

In the 1970s, Electro-Motive's Canadian subsidiary, General Motors Diesel, built a variation of the GP40-2 for Canadian National and Toronto's GO Transit that used a full-width nose section and a four-piece windshield. Sources vary, and this model is sometimes described as GP40-2W, GP40-2L or just as a GP40-2 with no suffix to distinguish it from models with the standard cab. Canadian National routinely operated its wide-nose GP40-2s with the conventional cab variety, as well as other diesels. In addition to operating in Canada, some were cleared for international service and were regularly assigned to service on Central Vermont and other American subsidiaries.

CHAPTER 8

THE
UNITED STATES
MAIL

For almost 140 years, the railroads carried the mail, and a whole
system grew up to maintain the postal service. Special vehicles and
equipment were produced, and the mail train was always the fastest
on the line. A corps of dedicated workers, who took pride in their
challenging task, served in the traveling Railroad Post Offices.

From early years, the value of railroads in carrying mail was
recognized. On July 7, 1838 an Act of Congress declared
every American railroad to be a postal route. But the
provision of proper facilities for postal work took longer. By
providing cars in which mail could be sorted for local

**Above: A mail catching device picks up mail on the move.
Left: Smoke and steam make a living black-and-white
composition which conveys much of the railroad locomotive's
enduring appeal. However, pollution was the result.**

destinations as the train went along, Canada took the lead,
though its developments were owed to Great Britain,
pioneer of the postal train. In 1862 the sorting of letters on
American trains began, starting on the Hannibal & St
Joseph line's overland mail train running between the
Missouri towns of St Joseph and Quincy. The service was
gradually extended, particularly under the management of
Colonel George S. Bangs in 1871. In 1874 he was
responsible for the introduction of the first New York-
Chicago mail-only train, in association with the Vanderbilt

99

railroad empire, which built and operated the train. In addition to its crew, the train was staffed by post office employees. The run was accomplished within 24 hours. Letters written in Chicago on Monday afternoon were being read in New York on Wednesday morning: a dramatic speeding up of business deals became possible.

But in his determination to run the finest rail borne postal service in the world, Bangs was frequently frustrated by the Post Office, whose political management was open to pressures from less efficient roads than those which Bangs would have chosen to work with. Congress threw its own spanner in the works in 1876 by reducing the charges

Presidential Special—In 1953, former President Harry S. Truman speaks from the end platform of the Baltimore & Ohio *National Limited* on leaving Washington, DC for his home town, Independence, Missouri.

payable to railroads for carrying mail. The New York Central took off its mail special, as did the Pennsylvania Railroad, which had followed its rival in building specialized sorting cars. In 1877 they were restored, along with extra funding for trunk mail, and the service continued to expand. By 1888 it was calculated that postal clerks traveled a total of 122,031,104 miles (196,384,655km) a year, and the railroads distributed 6,528,772,060 items of standard mail.

A Vital Industry

In this pre-telephone era, with the economy expanding mightily, the mail was a vital thing, and a mail train took priority over every other regular service. Its status was shown by the externally elaborate cars built by the New York Central in the late 1880s, painted white, highly varnished, and decorated with cream tints and gilt.

Class K9 4-6-0

Plant System (Savannah, Florida & Western Railway): 1901

Boiler pressure: 180psi (12.6cm²)	**Cylinders:** 19x28in (487x718mm)
Driving wheels: 72in (1846mm)	**Grate area:** 3sq ft (3m²)
Heating surface: not known	**Tractive effort:** 21,240lb (9633kg)
Total weight: 252,900lb (114.7t)	

This class was built for high-speed passenger work by Alco's Rhode Island Locomotive Works. A speed of 193kph (120mph) was claimed (but not substantiated) for No 111 in 1901.

The Seaboard Line and the Plant System were competing for the US Mail contract from Washington to the West Indies. An eight-car mail train was split between the two lines at Savannah, and the first to reach its own terminus at Jacksonville, Fla, was to get the contract. The Plant System's first engine, No. 107, was delayed by a hot axle

Built by the Schenectady works in 1901, this Chicago & St Paul 4-6-0, No. 307 of class G2, for fast passenger work, is a close cousin of the Plant System's K9. Its big roof-ventilated cab, with protective curtain, is a notable feature.

box. No. 111 took over the train and it ran from Jesup to Jacksonville, 186km (115 miles), averaging 124kph (77mph). No. 111 was broken up in 1942.

Emblazoned with "United States Post Office" and "The Fast Mail Train," and the company names "New York Central" and "Lake Shore," they were also individually named after state governors and cabinet members.

This train, like many others, was fitted with mail catchers, a pouch which could be swung out to pick up or drop mail bags at specific points without requiring the train to stop. Three different postal crews worked between New York and Chicago, changing at Syracuse and Cleveland, and supplemented westbound by a Chicago crew which came on Elkhart, Indiana, specifically to sort mail for Chicago.

Mail bound for destinations further west was transferred at Chicago where the Chicago, Burlington & Quincy, and the Chicago, Milwaukee & St Paul railroads had their own postal trains waiting.

Paying its Way

The railroad companies were paid a basic rate, dependent on the volume of postal traffic, but special funds were available to the Post Office to pay for fast mail trains on lines where the volume was not great enough for the normal service to pay its way. Thus the Jacksonville, Tampa & Key

K4 4-6-2

Pennsylvania Railroad (PRR): 1914

Boiler pressure: 205psi (15kg/cm²)		**Cylinders:** 27x28in (692x718mm)	
Driving wheels: 80in (2051mm)		**Grate area:** 69.9sq ft (6.5m²)	
Heating surface: 4041sq ft (375m²)		**Superheater:** 943sq ft (87.6m²)	
Tractive effort: 44,460lb (20,163kg)		**Total weight:** 309,890lb (140.5t)	

During the mid-30s streamlining vogue, five of the class were streamlined, but the cladding was removed in the early 1940s.

"An engine among engines" wrote A.F. Staufer, author of *Pennsy Power*, and indeed this was one of the largest and most successful classes of "Pacific" among the railroads of the world. The brief given to motive power chief J.T. Wallis was to produce a main passenger engine for the line. The prototype of the design was built in 1914. Based on the E6 "Atlantic" type, it was a compact locomotive even by the American standards of the time, but with a tractive effort rated at 44,460lb (20,166kg) it had ample power packed into it. It was superheated but hand-fired, and a screw reverser was fitted. Line production began in 1917. Only minor changes were made in the first 14 years, testifying to the thoroughness with which the design had been prepared and tested at the Altoona test plant and on the road. They gave excellent main line service through the 1920s and 1930s, lasting on secondary duties into the 1950s. Eventually, 425 K4s were built, all but 74 of them at the the railroad's Juniata shops; the others were built by Baldwins. The decision to order a further 100 in 1927 and 1928 aroused controversy: critics said a more powerful "Hudson" type should have been brought in. By the mid-

1930s, all K4s were fitted with power reversers and automatic stokers: that 70sq ft (6.5m2) grate was a very big one for a fireman to keep supplied on a long run. Over the years, eight tender types were fitted, ranging from type 70-P 75, holding 12.5 tons (12.7t) of coal and 5800gals (21,198l) of water, to 130-P 75 with almost double the capacity.

The K4 could maintain 60–75mph (96–120km/h) with a 1000 ton (1016t) train over level or gently rolling terrain; its top recorded speed of 92mph (148km/h) was achieved in test operations with No 5354. As cars became heavier, they were often used in double-headed formation. In 1917, air conditioning had not figured among the luxuries provided for passengers, but 20 years later, air conditioned cars were helping to maintain the "Limited's" prestige. K4s hauled this great train in four stages between New York and Chicago: Manhattan Transfer to Harrisburg (187 miles/301km); Harrisburg to Pittsburgh (245 miles/394km); Pittsburgh to Crestline (189 miles/304km); Crestline to Chicago (279 miles/ 449km). The last of the class in passenger service, No. 5351, was retired in November 1957. The first of the K4s, No. 1737, was due to be preserved, but its condition was too bad, and by a piece of engineering sleight of hand its plates were transferred to No. 3750.

1400 class 2-8-2

Missouri Pacific Railroad (MoPac): 1923

Boiler pressure: 200psi (14kg/cm²)		**Cylinders:** 27x32in (685x812mm)	
Driving wheels: 63in (1599mm)		**Grate area:** 66.7sq ft (6.2m²)	
Heating surface: 3900sq ft (369.6m²)		**Superheater:** 1051sq ft (97.6m²)	
Tractive effort: 62,950lb (28,548kg)		**Total weight:** 305,115lb (138.4t)	

A standard freight type on the MoPac until the end of steam, with 171 built, it handled virtually every kind of freight service from long-distance fast freight to cattle cars or perishable goods. It was built by Alco, with the drive on the third set of coupled wheels, and a slightly tapered round-top boiler, and about half were fitted with steam boosters to the trailing wheels, adding a tractive effort of 4475lb (2030kg) on starting. Most were coal burners, though some were oil-fired. The bogie tenders had a brakeman's cabin built over the water tank. They survived in large numbers into the 1950s, by which time pick-up freights and yard duties were their main tasks.

In the livery of the Louisville and Nashville Railroad, an associate company of the Missouri Pacific, class 1400 No. 1906 stands at the head of a mixed freight. Sister L&N engine No. 1901 stands on an adjacent road.

West and South Florida railroads, not high volume lines, received $44,000 in 1889 to run a high speed train each day. Passengers of course benefited, though usually they were made to pay extra.

Government regulation of the mail service was close, as befitted an exercise that was costing $51,008,911 in 1907, five-eighths of the total cost of the postal service. Companies were forbidden to leave mail behind; the construction of postal cars was to official specification, and the central passenger terminals had to be used for postal services.

The Post Office specified which trains should carry the mail, and also kept a close watch on speed and reliability. The speed of the mail train became a matter of popular legend. "Legend" it often truly was, as maximum speeds were not recorded. Punctuality was what the Post Office measured, though the timetable was often quite demanding. There was a famous occasion in 1901 involving the Florida lines. Post to and from the United States to the West Indies went by train

"Chicago—Railroad Center of the World," announces this publicity shot of a line-up of Central Illinois steam power on the lakeside tracks. The city area had around 5700 miles (9175km) of railroad track, used by 35 railroad companies.

Expensive Breakfast on the Penn

The old adage goes, "Nothing is finer than dinner in the diner"; however, the price for that dinner was usually higher on board the train than it was in a regular restaurant. The dining car was a convenience and a luxury, not a necessity of travel.

One traveler writing in the May 1904 issue of *Railway and Locomotive Engineering* described her experience on a train of the great Pennsylvania Railroad: "… Being very anxious to see the Horseshoe Curve, I traveled over the Pennsylvania to Chicago, on the finest train they run. The man who fashioned that horseshoe surely whistled the 'Anvil Chorus' when he had finished. It is a wonderful piece of engineering.

"It was very nice to travel on this limited train, but it had its drawbacks; unless limited to time, I would not care to do it again. My 'grumbling' is, however, confined to the meal business and overheated cars. The dining car service is, I believe, operated by the Pullman Company. I want to say most emphatically the 'dollar a meal' system ought to be abolished. Who wants to eat a dollar breakfast? Then comes luncheon and dinner; I am quite willing to pay a dollar for my dinner, but I am not willing to pay a dollar for each of these meals and be glared at by a waiter because, in his eyes, my tip is too small, and be given a finger bowl the water in which has been used by someone else. I am very certain the Pennsylvania Railroad would not tolerate this.

"Many lines for traveling northwest are offered one in Chicago; as I could go by one only, I chose the CB&Q, one of their finest trains—splendidly equipped cars, well lighted, but overheated. On my return I bought my ticket via the Chicago, Milwaukee and St Paul—I am not handing out bouquets, but if I were, I might select a few flowers to give the CB&Q, but the biggest, choicest bunch would be offered the 'St Paul.' It will be pleasant to remember that trip all my life: the roadbed is smooth, the cars are the very finest, the attendants—conductors, porters, waiter and the men in charge of the dining cars—most kindly and attentive. The food is excellent, abundant, and carefully served; the 'tips' it suited me to give were accepted in a nice manner, the men seemed pleased.

"Here I want to say that where railway companies operate their own dining, parlor, and sleeping cars, the service is the best, one's comfort the greatest, the employees act as if they wanted to please their 'road' by doing well by its patrons, and I think the traveling public recognizes this."

Nearly one hundred years later, this rail traveler's observations on quality of service could easily be applied to other modes of transportation offered today—a lesson, it seems, to be learned again and again.

between Washington, DC and Jacksonville, Florida, where it was transferred to ships. In that year, the Plant System (Savannah, Florida & Western Railroad) and the Seaboard Line companies were competing for this US Mail contract. The 4-6-0 Class K9 locomotive of the Plant System was built for high-speed passenger work by Alco's Rhode Island Locomotive Works, and No. 111 was particularly fast.

In March the Post Office intended to award the mail contract to the line which could provide a faster service. To test this, an eight-car mail train was split between the two companies at Savannah, and the first to reach its own terminus at Jacksonville, was to get the contract. The Plant System's first engine, No. 107, was delayed by a hot axle box. No. 111 took over the four-car train and ran from Jesup, Georgia to Jacksonville, 115.9 miles (186.5km), at an average of 77.3mph (124.3km/h), including a reputed but unsubstantiated maximum of 120mph (193 km/h) attained between the Georgian towns of Screven and Satilla. The Plant System won the race and duly obtained the contract.

In 1907 the railroads had 1286 postal cars and a further 3400 passenger cars with separate postal compartments, operating a total of 3224 scheduled service routes, the great majority being combined with passenger services. This general level of service continued into the 1930s, when the reduction of passenger services and the availability of road vehicles began the decline of rail borne mail. But railroad distribution of mail continued on some lines until the end of the 1960s, after when all post went by road and air. The railroads' national parcels distribution system, whose own origins went back to before the days of Wells Fargo and the beginning of American Express, and which became the Railway Express Agency in 1929, carried on in much reduced form until 1975.

Class M1 4-8-2
Pennsylvania Railroad (PRR): 1923

Boiler pressure: 250lb (17.5kg/cm²)		**Cylinders:** 27x30in (685x761mm)	
Driving wheels: 72in (1827mm)		**Grate area:** 66.8sq ft (6.2m²)	
Heating surface: 4087sq ft (379m²)		**Superheater:** 1051sq ft (97.6m²)	
Tractive effort: 64,550lb (29,274kg)		**Total weight:** 560,000lb (254t)	

The drawing shows a locomotive of class M1a, No. 6707, built by Baldwins to PRR specification in 1930. Typical features include the wide saddle-type sandbox, power reversing gear, and the Belpaire firebox.

The first engine of the "Mountain" wheel arrangement was built in 1911 by Alco (at Schenectady, New York, for the Chesapeake & Ohio Railway) to haul passenger trains over its Clifton Forge Division in the Allegheny Mountains. At the time, it was claimed as the most powerful non-articulated engine in the world. The design was recognized as valuable where adhesion and tractive power were needed as well as speed. In 1918, it was one of eight standard types designated by the wartime US Railroad Administration, and many were built for lines with mountain sections. The Pennsylvania Railroad built its first as a test engine, at its Juniata workshops in Altoona, and 200 others of Class M1 followed. Following American practice, it was a two-cylinder simple, with Walschaerts valve gear operating piston valves. The boiler tapered up from 84.5in(2144mm) behind the chimney to 96in (2436mm) and the long Belpaire firebox was supplied by duplex stokers. The running plate was stepped up to accommodate the air compressor equipment. On these locomotives, braking power was as vital as traction, as they negotiated the long descents with trains of 140 coal hopper cars loading up to 4700 tons (4776t).

The 4-8-2 remained popular in the United States and Canada until the end of the 1920s, when most lines took up the 4-8-4, with its even bigger firebox. The M1s were withdrawn in 1950.

CHAPTER 9

POWER
INNOVATIONS AND
WORLD WAR I

Significant design innovations led to yet-bigger locomotives in the
early twentieth century. American involvement in World War I
brought new challenges to the railroad companies. However, a
failure to meet these challenges meant the railroads experienced
their first taste of state control as the federal government took over.

From very early years North American steam locomotive building had followed its own course, producing a series of "world's biggest" or "most powerful" locomotives from the first 4-4-0 on. A vigorous export industry had also

Above: "Punch the ticket, punch with care; Punch in the presence of the passen-jare…" The train conductor had a highly responsible task, as ticket fraud was rife.
Left: Steam sits on the side-track as the conquering diesel-electrics power through on the main line.

developed. But in the early twentieth century, two innovations, both from Europe, would have a profound impact on the American locomotive. The first was the articulated engine, the brainchild of the Swiss-French engineer Anatole Mallet.

Two power units under a single large boiler resulted in an engine of exceptional tractive effort that could also negotiate tight curves. Mallet was also a pioneer of compound expansion, in which the boiler steam was used to maximum effect, first in high-pressure, then in low-

Boxcab Class EF-1

Milwaukee Road: 1914

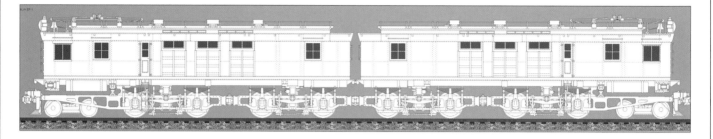

The EF-1 box-cab. Designed for slow haulage of heavy trains up-grade, and slow descents, it employed regenerative braking to draw energy from the wheels.

Milwaukee Road's first electric locomotives were massive EF-1 boxcabs, each consisting of two units semipermanently coupled with a 2-Bo-Bo+Bo-Bo-2 wheel arrangement. Used to haul freight up mountain grades as steep as 2.2 per cent, they featured regenerative braking (which turned traction motors into generators).

Type: 2-Bo-Bo+Bo-Bo-2, freight electric
Power: 3000V DC from overhead wire
Output: 3000hp (2235kW)
Tractive effort: 112,750lbf (501kN)
Max. operating speed: n/a
Weight: 576,000lb (261t)
Max. axle load: 56,250lb (26t)
Overall length: 112ft (34.138m)
Gauge: 4ft 8.5in (1435mm)

Below: Avalanche slopes as well as snowdrifts required the building of snowsheds, like this one on the Southern Pacific's Ogden line, in a 1907 illustration. Their wooden construction presented a different danger—that of fire.

pressure, cylinders. The Baltimore & Ohio was first to operate the Mallet type, in a famous locomotive, the 0-6-6-0 "Old Maud" of 1904, but many others would follow on this and other lines. The second innovation was the superheater, first developed by Wilhelm Schmidt on the Prussian railroads of Germany. This device reheated the steam produced by a boiler, increasing its temperature to between 500° and 750°, dramatically increasing its expansive power. One third as much steam again from every pound of coal was welcome news to railroad operators. From around 1910 virtually every new locomotive was superheated, and many—recently constructed in the building boom of 1902 to 1905—underwent conversion.

Big Business

Locomotive building was a major industry, with Baldwin Locomotive Works being the world's largest plant. In 1900 eight of its smaller competitors merged to form the American Locomotive Company (Alco). Steam was the unchallenged source of motive power, and over 40,000 locomotives ran in the United States; around one to every 48 miles (77km) of track.

In fact, of course, there was a massive concentration of locomotives in and around the major cities and railroad junctions, which by now had vast switching and train-marshaling yards. More than half the locomotive stock was to be found in the northeast.

But steam was not quite universal. In 1894 and 1895 the Baltimore & Ohio railroad had installed an overhead electric power line in its smoke-filled tunnel under the city of Baltimore, and electric locomotives pulled the trains, including their steam locomotives, through it with a much greater degree of safety and comfort for crews and passengers. General Electric was the builder of these engines. The Baltimore & Ohio installation was studied with great interest.

MP54 EMU
Pennsylvania Railroad (PRR): 1914

In 1915 the Pennsylvania Railroad began electrifying its intensive Philadelphia area suburban services using a 11kV AC overhead system. The first route under wire was the famous Main Line from Broad Street to Paoli. To provide service on the electric lines, the

Type: Suburban passenger electric EMU
Power: 11,500V at 25Hz alternating current
Output: 400hp (298 kW) per car
Max. operating speed: 65mph (104km/h) with some cars 80mph (128km/h)
Weight: 130,000lb (59t)—varied among different classes
Overall length: 64ft 6in (19.65m)
Max. axle load: n/a
Gauge: 4ft 8.5in (1435mm)

A three-car set of Pennsylvania MP54s heads towards Newark, New Jersey, on the PRR high line in 1961. This type of electric multiple unit worked PRR rails for more than five decades.

railroad's Altoona shops rebuilt steel P54 passenger cars into MP54 electric multiple units using Westinghouse electrical components. Each car used a single pantograph and one powered bogie with two AC traction motors. The ends of the cars were equipped with running controls and a pair of porthole-style windows, giving the MP54s a characteristic "owl-eye" look. Hundreds of MP54s were built and, after the electrification of the New York–Washington DC route, were a common sight on the railroad's electrified lines.

'Bi-Polar', Type EP-2
Milwaukee Road: 1919

Milwaukee Road's westernmost electrification crossed the Washington Cascades. For passenger traffic, Milwaukee turned to General Electric, and, in 1919, it built five massive three-piece articulated electrics using a 1-Bo-Do-Do-Bo-1 wheel arrangement. These were powered using state-of-the-art gearless two-pole, or "Bi-Polar," motors whereby

Type: 1-Bo-Do-Do-Bo-1 passenger electric
Power: 3000V DC from overhead
Tractive effort: 42,000lbf (187kN) at 27mph (43km/h)
Max. operating speed: 70mph (112km/h)
Weight: 530,000lb (240.4t)
Overall length: 76ft (23.164m)
Max. axle load: 38,500lb (17.5t)
Gauge: 4ft 8.5in (1435mm)

General Electric built five massive Bi-Polar electrics for Milwaukee Road's Pacific electrification. Although the locomotives were withdrawn in the 1950s, one has been preserved for display in St Louis.

the armatures were mounted on the driving axles.

The EP-2 types featured a distinctive exterior design with a center-cab arrangement and rounded hood sections at both ends. These 12-motor machines were extraordinarily powerful for the period, and Milwaukee Road demonstrated this power by staging a well-publicized "tug of war" between a Bi-Polar electric and a pair of steam locomotives—the electric won.

The "Bi-Polars" were withdrawn in the 1950s, and Milwaukee's Washington electrification discontinued in 1972.

The Rise of Electric

Many municipalities were beginning to chafe at the presence of steam locomotives in town and city streets. The New York Central, prompted both by demands from the city council and by a horrific collision in the smoke-filled Park Avenue tunnel in 1902, installed a third-rail electric system in 1904 to serve its new Grand Central Terminal. In 1910 the Pennsylvania Railroad developed its own DD1 side-rod driven electric locomotives to haul long distance trains from Penn Station to Manhattan Transfer, where steam power took over. Electric traction's role was seen by most railroads as exclusively short haul in places where the steam locomotive was at a disadvantage or forbidden by local ordinance.

It was seen as a slow speed form, and the overhead catenary or third rails were expensive to install. More extensive use was pioneered by the Milwaukee Road from 1919 when its long haul route through the Cascade Mountains in Washington State was electrified, using a quintet of triple-unit bipolar motors. They had a long career, into the 1950s, but the venture was not imitated by other mountain lines in North America (the line was converted to diesel in 1973).

World War I and Federal Control

Even before the United States entered World War I in April 1917 (Canada, then part of the British Empire, had been involved from the start), the railroads were busy carrying war supplies. With America now a combatant power, this activity greatly increased, and the pressure on all lines leading to Atlantic ports became intense. But as freight traffic on the eastern seaboard leapt up, so shippers in the

CNJ-1000 Central
Railroad of New Jersey: 1925

By the mid-1920s, a market had developed for diesel-powered switchers in large cities where anti-smoke legislation discouraged the use of steam locomotives. Ingersoll-Rand teamed up with locomotive producers Alco and GE, and built a prototype diesel, which they demonstrated in 1924. Several railroads were interested in the slow-speed, low-output switchers. In 1925 Central Railroad of New Jersey bought the first of these, which was built as a "stock" locomotive at the end of 1924. It was numbered 1000 and assigned to CNJ's isolated waterfront trackage in the Bronx, New York City. After more than 30 years of regular service, CNJ 1000 was retired and preserved at the Baltimore & Ohio Museum in Baltimore, Maryland.

Type: Bo-Bo, diesel-electric
Power and output: Ingersoll-Rand 6-cyl engine producing 300 hp/229 kW
Tractive effort: 30,000lbf1 (33kN) starting TE
Max. operating speed: N/A
Weight: 120,000lb (60t)
Overall length: 32ft 8in (9.95m)
Gauge: 4ft. 8.5in (1435mm)

Compared with modern diesel engines, the prime mover in CNJ 1000 was heavy and ponderous. Later locomotives used compact high-output diesels originally designed for marine applications.

"Berkshire" 2-8-4

Illinois Central Railroad: 1925

Boiler pressure: 240psi (16.8kg/cm²)		**Cylinders:** 28x30in (710x761mm)	
Driving wheels: 63in (1599mm)		**Grate area:** 106sq ft (9.84m²)	
Heating surface: 5157sq ft (479m²)		**Superheater:** 2111sq ft (196m²)	
Tractive effort: 69,400lb (31,473kg)		**Total weight:** 385,000lb (174.6t) (engine only)	

William E. Woodard, Lima Locomotive Company's chief engineer, led the design of the first 2-8-4. Built by Lima as an experiment and showpiece, it was sold later to the Illinois Central. The intention was to obtain high horsepower and economical use of fuel. In this it was largely successful and in its design details was a model for all other "super-power" engines to come. It was a two-cylinder, simple expansion locomotive, with a long firebox nearly a quarter the length of the boiler, supported by the four-wheel truck. The truck also had a steam booster, giving an additional 13,200lb (5986kg) of

A later "Berkshire", No. 2746, of the Chesapeake & Ohio Railroad, built in 1946, wheels a mainline freight under a signal gantry in 1948. The railroad had altogether 90 of these great locomotives, built between 1943 and 1947.

tractive effort at low speed. Lima "super-power" led the way to a reassessment of steam performance: not simply brute dragging force, but force per unit of time, measured in horsepower in the cylinders and at the drawbar.

9000 class "Union Pacific" type 4-12-2
Union Pacific Railroad (UPR): 1926

A 4-12-2 rolls its load across the plains: UP 9007 at Archer, Wyoming, on September 4, 1955. The westbound freight consists of 102 cars; the train is traveling at 25mph (40km/h).

Boiler pressure: 220psi (15.5kg/cm²)	
Cylinders: 27x32in (685x812mm); inside cyl 27x31in (685x787mm)	
Driving wheels: 67in (1700mm)	**Grate area:** 108.25sq ft (10m²)
Heating surface: 5853sq ft (543.8m²)	**Superheater:** 237.8m² (2560sq ft)
Tractive effort: 96,650lb (43,832kg)	**Total weight:** 782,000lb (354.6t)

Built by Alco's Brooks Works, these were until 1934 the longest and largest non-articulated locomotives in the world. The coupled wheelbase was 30ft 8in (9340mm). Eighty-eight were built and a company statement said the aim was "to haul mile-long freights at passenger train speeds".

Unusual for the United States, they were three-cylinder engines, though employing simple expansion. The first and last sets of coupled wheels were allowed lateral play—the fourth was originally flangeless, but this was later found to be unnecessary. Though no other lines used them, the 4-12-2s ran on the Union Pacific until 1956. They represented the maximum power to be got from a rigid-framed locomotive. Originally deployed on the the railroad's main line through Wyoming, they later worked in Kansas and Nebraska. The first engine, No. 9000, is preserved.

midwest were left with insufficient cars to move their produce. To help with coordination, the railroads set up their own Railroad War Board, but the old habits of company self-interest and regional cartels could not be shaken off.

Coal and grain stockpiles mounted, and normal distribution patterns were hopelessly disrupted. While the companies argued over responsibility, the federal government used its emergency powers to take over control of the entire railroad system beginning January 1, 1918.

William Gibbs McAdoo, Secretary of the Treasury, became Director-General of the Railroad Authority. Though it has been described as "nationalization," it was not—the railroads remained under private ownership and the rights of bondholders and shareholders were protected.

Under the McAdoo regime, railroad workers' pay went up sharply, as did passenger and freight rates. For just over two years, the vast network was treated as a single system. The congestion was eased, and under centralized direction, and with regional operating chiefs, the railroads provided an

Switching Engine 0-6-0
State Belt Railroad of California: 1927

Boiler pressure: 190lb (13.3kg/cm²)	**Cylinders:** 20x24in (508x609mm)
Driving wheels: 51in (1295mm)	**Grate area:** 33.1sq ft (3m²)
Heating surface: 1564sq ft (145.3m²)	**Superheater:** 435sq ft (40.4m²)
Tractive effort: 30,400lb (15,000kg)	**Total weight:** 147,700lb (67t)

Switching engines carried out the train marshaling operations at terminals, and in carriage and freight yards, and often also hauled local pick-up freights from factory sidings and local depots. By this time, some were very large 10-coupled engines, with boosters on the tender wheels, needed to move trainloads of 1 mile (1.6km) or more in length. More typically, switchers were of 0-8-0 or 0-6-0 wheel arrangement, often modified from "Consolidation" or "Mogul" types. Not normally used on the open road, and restricted to low speeds, they were not considered to need front trucks: good adhesion, with the weight on the driving wheels, and a tight turning circle were more important: frame length of these engines sometimes extended to more than double their coupled wheelbase. A Baldwins 0-8-0 switcher of the Illinois Central, also built in 1927, 36ft 8in

Yolo Shortline 0-6-0 No. 1233 on the open road. Like the Southern Pacific class S-14 0-6-0, this engine has a Vanderbilt tender rather than the typical sloping switcher tender.

(11,167mm) long, had a wheelbase of only 15ft (4568mm). With the American aversion to using tank engines, they usually had tenders, often sloped down toward the rear to give the driver a better view when reversing. By 1927 power-operated reversing gear, long pressed for by the labor unions, was almost always fitted in switchers, a great relief to drivers. Being relatively straightforward engines, and running up modest mileages, switchers often had a long working life, and examples from the early twentieth century survived on many lines into the last days of steam.

TRAVELERS' TALES
Private Cars

It was not only the railroad magnates who traveled in private cars. From the 1870s until World War II, every self-respecting business tycoon had to have one—or several. Pullman also had private rental cars available for those who were merely rich.

Attached to scheduled trains, or running as specials, the private cars reached a standard of opulent display which has never been rivaled unless perhaps on the same owners' private steam yachts.

Gold taps; gold table services; French chefs in the kitchen; organs in the parlor, which might also have an open fire burning aromatic logs; marble baths in the bathrooms—plutocrats competed to have the most sumptuous home on wheels. Each car had its name, often with a hint of advertisement, like Henry Ford's *Fair Lane*.

Personalization sometimes took odd forms: Jay Gould, a martyr to stomach ulcers, had a cow car included in his train, whose passenger provided milk of just the right kind to suit the great man's delicate digestion. Guests of the beer king Adolphus Busch found his product, suitably chilled, piped into each stateroom in his car *Adolphus*. In the 1880s a car might cost $30,000, but the ante steadily rose. By the late 1920s private cars were being built for $300,000 and more.

effective service. The Railroad Authority interpreted its remit widely. An engineering committee was set up to design a range of twelve "standard" locomotive types, using eight different wheel arrangements, that would suffice to cover all requirements from long haul expresses to yard switching. More than 1800 Railroad Authority locomotives were built.

A Return to Private Hands

Many people, both railroad workers and members of the public, observed that government control provided an effective railroad system, without the rivalries, restrictive practices, financial manipulations, and downright chicanery of the companies. But the Railroad Authority was a child of emergency, and its wide powers, overriding the innumerable individual state laws and regulations affecting railroads, could hardly be retained in peacetime.

In 1920 the railroads were returned to the private sector, amid controversy over whether the Railroad Authority had been a good thing or a bad thing, and with an instant clamor for reparations against the deterioration of tracks and equipment during federal control.

In fact, track and equipment on many lines had been substantially upgraded by this time. The matter was summed up by Walker Hines in his comprehensive and authoritative history of wartime operations in the United States and Canada: "The increased cost of railroad operations during the period of federal Control was due to the War and could not have been avoided by any other means of control. If private control had been retained, the increased cost of railroad operation would still have had to be met … In that event, if the entire burden could not have been placed on the public through increases in rates, it would have been met through a combination of impaired service to the public and of losses to the railroad security holders, and this would probably have involved some form of government subsidy so as to place part of the burden on the public treasury."

He added: "… the Government's temporary operation of the railroads accomplished with credit the objects which made resort to it imperative. The war needs for transportation were met and railroad security holders protected from a large part, though by no means all, of the injurious consequences of the War."

CHAPTER 10

THE INTER-WAR YEARS

It seems that steam locomotives could not be made more powerful
and efficient—and then came the concept of "Super-Power."
However, the supremacy of steam traction, after a hundred years,
now began to face serious challenges from the internal combustion
engine, as a new generation of industry moved into rail transport.

Though some companies ordered standard Railroad
Authority locomotive types after 1920, the attempt to
impose standardization was generally ignored. In any case,
the immediate post-war slump brought a fall in traffic and
in orders for new locomotives and rolling stock. There was

**Above: At an important junction or depot, the signal cabins could
hold hundreds of levers controlling switches and signals.
Left: In the 1930s, the Rio Grande company rebuilt several
Western Pacific dining cars, fitting plush, modern interiors.**

also a sense of frustration relating to motive power. The
commercial managers wanted to get longer and heavier
trains, pulled at higher speeds, and at less cost per ton-mile.
They were influenced both by operating costs and by a new
sense of competition. The internal combustion engine had
made dramatic progress in the war and huge numbers of
army surplus trucks were available cheap. It did not take a
business genius to see the likelihood of competition, at least
in local freight and passenger transport. For the designers, it
was something of an impasse. The adoption of

Class J1 "Hudson" 4-6-4
New York Central Railroad (NYC): 1927

Class J-1 No. 5271 poses with a 10-car train, typical of the New York Central's expresses, around the year 1935. The rugged building style, hidden in later streamlined engines, is visible here.

Boiler pressure: 225psi1 (5.75kg/cm²)	**Cylinders:** 25x28in (634x711mm)
Driving wheels: 79in (2005mm)	**Grate area:** 81.5sq ft (7.6m²)
Heating surface: 4187sq ft (389m²)	**Superheater:** 1745sq ft (162.1m²)
Tractive effort: 42,300lb (19,183kg)	**Total weight:** 565,200lb (256.3t)

The first 4-6-4s were significantly more powerful than the "Pacifics," which they replaced on such New York Central express services as the "Empire State." Built by Alco, the J1 class totaled 225. The type developed rapidly: by 1930, with the J1c, the boiler pressure had gone up to 275psi (19.3kg/cm2) and the cylinders had been modified to 22.5x29in (571x736mm) for better tractive effort. All were booster-fitted on the rear bogie, whose rear wheels at 51in (1294mm) were 15in (381mm) bigger than the front pair. From 1937, a considerably altered "Hudson," classed J3, appeared, 10 of them streamlined for high-prestige duties.

The 4-6-4 proved excellent for high-speed passenger express work. The fastest was probably the F6 "Hudson" built by Baldwins for the Chicago Milwaukee St Paul & Pacific Railroad in 1930. In July 1934, No 6402, hauling the 9 a.m. "Milwaukee Express," ran between Chicago and Milwaukee at an average 76.7mph (123.4km/h), and maximum 103.5mph (166.5km/h).

superheating, almost universal by 1911, had helped to produce more efficient locomotives, but more was still being demanded. Other ancillary equipment—including feedwater heaters, lubricating systems, and pumps of various kinds—had been brought to a state of high reliability. None of this was enough. Various essays at giant locomotives, like the famous Erie "triplex" 2-8-8-8-2 of 1914, and the Virginian 2-10-10-2 of 1918, had proved to be failures, incapable of providing enough steam to generate the required power. Double-heading of trains, though common, was very expensive and made heavy demands on the locomotive stock.

Plainly, the buck stopped with the designers, and particularly with the three major locomotive builders, Baldwin, Alco, and Lima Locomotive Works. Each struggled to respond to the situation. Their problem was that locomotives had reached their natural physical limits:

there was simply not room for wider boilers or bigger cylinders. Both Alco and Baldwin experimented with three-cylinder engines, despite the long established American distrust of crank axles. As its 60,000th locomotive, Baldwin built a demonstration engine, a three-cylinder compound 4-10-2, but it remained unique (it is preserved at the Franklin Institute, Philadelphia).

New Designs

The company that showed the way forward was Lima. In 1921 it was virtually shut down, with an empty order book. It had grown by building the specialized patent "Shay" geared locomotives for logging lines, but from 1916 with a new design chief, William E. Woodard, it went for a share of the "Class One" market—the big main line railroads. In May 1921 his assistant, Herb Snyder, presented a paper to the American Society of Mechanical Engineers, boldly entitled: "The Need for Improvement in the Design of Present-Day Locomotives." Woodard was aided by the fact that Lima's owners also owned a number of equipment suppliers: the Franklin accessory supply company, the American Arch Company, and the Locomotive Superheater Company—all would contribute to, and benefit from, the new approach. In 1925 he produced a new design, the first 2-8-4 locomotive. Built as a speculative exercise, it was

known as the A-1. Everyone in the works was highly enthusiastic. The plant manager, John H. Wynne, wrote to his father on February 8, 1925: "She is a beauty. She has an automatic stoker, feedwater heater, power reverse gear, cast steel cylinders (iron bushed) with outside exhaust pipes, a four-wheel trailer with booster engine attached…and a firebox almost as large as your front room!" Their beauty was a "tramp," out to charm the susceptibilities of motive

"Cab-first" Class AC-5 4-8-8-2

Southern Pacific Railroad (SPR): 1928

The view was fine, but crews worried at first about collisions. Southern Pacific No. 4100 belonged to class AC-4, identical in leading dimensions with AC-5. AC-4 was numbered 4100–4109; AC-5, 4110–4125.

The "cab-first" concept goes back to railroads in Germany and Italy, but the Southern Pacific Railroad took it up in the biggest way. In the long snow-sheds and tunnels of its Sierra Nevada line, an engine whose cab was free from back-blown smoke was a great boon to the crew. Between Truckee and Blue Canyon, there were 38 miles (61km) of snow-sheds, designed to prevent drifts 50–200ft (15–60m) deep from blocking the line. As the engines burned oil, the problem of access to the fuel supply was easily dealt with: oil and water were towed in a 12-wheel double bogie tender, with oil supplied at 5lb (2.2kg) pressure to the burners. The first AC (articulated consolidation) locomotives had been Mallet compounds turned back-to-front in 1910; these were rebuilt from 1927 as simple expansion engines, and the AC-5s were four-cylinder simples from the start, of greater mechanical dimensions than the AC-1s. Ten of this new type were built by Baldwins in 1928, with a further

16 in the following year, and 25 more in 1930, when the boiler pressure was raised to 250psi (17.5kg/cm2). In all, the railroad had over 200 AC locomotives, constructed up to 1937, of which only class AC-9 was not cab-forward. Their original intended route was the mountain stretch between Roseville, California, and Sparks, Nevada, but they were also used on other divisions of the Southern Pacific where their power and smoke-free driving position were of value. Like the Italian class 671, these locomotives ran permanently "backward." The last in action was 4274 in December 1956.

Boiler pressure: 235psi (16.5kg/cm²)	**Cylinders:** 24x32in (609x812mm)
Driving wheels: 63.5in (1612mm)	**Grate area:** 139sq ft (12.9m²)
Heating surface: 6505sq ft (604.1m²)	**Superheater:** 2988sq ft (277.5m²)
Tractive effort: 106,300lb (46,848kg)	**Total weight:** 614,000lb (278.4t)
	(engine only)

"Northern" Class S1 4-8-4
Great Northern Railroad (GN): 1929

The 4-8-4 first ran on the Northern Pacific Railroad in 1927, but when the Great Northern's new train, *The Empire Builder*, cut five hours from the transcontinental schedule, six of this configuration were built by Baldwins for the long haul over the continental divide in Montana. The maximum westbound grade was 1.8 per cent and they took 14-car trains up without assistance, enjoying a tractive effort 22 per cent greater than that of the 4-8-2 "Mountain" types they replaced. The boiler was of 98in (2487mm) diameter and had a Belpaire firebox. Both front and rear bogies ran in outside frames, and all axles had roller bearings. As often with American engines, compressor pumps were mounted on the smoke-box front. Apart from one, No. 2552, they were oil burners, with tenders of the "Vanderbilt" type, running on two six-wheel bogies, and holding 5800gal (21,955l) of oil and 22,000gal (83,278l) of water. These

A Toronto landmark rises behind the preserved CPR 4-4-4 No. 2928 of class F-1a, standing in the city's main station.

Boiler pressure: 250psi (17.5kg/cm²)	**Cylinders:** 28x30in (710x761mm)
Driving wheels: 73in (1853mm)	**Grate area:** 94sq ft (8.7m²)
Heating surface: 4560sq ft (423m²)	**Superheater:** 2028sq ft (188.3m²)
Tractive effort: 67,000lb (30,385kg)	**Total weight:** 847,900lb (418.7t)

"Northerns" 16ft (4874mm) high and 108ft 7in (33,071mm) long, were imposing engines and the company exploited them vigorously for their promotional value as well as for their service in action. But with the arrival of the GN's class S2 4-8-4, with 2030mm (80in) driving wheels, they were soon switched to freight haulage, and the S2s took over the passenger express work.

Class Z-5 2-8-8-4

Northern Pacific Railroad (NP): 1930

Boiler pressure: 250psi (17.5kg/cm²)		**Cylinders:** 26x32in (660x812mm)	
Driving wheels: 63in (1599mm)		**Grate area:** 182sq ft (17m²)	
Heating surface: 7673sq ft (712.6m²)		**Superheater:** 3219sq ft (299m²)	
Tractive effort: 140,000lb (63,492kg)		**Total weight:** 1,010,475lb (499t)	

Until the advent of the Union Pacific "Big Boys" in 1941, this was the biggest locomotive in the world, and in terms of grate area, evaporative heating surface and superheating surface, they were never exceeded. The prototype was built by the American Locomotive Company in 1928; and 11 were ordered in 1930, but from Baldwins. These "Yellowstones" were designed to haul 4000-ton (4064t) freight trains on the 216-mile (347.6km) sector of the transcontinental route through the "Badlands" between Mandan, North Dakota and Glendive, Montana, up grades of 1.1 per cent. They worked into the late 1940s. The engines stood 17ft 2in (5228mm) from the rails to the chimney lip, and were built Mallet-fashion, with the pilot and front coupled wheels forming an articulated truck; the rear coupled axles fixed to the frame, and a

Northern Pacific Z5 No. 5006 stands at Livingston, Montana, on June 10, 1941. Just out of shops, provided with a new frame and roller bearings, its function here is as a helper engine.

pivoted four-wheel trailing truck, but the four cylinders were simple-expansion only. The long firebox was intended to burn lignite, or "Rosebud coal," from a Northern Pacific-owned mine. A booster engine was fitted to the trailing truck to assist with starting off, and delivering an additional 13,400lb (6077kg) of tractive effort. All were later fitted with roller bearings, something in which the railroad was a pioneer. Cladding was applied to the boiler from a point between the chimney and the first dome, giving it a smooth skin in contrast to the exposed pipework around the smokebox.

power superintendents. It made full use of all recent improvements in steam locomotive technology, from the single cast steel frame to a two-cylinder, simple expansion locomotive, with a long firebox nearly a quarter the length of the boiler, supported by the four-wheel truck. Tested in April 1925 on the Boston & Albany line through the Berkshire Mountains, the 2-8-4 took a 2296-ton (2333t) train east from Selkirk Yard to North Adams Junction in 10 minutes less than its H10 predecessor with a train of 1691

tons. It was also considerably more economical with fuel. The case for "super-power" was proved. Indeed, even while the A-1 was still being tested, the same concepts, plus a combustion chamber, were built into ten 2-10-4s ordered in 1925 by the Texas & Pacific Railroad.

Super-power was based on a new proportion of firebox (with a combustion chamber reaching forward into the boiler space), boiler, and superheater. It prompted a reassessment of steam performance: not simply brute

P5

Pennsylvania Railroad (PRR): 1930

In fact, only one true P5 was built, the Pennsy's No. 4700, seen here with pantograph raised, as all subsequent locomotives of the class incorporated certain alterations as P5a.

Type: 2-Co-2, mixed-traffic electric

Power: 11,500 V at 25Hz AC from overhead

Output: 3750hp (2794kW)

Tractive effort: 57,250lbf (254kN) starting TE

Max. operating speed: Originally intended for 90mph (144km/h); later limited to 70mph (112km/h)

Weight: 392,000lb (178t)

Overall length: 62ft 8in (19.101m)

Max. axle load: 77,000lb (35t)

Gauge: 4ft 8.5in (1435mm)

In the 1920s, the Pennsylvania Railroad set out to electrify its busy multiple-track New York to Washington, DC main line. Known for its home-built locomotive designs, it began to build a fleet of electrics for service on this route.

The P5 Class was a boxcab that used a 2-Co-2 wheel arrangement, making it effectively an electric version of the K4s Pacific type. Although intended for fast passenger service, the P5 was plagued by lateral swaying and cracked axles, so the Pennsylvania Railroad relegated the P5s to freight service.

dragging force, but force per unit of time, measured in horsepower in the cylinders and at the drawbar. The four-wheel truck, allowing for a bigger and heavier firebox, was to become standard in large locomotives. Lima's pioneering work set the pattern for the final decades of American steam, and also resulted in a satisfactory growth of market share for the smallest of the big three constructors.

In 1926 the Union Pacific Railroad acquired the first of eighty-eight 4-12-2s of the 9000 class from Alco's Brooks Works. These were until 1934 the longest and largest non-articulated locomotives in the world. The length of the coupled wheelbase was 30ft 8in (9.3m). A company statement announced the aim as "to haul mile-long freights at passenger train speeds."

Unusually, they were three-cylinder engines, and in a rare employment of overseas technology, the British Gresley

EP-3
New Haven Railroad: 1931

Type: 2-Co-Co-2, passenger electric
Power: 11kV alternating current at 25Hz from overhead, or 660V DC from third rail
Tractive effort: 68,500lbf (304kN) starting TE
Max. operating speed: 80mph (128km/h)—one unit modified for 120mph (192km/h) running in tests
Weight: Approx. 404,000lb (183t)
Overall length: n/a
Max. axle load: 46,000lb (21t)
Gauge: 4ft 8.5in (1435mm)

General Electric built 10 box-cab electrics for the New Haven Railroad in 1931 which used a 2-Co-Co-2 wheel arrangement. Designated EP-3, these electrics were regularly used to haul long-distance and suburban passenger trains over the railroad's four-track electrified mainline between New Haven, Connecticut, and its two New York terminals, Grand Central and Penn Station. They would also be used on electrified branches, such as the line to Danbury, Connecticut. In 1938, General Electric built six EP-4 electrics that were mechanically similar, but featured a double-ended streamlined carbody. During World War II, General Electric and Westinghouse divided an order for 10 additional streamlined freight electrics, designated EF-3. Most were displaced in the late 1950s by new Electro-Motive Division's FL9s.

A Milwaukee Road "Little Joe" and box-cab electric are seen here wearing the railroad's maroon and orange livery. This particular livery was also featured on Milwaukee Road diesel electrics in the 1950s.

A New Haven EP-3 electric rolls through Mott Haven Yard over the New York Central route from Grand Central Terminal. These electrics operated off both third-rail and overhead electrification.

conjugated valve gear was used. The 4-12-2s were successfully employed on the Union Pacific until 1956, and the first engine, No. 9000, is preserved. With a tractive effort of 96,650lb (43,832kg), they represented the maximum power to be got from a rigid-framed locomotive.

Arrival of the "Big Boys"

Three years later another railroad with long haul routes across wilderness and mountainous terrain introduced what was, until the advent of the Union Pacific "Big Boys" in 1941, the biggest locomotive in the world. In some respects, such as grate area, evaporative heating surface, and superheating surface, it was never exceeded. This was the Class Z-5 2-8-8-4 of the Northern Pacific Railroad. A prototype was built by the Alco in that year, and in 1930 a production run of 11 was ordered—though from Baldwin rather than Alco. Known as the "Yellowstones," they were designed to haul 4000-ton (4064t) freight trains on the

216-mile (347.6km) sector of the transcontinental route through the Badlands between Mandan, North Dakota, and Glendive, Montana, up grades of 1.1 percent.

The Yellowstones worked on such tasks into the late 1940s. They were built Mallet-fashion, with the pilot and front coupled wheels forming an articulated truck; the rear coupled axles fixed to the frame, and a pivoted four-wheel trailing truck, but the four cylinders were simple-expansion only. The immense firebox of over 200sq ft (18.6m2) was intended to burn lignite, or "Rosebud coal," from a Montana mine owned by the Northern Pacific Railroad.

Engines of the Yellowstone configuration were the biggest steam power on several major railroads, including the Baltimore & Ohio and the ore-hauling Duluth, Missabe & Iron Range Railway, and were built into the 1940s. They established the double set of simple-expansion cylinders as the standard for the biggest and most powerful locomotives. Everything on the largest possible scale, well built from

4-8-0

Delaware & Hudson Railroad (D&H): 1933

Boiler pressure: 500psi (35kg/cm²)

Cylinders: hp 20x32in (507.6x812mm); intermediate 27.5x32in (698x812mm); lp 33x32in (837.5x812mm)

Driving wheels: 63in (1599mm)

Grate area: 75.8sq ft (7m²)

Heating surface: 3351sq ft (311m²)

Superheater: 1076sq ft (99.9m²)

Tractive effort: 108,000lb (53412kg)

Total weight: not known

The Delaware & Hudson 4-8-0 *L.H. Loree*, on view at a public exhibition in 1933. The rods of the tender booster engine can be seen. For Loree, it was something of a personal quest to develop a "new generation" of steam power.

Under its President, L.H. Loree, the Delaware & Hudson pursued a progressive design and maintenance policy. At this time railroads in several countries were experimenting with very high pressure.

This locomotive, named for Loree, was the third in a Delaware & Hudson series begun in 1924. It was a four-cylinder triple-expansion

compound, with front and rear cylinders driving the same set of coupled wheels. The high-pressure cylinder on the right of the cab discharged to the intermediate-pressure cylinder on the left, and the steam finally was piped to the two front low-pressure cylinders.

Rotary cam poppet valves were also fitted, and the firebox had over-fire air jets to improve combustion. A six-wheel rear bogie on the tender was fitted with a booster engine. With so many innovative features, it unsurprisingly remained a one-off. Fortunately, the railroad also possessed a stud of well-designed and maintained conventional locomotives.

Above: Four locomotives in front and one behind give their utmost in hoisting the San Francisco–Chicago Express over Soldier's Summit, on the Denver & Rio Grande line, in the Wasatch Mountains between Ogden and Green River.

first-class materials, utilizing all that was known of efficient steam circulation, ensured that they did a very effective job. In terms of their own tonnage, and the tonnage they could move, they overshadowed all other locomotives.

The 4-8-4 "Northern"

Probably the most important and successful locomotive type of the decade was the 4-8-4 "Northern," first built for the Northern Pacific in 1927. More than a thousand were at work on a variety of roads by 1940. Engines of this wheel configuration seemed to work as effectively on express passenger as on fast freight trains. With wheels of a diameter up to 80in (203cm), they could be very fast, but also ran

Right: Richmond, VA, was the only place in the world where three main lines crossed one another at different levels: the Chesapeake & Ohio at the top, the Seaboard Air Line in the middle, and the Southern Railway at ground level.

with great smoothness and stability. Among the high-speed versions were the Union Pacific's semistreamlined GS type operating the San Francisco-Los Angeles "Daylight" streamlined train. But it is unlikely that any 4-8-4 has exceeded the speeds attained by the Milwaukee Road's F7s.

With their streamlined front and boiler casing that also covered the cylinders, the F7s exemplified the tendency of designers in the mid-1930s to play down the "steamy" aspect of their passenger engines, but the wheels and running gear were left uncovered for easy access. They ran their 12-car, 550-ton (559t) trains at an average of 66mph

Timken's Alco-built "Four Aces" demonstration locomotive with roller bearings on all axles is pulled along the rails by three women, in this famous scene photographed at Chicago in 1930.

(106km/h) including five stops, between Chicago and St Paul. There is one verified account of 120mph (193km/h) averaged over a 5mile (8km) stretch, but no authenticated maximum speed above this. In 1940 they did, however, operate the fastest scheduled steam service anywhere, on the "Hiawatha's" Wisconsin Sparta-Portage sector, 78.5 miles (126.3 km) run at an average of 81.25mph (130.75km/h).

Railroad engineers were keenly aware of new technologies. The advantages of tapered roller bearings, already used in the automobile industry, were introduced to the American railroads in 1930, when the Timken Roller Bearing Company sponsored a demonstration locomotive. Apart from having roller bearings fitted on all axles, it was a standard Alco Schenectady-built 4-8-4 "Northern." It was given the road number 1111 and consequently known as the "Four Aces." Fifty-two manufacturers of special parts supplied their products at no charge until the locomotive had run 100,000 miles (160,930km). Thirteen railroads tested it over the next two years. The case for roller bearings was well and truly made.

Diesel and Electric

More radically, the two biggest builders, Alco and Baldwin, both constructed experimental locomotives using internal combustion engines, in 1924 and 1925 respectively. These were intended as switching engines. Typically the switcher stood around doing nothing for lengthy periods, and its main task was to move loads at very slow speeds. A locomotive whose power could be turned on and off, and which could be geared down to provide heavy traction at minimal speed was an attractive prospect. But the pioneer diesels were expensive and temperamental, and required their own fueling and maintenance facilities. Even by 1936, only 190 or so were working on American railroads. The

Burlington's *Zephyr*
Burlington Railroad: 1934

Burlington's shining *Zephyr* emerged from the depths of the Great Depression, dazzled the American public, and forever changed both passenger travel and the state of motive-power on American railroads. In the 1920s, railroad passenger services had been hit hard by highway transport and air travel. The Depression aggravated the situation, and many railroads saw passenger numbers plummet. In order to reverse this trend, two large Western railroads, Union Pacific, and the Chicago, Burlington & Quincy, decided to introduce flashy new services using all-new lightweight trains.

In April 1934, Burlington debuted the sleek, streamlined, stainless-steel *Zephyr*, a lightweight three-car articulated passenger train powered by a state-of-the-art Winton diesel engine with electric traction motors. The *Zephyr* was the result of pairing modern vehicular construction techniques with recently developed high-output diesel engines. In 1930 automotive manufacturer General Motors had purchased both Winton Engine and one of its largest customers, rail car manufacturer Electro-Motive. In 1932, the German "Flying Hamburger" trains set an important precedent, demonstrating that a streamlined diesel-powered railcar could offer fast service and attract passengers.

The *Zephyr* was capable of speeds well in excess of 100mph (160km/h) and could run for hundreds of miles without the need to stop for water or fuel. This permitted Burlington to trim running times. Based on the success of the first *Zephyr* (a train later known

The success of the *Zephyr* inspired other railroads to order streamlined trains. Boston & Maine's *Flying Yankee*, seen here at Old Orchard Beach, Maine, was a near copy of the *Zephyr*.

Type: Diesel-electric powered streamlined articulated high speed train
Power and output: Winton 201E diesel producing 600hp (44kW)
Tractive effort: n/a
Max. operating speed: 116mph (186km/h)
Weight: 175,000lb (79t)
Overall length: 196ft (59.741m)
Gauge: 4ft 8.5in (1435mm)

as *Pioneer Zephyr*), Burlington ordered a whole fleet of similar diesel streamliners. These trains were longer and had more passenger capacity than the *Pioneer Zephyr*. The streamlined trains were a spectacular success. Both Burlington and Union Pacific experienced dramatic increases in passenger numbers. After World War II, the streamlined lightweight train enjoyed renewed interest and hundreds of conventionally coupled, locomotive-hauled streamlined trains appeared. The Budd company grew to be one of the largest producers of new passenger equipment. The early diesel trains helped to establish Electro-Motive's reputation as a locomotive manufacturer. Twenty-five years after the *Zephyr's* debut, the diesel reigned as the premier motive power on American lines, and Electro-Motive had become America's largest locomotive maker.

M-10000
Union Pacific: 1934

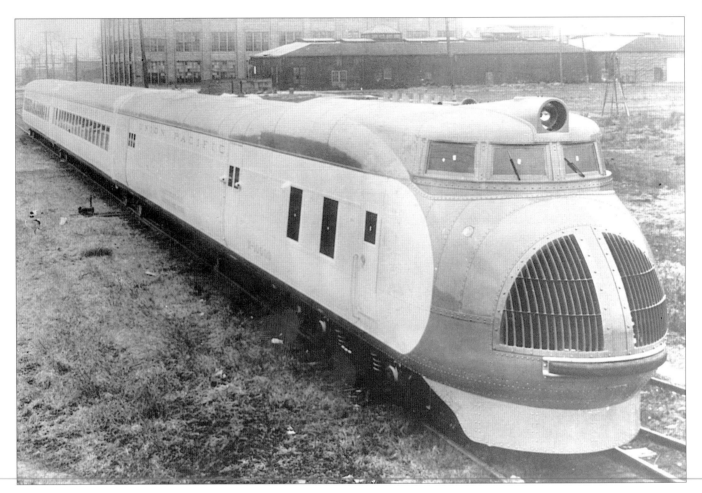

In the early 1930s, the Electro-Motive Corporation, a gas-electric motorcar producer that had recently been acquired by the automotive giant General Motors, set out to change the face of American railroading.

The Great Depression, combined with the advent of private automobiles and airline travel, resulted in a precipitous decline in railroad passenger traffic. Two lines, Union Pacific and Burlington, set out to reverse this negative trend with the introduction of new fast passenger trains. Union Pacific worked with passenger car manufacturer Pullman to construct a three-car aluminium articulated streamlined train. Completed in early 1934, this train was powered by a Winton distillate engine with electric transmission. (A distillate engine required a spark plug for ignition and is not a diesel.) Numbered the M-10000, and originally known as the *Streamliner*, the train was painted in a flashy mustard and brown color scheme and sent on a nationwide publicity tour by Union Pacific. It was America's first streamlined passenger train

The automotive industry origins of the M-1000 show in the train's design, complete with radiator grill and fender. Its form somewhat anticipates the Japanese bullet train of the 1970s.

Type: Distillate-electric powered streamlined articulated high speed train
Power: Not known
Tractive effort: n/a
Max. operating speed: 111mph (178km/h)
Weight: 170,000lbs (77t)
Overall length: 204ft 6in (62.331m)
Gauge: 4ft 8.5in (1435mm)

and helped to spur a national interest in railroad streamliners.

Later, Union Pacific assigned the M-10000 to service as its City of Salina (Kansas). The train was too small for long-haul service; however, Union Pacific was to order a fleet of similarly styled, streamlined diesel trains for its long distance services.

Canadian National Railway's 303-ton (308t) double-unit diesel-powered road engine of 1929 has already been mentioned.

Electric traction, by now increasingly common in Europe, was still in very limited use in North America. The coal-hauling Virginian Railway installed an overhead wire system in 1925, over the 123 mile (198km) route between Mullens and Roanoke, and bought twelve massive triple-unit boxcab EL-3A types from Baldwin-Westinghouse to operate the trains—which they did right up to the 1950s. A major project was launched by the Pennsylvania Railroad in 1928, when, after electrifying its Philadelphia local services,

Class S-3 2-8-4
New York Chicago & St Louis Railroad (Nickel Plate Road): 1934

Boiler pressure: 245psi (17kg/cm²)	**Cylinders:** 25x34in (634.5x863mm)
Driving wheels: 69in (1751mm)	**Grate area:** 90.3sq ft (8.4m²)
Heating surface: 4772sq ft (443.2m²)	**Superheater:** 1932sq ft (179.4m²)
Tractive effort: 64,100lb (29,070kg)	**Total weight:** 444,290lb (201.5t)
	(engine only)

Lima Works built 70 of the S-3 "Berkshire" for the Nickel Plate Road, essentially similar to a range of others built during the 1930s for other lines with heavy freight traffic, all two-cylinder simples, fitted with the American standard Type E superheater. Differences in dimension and detail were relatively small. Some types had trailer boosters. Engines of this configuration were the backbone of general long-distance freight. They normally ran with 12-wheel tenders with a capacity around 20,000gals (75,708l) of water and 22 tons (22.35t) of coal. The Nickel Plate's first 15, of 1934, were

Nickel Plate S-3 2-8-4 No. 779, photographed at the "Wheels" pageant in Chicago, 1949. The split-new locomotive had arrived from Lima Works just in time for the show.

classed as S-1. Over a fifteen-year period, virtually nothing changed in the design of the S-3: for the line's purpose, a sufficient point of steam development had been reached. Forty were built up to 1943, then ten S-2s followed in 1944 and ten S-3s in 1949. Dimensions are for S-3.

Class A 4-4-2
Chicago Milwaukee St Paul & Pacific Railroad (CMStP&PRR): 1935

America's "Super-Atlantic," No. 2 of Class A. Despite their distinctive appearance and exceptional performance, none of the four were preserved. All were cut up in 1951 and 1952.

Boiler pressure: 300psi (21kg/cm²)	**Cylinders:** 19x28in (483x711mm)
Driving wheels: 84in (2134mm)	**Grate area:** 69sq ft (6.4m²)
Heating surface: 3245sq ft (301.5m²)	**Superheater:** 1029sq ft (96m²)
Tractive effort: 30,600lb (13,900kg)	**Total weight:** 537,000lb (265.18t)

It is 2.21 pm by the station clock at Milwaukee, Wisconsin, and "Atlantic" No. 4, *Chippewa*, is coupled up to the "Hiawatha." The "hoghead," American railroad slang for the driver, looks all set to let her roll for Chicago.

Travelers between Chicago and Minneapolis–St Paul had a choice of three routes, which competed fiercely, offering high standards of speed and service. There was no climbing to do, so high speeds were possible, and Alco built four specialized oil-burning loco-motives with streamlined casings to pull the "Hiawatha" flyer on a timing of 6hrs, 30mins for its 412mile (663km) route, averaging a speed of 66mph (106km/h). On a test outing, one made one of the fastest-ever steam runs, 141 miles (227km) from Milwaukee to New Lisbon in 113 minutes. The "Hiawatha" timing was later cut to 6hrs, 15mins, despite five intermediate stops. Sustained speeds in excess of 100mph (161km/h) were necessary to maintain time. Engine and train were painted in a striking livery of yellow, orange, maroon and brown. It was not a lightweight train: with nine cars, it weighed 412.5 tons (419.1t). These were the biggest, heaviest "Atlantics" built, and larger tenders later increased their weight. In 1938 the streamlined F7 4-6-4s replaced them, able to maintain the schedule with a 12-car train, and from 1940 the Atlantics were diverted to the new "Mid-West Hiawatha" operating between Chicago, Omaha, and Sioux Falls.

By 1948, diesel locomotives had taken over, and the 4-4-2s, not adaptable to other types of use, were retired by 1951, their prestige and superb performance forgotten; all were scrapped.

The dash of the steam-powered express is captured in this view of the New York Central's "Twentieth Century Limited" sweeping under the "cut-off" bridge over the Hudson at Castleton, NY.

it began to install electric traction on its New York-Philadelphia-Washington main line. An eventual result of this was the celebrated GG1 class 2-Co-Co-2 locomotive of 1934, built at the line's own workshops at Altoona, Pennsylvania; its final version was styled by Raymond Loewy. Some of these survived in main line service until 1983. Meanwhile, in 1931 the New Haven Railroad also showed the value of electric locomotives in running high-density rapid transit on its two lines into New York City. Railroad shares plunged with every other financial security in the Wall Street Crash of 1929, and, despite the ventures of the Pennsylvania and New Haven railroads, the ensuing years of

the Great Depression were a tough and troubled time for railroad operation. Services were cut back, staff were laid off, and maintenance work on buildings and equipment was pared down. Competition from trucks and newly formed airlines made the railroad's situation even worse. In 1935, when a hurricane wrecked the Florida East Coast Railroad's 114-mile (183km) series of viaducts along the Florida Keys, a highway was built as a replacement.

WORKING ON THE RAILROAD

The Locomotive Stylists

In 1928 a German immigrant to the United States, Otto Kuhler, greatly admired the New York Central's new J-1 4-6-4 "Hudsons" and began sketching ways in which their long, powerful lines could be smoothed off and yet emphasized. Product styling was a driving force of new industry, from radio to automobiles; and Alco was sufficiently impressed to hire him as a design consultant. Kuhler was the pioneer of American railroad streamlining, and designed the "Hiawatha" trains.

Another prominent designer was Raymond Loewy, with the Pennsylvania Railroad. Loewy's approach was thorough, beginning with a clay model, and later he used wind tunnel tests in order to tackle problems like low-hanging smoke. He was responsible for the external

styling of the electric GG1 and for the Pennsy's last great steam locomotives, the "duplexes" with double sets of cylinders and driving wheels set in a rigid frame; the T1 4-4-4-4—described by one railroad historian as "impressive in every way except grate area and boiler capacity"; the 4-4-6-4 Q2s; and the solitary 6-4-4-6 S 1.

All were gone by 1953, most of them with less than ten years' service. Their visual impact, especially at speed, was awesome. Loewy recalled standing at Fort Wayne station: "120 miles an hour. . . It flashed by like a steel thunderbolt; the ground shaking under me . . . I felt shaken and overcome by an overwhelming feeling of power, by a sense of pride at the sight of what I had helped to create ."

Class J3 4-8-4
Chesapeake & Ohio Railroad (C&O): 1935

Boiler pressure: 245psi (17.2kg/cm²)	**Cylinders:** 27.5x30in (699x762mm)
Driving wheels: 72in (1829mm)	**Grate area:** 100sq ft (9.3m²)
Heating surface: 5534sq ft (514m²)	**Superheater:** 2347sq ft (218m²)
Tractive effort: 67,187lb (33,179kg)	**Total weight:** 476,280lb (216t) (engine only)

Fifteen of these passenger engines were built by Lima between 1935 and 1948; the later ones classed as J3a had roller bearings and other improvements but the same dimensions. The last to be built, No. 614, which had been preserved for special excursion work, was hastily overhauled and used for the ill-judged ACE (American Coal Enterprises) display runs in the winter of 1984–5.

This scheme, intended to promote the production of new-generation, "clean coal" steam locomotives, though initially backed by the Chessie System and American coal interests, expired in 1985 without having produced a prototype engine, though plans for an

The preserved Chesapeake & Ohio No. 614 restarts its train after a signal stop. The steam-pipe to the rear truck booster engine can be seen. With an extra 5600kg (15,000lb) of weight compared to a two-wheel truck, the four-wheel version could support an additional 20,500kg (55,000lb) of engine weight.

ACE 3000 and 6000 had been drawn up. Unfortunately, the J3, not properly adapted, put up anything but a "clean" performance, and on one demonstration trip in January 1985 it also, embarrassingly, ran completely out of coal.

Canadian Excellence

Nevertheless, there were some bright spots, where exceptional performance, usually sparked off by inter-company competition, could be found. One of these was the Canadian National Railway's "Intercity Limited" from Toronto to Montreal. The alternative routes between these cities was the cause of a needle match between the Canadian National and Canadian Pacific. The Canadian Pacific had the longer road at 340 miles (547km), but for an exhilarating period between 1930 and 1933, it provided the world's fastest train over a distance exceeding 100 miles (161km), from Smiths Falls, Ontario to Montreal West, 124 miles (199km) at an average speed of 68.9mph (110.9km/h).

Between 1930 and 1933, Canadian National's Toronto to Montreal run was reduced to six hours, while the Canadian Pacific took fifteen minutes more. Then, from April 1933, the two lines pooled the service and the schedule was

"Union" class 0-10-2
Union Railroad:
1936

Boiler pressure: 260lb (18.25kg/cm²)	Cylinders: 28x32in (711x812mm)
Driving wheels: 61in (1548mm)	Grate area: m²)
Heating surface: m²)	Superheater: m²)
Tractive effort: 90,900lb (41,220kg)	Total weight: 644,510lb (292.3t)

By this time, big American locomotives were in a class of their own, rivaled only by the attempts of the Soviet railroads to outbuild their capitalist rivals. This class, though only three in number, is interesting partly because it can be more easily compared to European and other 10-coupled types. The Union Railroad was a short but strategically placed line, providing links between six trunk line railroads in the busy Pittsburgh area. It had less than 45 miles (72km) of track, but the usage was extremely intensive and some of the lines were steeply graded. To provide greater traction than the company's 2-8-0s, this engine was commissioned from Baldwins, the first 0-10-2. The wheelbase was also restricted by the need to fit the same turntables as the 2-8-0s. Since the locomotive would only ever operate at low speeds, a leading truck was dispensed with,

The Union 0-10-2s were sold to the Duluth Missabe and Iron Range Railroad, which ran them at its Lake Superior dockside yards until 1958. Here No. 605 stands in store at Proctor, Wisconsin.

though the end product looked oddly like an engine that had managed to mislay its front carrying wheels. To assist moving of heavy trains up the grades, a booster was fitted to the leading tender truck, whose wheels were coupled. It added a tractive force of 17,150lb (7780kg) to the locomotive's effort. The short-distance working of what was essentially a giant switching engine meant that the tender, though large by non-American standards, holding 14 tons (14.2t) of coal and 10,000gals (37,854l) of water, was quite a small one.

"Challenger" class 4-6-6-4
Union Pacific Railroad (UP): 1936

Both the Union Pacific and Northern Pacific put locomotives of this configuration on the road in 1936. They were two-in-one articulated engines, with a single huge boiler supplying steam to two power units, based on the Mallet principle, but with simple-expansion cylinders only. Walschaerts valve gear actuated the piston valves, and the cylinders drove the third pair of coupled wheels. Both on the Union Pacific and Northern Pacific engines, the front cylinders were positioned further ahead of the coupled wheels than the rear ones; with an extra-long piston rod taking up the space. The Union Pacific engines, named "Challengers," were designed as mixed-traffic engines, though most of their activity was on fast freights. Considered as passenger engines, they were the largest and most powerful ever run. Forty were ordered from Alco in 1936; a further 65, incorporating some modifications, were built between 1942 and 1945. The type proved excellent for high-speed freight trains, and other lines quickly followed the example. Baldwins built 4-6-6-4s for the Denver & Rio Grande Western in 1938, and for the Western Maryland in 1939. But the "Challengers" were the only ones to operate regular passenger services, notably between Salt Lake City, Las Vegas, and Los Angeles.

Some were converted to oil-burning, but the great majority were coal burners, the huge grates fed by automatic stokers. They remained in service until 1958, by which time the Union Pacific's diesel program had advanced far enough to deprive them of any suitable duties. One is preserved in working order (No 3985).

The long piston-road of the front cylinder and the massive dimensions of the boiler are clearly visible in this imposing shot of preserved Union Pacific No. 3985.

No. 3985 gets on the move, heading toward San Jose for a railroad history convention in 1992. The length of the boiler severely limited the engineer's forward look-out.

Boiler pressure: 255psi (17.9kg/cm²)	**Cylinders:** 21x32in (533x813mm)
Driving wheels: 69in (1753mm)	**Grate area:** 108sq ft (10m²)
Heating surface: 4642sq ft (431m²)	**Superheater:** 1741sq ft (162m²)
Tractive effort: 97,400lb (44,100kg)	**Total weight:** 1,071,000lb (486t)

The huge size of the "Challengers" is appreciated when one realizes that the driving wheels are as tall as the average man.

promptly extended to 6 hours, 30 minutes. On certain routes, speeds in excess of 100mph (161km/h) were a daily occurrence. One of these was the Chicago, Milwaukee, St Paul & Pacific Railroad. Travelers between Chicago and St Paul had a choice of three routes, all competing fiercely and offering the highest standards of speed and service. With no climbing to do, high speed was possible.

Alco built four highly specialized oil burning locomotives, the Class A 4-4-2, to pull the Hiawatha flyer, on a timing of 6 hours, 30 minutes for its 412-mile (663km) route, giving an average running speed of 66mph (106km/h). The Hiawatha timing was later cut to 6 hours, 15 minutes, despite five intermediate stops. Sustained speeds in excess of 100mph (161km) were necessary to maintain time. The engines were fitted with streamlined casings, and they and their trains were painted in a striking livery of yellow, orange, maroon, and brown. It was not a lightweight train: with nine cars it amounted to 412.5 tons

(419t). These were the biggest and heaviest "Atlantics" ever built, and when replaced by the similarly styled F-7 4-8-4s already referred to, they ran other express services westward from Chicago.

Speed and Efficiency

During the 1930s, in response to the call for greater tractive power combined with higher speed, the designers' answer was to provide locomotives of such power that their relative inefficiency at low speed did not hinder them from getting massive train weights on the move. Designers had ceased to be simply concerned by how many tons a locomotive could pull, probably at a low speed.

Driven by the demands of commercial and traffic managers who wanted to combine haulage power with speed and efficiency, they were thinking in terms of what horsepower could be developed by a really big, hard working locomotive. Performance of this kind was

---

TRAVELERS' TALES
The Footplate Rider

From the 1920s to the 1960s, the French banker Baron Gérard Vuillet was an ardent rail enthusiast. His international business connections with railroads won him many invitations to indulge his passion for footplate riding. On June 15, 1937, he rode on "Atlantic" type "Hiawatha" No. 4 of the Milwaukee Road, heading one of the fastest trains in the world, No. 101, over the 409.8 miles (659.4km) between Chicago and St Paul. The Baron, a keen recorder of locomotive performance, was highly impressed:

"For the 409.8 miles the net running time, including all regular slacks, was 5hr 40min, equivalent to a speed of 72.4mph. The run consisted mainly of a series of extremely energetic recoveries from slacks, requiring very hard work. Thus when recovering from the pwr [permanent way repair] slack at Ranney between Chicago and Milwaukee, from a speed of 60 mph, 70 mph was reached in 1 min 10 sec, 76mph in 2min

10sec, 80mph in 3min 10sec, 85mph in 4min, 90mph in 5min 20sec, 95mph in 7min 10sec, and 100mph in 8min 10sec. This acceleration took place on a slightly rising gradient of 1/3333. Twelve miles were then run at a speed varying between 97 and 106mph. On level track the sustained speed was 100.7mph, with the boiler pressure maintained at 295lb and water level unvarying at half a glass. The steam-chest pressure was 280lb per in2, the steam temperature 690oF. The engine was cutting off at 28% with a back pressure of 16lb per in2. Two shovelfuls of sands were thrown into the firebox when the engine started to accelerate, the fierce blast drawing the sand through the tubes and thus cleaning them; this was quite usual on oil-fired engines. The locomotive rode remarkably well. At 96mph I wrote my notes conveniently standing up and not leaning against anything. At 106mph I took them quite comfortably, sitting down."

Electro-Motive EA
Baltimore & Ohio Railroad: 1936

Baltimore & Ohio's EA featured a smoother streamlined treatment than later E-units. This locomotive was powered by a Winton 201A diesel engine, while later models used the more successful 567 engine.

Type: A1A-A1A, passenger diesel-electric

Power and output: A pair of Winton 12-cylinder 201-A diesels producing 1800hp (1343kW)

Tractive effort: 48,600lb (216kN) starting TE

Max. operating speed: n/a

Weight: 285,000lb (129t)

Overall length: n/a

Gauge: 4ft 8.5in (1435mm)

Electro-Motive's initial success with diesel-powered articulated streamlined trains put it in a position to develop a passenger diesel independent of an articulated set. The control cab was elevated with a strengthened nose section placed in front, while the locomotive's body was designed as structurally integral framework using an attractive modern streamlined design, and the intake vents were located to the sides behind the cab. The first of the new and much improved locomotives was Model EA, Baltimore & Ohio No. 51, delivered in 1937.

exemplified by the Santa Fe Class 3765 4-8-4s built between 1937 and 1944, which ran the 1788 miles (2877km) from Kansas City to Los Angeles in 26 hours and at an average speed of 68.8 mph (110.7km/h), with nine crew changes on the way. They had driving wheels 80in (203cm) in diameter and a boiler pressure of 300psi (21 kg/cm2). A potential rival in speed to the F7 was the Class J 4-8-4 of the Norfolk & Western Railway. This line's real business was moving coal in vast tonnages. It did not run many passenger services and its stud of express engines was not large. Their quality was, however, first-class. Eleven of class J were built between 1941 and 1943 to handle the line's principal passenger trains, and one reached 110mph (177km/h) on a test run with 1025 tons (1041t) on the Pennsylvania Railroad, near Crestline, Ohio: at which speed its 70in (177cm) driving wheels were being turned at a rate which would have brought much greater speed with larger diameter. Speeds of up to 90mph (145km/h) in regular service with 14 or 15-car trains were also recorded. But the culmination of this approach was seen in the Union Pacific Railroad's Class 4000.

Big Steam

These articulated 4-8-8-4s were the "Big Boys"—the name was chalked on a smoke-box during construction by an unknown employee of Alco, and it stuck. The 25 engines of this class were the largest and most powerful steam locomotives ever built, surpassing the Northern Pacific Yellowstones of 1928 in weight and with a length of 132ft 10in (40.4m) compared to 122ft (37.1m); their nominal tractive effort, at 135,375lb (61,406kg), was slightly less. Although the Union Pacific was an early user of diesel locomotives for its passenger express trains, it did not begin

GS2 class 4-8-4
Southern Pacific Railroad (SP): 1937

Boiler pressure: 300psi (21.1kg/cm²)	**Cylinders:** 25.5x32in (648x813mm)
Driving wheels: 80in (2032mm)	**Grate area:** 90.4sq ft (8.4m²)
Heating surface: 4887sq ft (454m²)	**Superheater:** 2086sq ft (194m²)
Tractive effort: 71,173lb (32,285kg)	**Total weight:** 883,000lb (400.5t)

The "Daylight" name of the San Francisco–Los Angeles streamlined train referred to its ability to do the 470 mile (756km) run within daylight hours; GS2 locomotives supplied the power. The design was introduced in 1930, built by Baldwins; GS2, built by Lima, was the first to be streamlined and had other modifications. In total, 74 GS types were built, up to 1943. They were all oil-burners, and booster-fitted to help tackle the heavy 1 in 45 (2.2 percent) grade of Santa

The "Daylight Limited" restored – the replica train, hauled by preserved GS4 No 4449, swings round the bend at Brock, California.

Margarita Hill, up which they commonly hauled their 568 ton (577t) trains unaided. No GS2 survives, but a GS4 and GS6 have been preserved, the former in working order.

to use diesels for freight until 1947. In this department, steam was still unchallenged.

The frame was a single massive cast steel piece. Welding was extensively used in building, notably in the construction of the boiler, pressed to 300psi (21 kg/cm2)—the highest pressure used with a conventional "Stephenson" tubular boiler. Multiple jet exhausts fed out through a double chimney. All axles were fitted with roller bearings. A significant new feature was the redesign of the joint between the front truck and the frame, to allow lateral movement only. Any changes in gradient or unevenness in the track were absorbed by a highly effective suspension system. This solved what had been a problem with big articulated engines: the occasional tendency of weight to shift from one

Class F7 4-6-4
Chicago, Milwaukee, St Paul & Pacific Railroad (CMStP&PRR): 1937

Boiler pressure: 300psi (21kg/cm²)		**Cylinders:** 23.5x30in (597x762mm)	
Driving wheels: 84in (2134mm)		**Grate area:** 96.5sq ft (8.9m²)	
Heating surface: 4166sq ft (387m²)		**Superheater:** 1695sq ft (157m²)	
Tractive effort: 50,295lb (22,820kg)		**Total weight:** 791,000lb (359t)	

These were introduced to enable heavier trains to be hauled on the Chicago–Minneapolis–St Paul "Hiawatha" expresses, while keeping the exceptionally fast schedule on this competitive line. Other lines were using 4-8-4s for similar purposes, like the Union Pacific's semi-streamlined GS type operating the San Francisco-Los Angeles "Daylight" streamlined train. But it is unlikely that any 4-8-4 exceeded the speeds attained by the F7. With a streamlined front and boiler casing that covered the cylinders too, the F7s showed the tendency of American designers to play down the "steamy" aspect of their passenger engines, though the wheels and running gear were left uncovered for easy access. Unlike their 4-4-2 predecessors, they

The Class F74-6-4 was introduced to haul heavier trains in the cold north of the United States.

were coal-burning. They ran trains of up to 12 cars, 550 tons (559t) at an average of 66mph (106km/h), including five stops. There are accounts of these engines exceeding 120mph (193km/h), but none are authenticated. In 1940, however, they did operate the fastest scheduled steam service anywhere, on the "Hiawatha's" Sparta-Portage sector, 78.5 miles (126.3km) run at an average of 81.25mph (130.75km/h), an interesting comparison with the English "Cheltenham Flyer" of the 1930s on its Swindon–London stage.

Class J-3a 4-6-4

New York Central Railroad (NYC): 1938

Boiler pressure: 275psi (19.3kg/cm²)	**Cylinders:** 22.5x29in (571x736mm)
Driving wheels: 79in (2005mm)	**Grate area:** 82sq ft (81.9m²)
Heating surface: 4187sq ft (388.9m²)	**Superheater:** 1745sq ft (162m²)
Tractive effort: 43,440lb (19,700kg)	**Total weight:** 360,000lb (163.2t) (engine only)

Alco built 39 of this class, as well as another nine in streamlined form, tailored for the *Twentieth Century Limited*, representing the peak development of the New York Central's racing "Hudsons" and bringing the line's stock of the type to 275. In 1941, another two were streamlined to run the "Empire State Express." The streamliners' casing added only 5500lb (2494kg) to the engine

The "Empire State Express," still a steam-hauled flyer in February 1952, seen here at Dunkirk, New York, its un-streamlined J-class "Hudson" pumping a crisp white exhaust into the frosty air.

weight. A booster engine fitted to the trailing bogie could supply a further 12,100lb (5487kg) of tractive effort in starting.

set of wheels to the other with consequent loss of adhesion by the lightened wheels.

Although they worked on other parts of the Union Pacific system, the Big Boys were built chiefly for the mountainous Sherman Hill main line through the Wasatch Mountains between Ogden, Utah, and Green River, Wyoming, a 176-mile (283km) stretch rising from 1933ft (596m) to 8013ft (2444m), with a ruling grade of 1.14 percent. The 4000s could haul trains of up to 70 refrigerated fruit cars,

weighing 3200 tons, over this road without assistance. The Big Boys were immediately effective in service. The first batch, built in 1941, all achieved more than a million miles (1,609,000km). Wartime traffic gave them much heavier loads, and they often worked double-headed on immensely long trains. Their last revenue earning duties were in July 1959, and withdrawal was complete by July 1962.

In discussing locomotive operation in the inter-war years, it should be kept in mind that the majority of working

Class GS-6 4-8-4

Southern Pacific Railroad (SP): 1938

Boiler pressure: 260psi (18.2kg/cm²)	**Cylinders:** 27x30in (685x761.4mm)	
Driving wheels: 73.5in (1865.5mm)	**Grate area:** 90.2sq ft (8.4m²)	
Heating surface: 4852sq ft (450.6m²)	**Superheater:** 2086sq ft (193.75m²)	
Tractive effort: 64,200lb (29,115kg)	**Total weight:** 468,400lb (212.4t) (engine only)	

Although the 4-8-4 is associated mainly with passenger trains, a number of lines acquired freight or mixed-traffic versions, usually with high-speed freight in mind. The GS-6 was tasked with hustling perishable Californian fruit and vegetables eastward across the prairies in 40ft (12.2m) insulated and ice-packed refrigerator cars, each weighing up to 75 tons (76.2t) fully loaded, and with up to 30 in a trainload. In all, 23 were built, by Lima, the dimensions of this locomotive comparable interestingly with those of its express passenger sister of 1937. The nominal tractive force as stated by the builders was marginally less, and in most respects the engine was just slightly smaller. Notably the driving wheels were smaller and the steam pressure considerably lowered, reflecting a lower running speed. The freight model had more weight borne by the coupled wheels, 126.4 tons (128.4t) compared to the passenger engine's 123

For all their size, the American 4-8-4s had a certain muscular compactness, certainly compared to the articulated locomotives. SP No. 436, at San Francisco in June 1952, exudes power, but within a few years the Southern Pacific would scrap all its remaining steam engines.

tons (125t), a modest extra amount of adhesion in getting the drag on a lengthy train. Both were oil burners and were fitted with the same standard "Type E" superheater. Though the tenders, on two six-wheel bogies, were identical in appearance, the GS-6's carried slightly less water and slightly more oil. Despite its lowlier role, the GS-6 was subjected to similar semi-streamlined styling, though painted in glossy black rather than the "Daylight" livery.

engines predated 1925. Many smaller yard engines had been built before 1910. A Baldwin sponsored survey of 1939 suggested that as much as 90 percent of the American locomotive stock was obsolete. The railroads came to agree,

but their answer was not what Baldwin would have hoped for. Though the later 1930s saw significant developments in steam locomotive design and construction, the interest of the railroads was moving steadily toward the greater use of diesel power. A number of events came together to turn this interest into active decision. The first was the development of effective lightweight diesel engines. Work on this had been going on in a number of companies, including the Winton Engine Company. Then this business, together with the Electro-Motive Car Company, was purchased by General Motors in 1930. It was a step of great significance. Winton was working both on spark-fired petrol-distillate engines and on non-spark diesel engines. Realizing, perhaps a little ahead of their competition, that when the economy revived they would need something new to offer against road and air competition, the Union Pacific and Burlington railroads both worked with the engine builders to create entirely new trains.

The first to appear, in early 1934, was the Union Pacific's M1000, known as the "Streamliner," a three-car articulated set built of aluminum and using the distillate-powered engine. Used as an exhibition train, it drew huge crowds. Two months later came the silver, diesel-engined, three-car aluminum *Zephyr* on the Burlington Route, which was an even greater sensation. Capable of maintaining 100mph (161km/h), the streamlined trains drew a large increase in traffic. Other lines hastened to follow, like the Boston & Maine with its "Flying Yankee" set. The streamlined train became the latest thing and many express steam locomotives received a cosmetic makeover to give them a modern look.

The third significant development was the building by General Motors, in 1935, of its Electro-Motive Division facility at La Grange, Illinois. This plant was intended for volume production and nothing was left to chance when it came to promoting business. Glossy brochures, color advertisements in magazines, and a team of well-briefed salesmen set out to convince the railroads that the future lay with the internal combustion engine.

Cash-strapped companies could benefit from special deferred-payment or leasing agreements. In 1937 the EA type, Electro-Motive Division's first passenger locomotive, was introduced on the Baltimore & Ohio. Its air-smoothed boxcab design was new and lent itself to bright paint treatment. Like the streamliner units, it was obviously an up-to-the-minute product of the twentieth century.

Class E-4 4-6-4
Chicago & North Western Railroad (CNW): 1938

Competing for passenger traffic with the Milwaukee Road's "Hiawathas," the Chicago & North Western Railroad had to come up with something special, and had nine streamlined "Hudsons" built by Alco in a style not at all unlike the Milwaukee Road engines, also from Alco; but exposing the cylinders as well as the motion. A hard-coal burner, it had a smaller grate than the rival F-7 4-6-4, and larger-diameter cylinders gave it a higher nominal tractive effort (good for publicity), but the dimensions of the two were otherwise almost the same. In performance terms, the two types were evenly matched, though the Milwaukee Road set tighter schedules than the Chicago & North Western. But the E-4 could exceed 100mph (160km/h) with a 500 ton (508t) train on level track. Engines such as these achieved the peak of American steam performance. Major developments would have been needed to go beyond this point; and these, of course, never happened.

Boiler pressure: 300psi (21kg/cm²)		**Cylinders:** 25x29in (634.5x736mm)	
Driving wheels: 84in (2132mm)		**Grate area:** 90.7sq ft (8.4m²)	
Heating surface: 3979sq ft (369.5m2)		**Superheater:** 1884sq ft (175m²)	
Tractive effort: 55,000lb (24,940kg)		**Total weight:** 412,000lb (186.8t) (engine only)	

A rival of the CNW locomotive, the Reading's "Pacific" runs the "Crusader" between Philadelphia and New York, proclaiming "every modern travel luxury at the regular coach fare."

Demonstration engines ran for thousands of miles on many lines, winning praise from crews, lineside staff, and passengers. A range of switchers and road engines was being introduced to an appreciative market, when war broke out in Europe in September 1939.

Great Trains

Discussion of motive power has already shown that some remarkable trains ran in North America during the late 1920s and early 1920s, powered both by steam and diesel engines. Not every "Limited" or "Express" could claim the

Class FEF-2 4-8-4
Union Pacific Railroad (UP): 1939

Boiler pressure: 300psi (21kg/cm²)		**Cylinders:** 25x32in (635x813mm)	
Driving wheels: 80in (2032mm)		**Grate area:** 100sq ft (9.3m²)	
Heating surface: 393m² (4225sq ft)		**Superheater:** 1400sq ft (130m²)	
Tractive effort: 63,800lb (28,950kg)		**Total weight:** 908,000lb (412t)	

The period from 1939 to 1944 marked the real heyday of the 4-8-4 as a passenger engine. A Norfolk & Western Class J reached 110mph (177km/h) with a 1025 ton (1041t) train on level track, and similar feats have been ascribed to the Union Pacific FEF ("four-eight-four"), of which 45 were built, with variations of design, between 1938 and 1944, all by Alco.

These engines attained a peak of power and efficiency, ironically, just as the General Motors Electro-Motive Division diesels began to

Union Pacific No. 844 is the last locomotive of the final series, FEF-3. Built in 1944, preserved, restored, and still steaming, it attracts attention as it stands at Sacramento, California.

eat seriously into the domain of steam.

Streamlining was no longer enough, and the FEFs were free both of cosmetics and gadgets—they were merely superb two-cylinder simple-expansion steam locomotives.

Electro-Motive SW1
Various Railroads: 1939

Electro-Motive's model SW1 was one of the builder's more popular early switcher types. Powered by a six-cylinder 567 engine, the SW1 was designed for slow-speed assignments in freight and passenger yards. In Electro-Motive's original parlance, the initials SW indicated "six hundred horsepower, welded frame"; however, the SW designation obviously had connotations of "Switcher." Later, more powerful switchers retained the SW prefix in their model designations. Built between 1939 and 1953, the SW1 operated on many lines. It can be quickly identified from other switchers by its single, narrow exhaust stack, the large platform behind the cab, and the exterior sandbox, which is located below the radiator.

Electro-Motive's 600hp SW1 was a type used in passenger train coach yards. Chicago, Rock Island & Pacific No. 4801 is seen at Chicago's La Salle Street Station in November 1977.

Type: Diesel-electric
Power and output: Six-cylinder 567 engine producing 600hp (450kW)
Tractive effort: 24,000lbf (107kN) at 10mph (16km/h)
Max. operating speed: 80km/h (50mph)
Weight: 200,000lb (90.8t)
Overall length: 44ft 5in (13.53m)
Gauge: 4ft 8.5in (1435mm)

speeds reached by the fastest few, and not many had an all-Pullman consist. If train names were an almost essential way of identifying a specific service, they were also a fine imaginative opportunity for the publicity department. "Limited" meant restricted accommodation, perhaps first class only: it was advisable or necessary to book in advance. "Express," which originally meant a train intended for a single destination, very soon took on the notion of "fast" as

well. Most of the names were descriptive, like the Santa Fe's *California Limited*, which told where it was going, or coming from; or the *Daylight Limited* which announced its ability to run between San Francisco and Los Angeles within daylight hours.

In some of these cases, names like the *Kansas Cityan* suggested that the publicists weren't trying very hard. Other names played up modernity, like the New York Central's

Electro-Motive FT Four Unit Set
Various Railroads: 1939

By 1939, Electro-Motive had mastered the American passenger diesel and diesel switcher trade. The next market for it to tackle was the heavy freight locomotive business. It was in this area that the most amount of money could be made, as American railroads earned most of their money hauling freight and were looking for means to reduce their costs. Electro-Motive's FT freight diesel was the machine that railroads had waited for. A four-unit 5400hp (4023kW) demonstrator toured the United States in 1939 and 1940, proving that a diesel-electric could move heavy tonnage in demanding circumstances. In the following months and years, several major railroads jumped at the opportunity to buy FT freight diesels. Most FT diesels comprised two semipermanently coupled A-B units designed to form an A-B-B-A set. The "A" units featured an engineer's (driver's) cab, the "B" unit was a cabless booster. Initially the entire four-unit set was treated as a single locomotive because of concerns that labor unions would insist on putting a driver on each "unit" if they were treated as individual locomotives. With later "F" unit types, the semipermanently coupled arrangement was discontinued and normal couplers became standard.

Santa Fe's "F" units lead the "Super Chief" at Chicago in 1952. The success of the FT model led Electro-Motive to improve its "F" unit line by boosting output and improving reliability. The FT can be distinguished from other models by a row of four "porthole" windows on the locomotive's side. Later models such as these seen here only used two or three windows. Santa Fe operated the largest fleet of FTs. Unfortunately, color photographs of them are very rare, as many photographers were concentrating on capturing steam locomotives rather than diesels.

Type: Four unit diesel-electric in A-B-B-A configuration, all units using Bo-Bo wheel arrangement
Power and output: Each unit powered by an EMC 16-567 diesel rated at 1350hp (1007kW), for a total output of 5400hp (4023kW)
Tractive effort: 220,000lbf (978kN) starting TE
Max. operating speed: n/a
Weight: 900,000lb (400t)
Overall length: 193ft (58.826m)
Gauge: 4ft 8.5in (1435mm)

Twentieth Century Limited, or boasted the qualities of the road, like its Pennsylvanian rival the *Broadway Limited*. With the *San Francisco Chief* and *El Capitan*, the Santa Fe took on the feathers and golden sheen of the west's picturesque history. Some names were resonant but had no special relevance, like the Chicago-Vancouver *Mountaineer* operated by the Canadian Pacific and its American dependency, the Soo Line. Many a train could have carried that name.

Emblems of various kinds were popular. The *Maple Leaf* defined the Grand Trunk's Chicago-Toronto train. From the former city's Dearborn Station, the Chicago & Eastern Illinois's *Whippoorwill* ran to Evansville, Indiana, and the *Meadowlark* to Cypress, California. It also operated the

Silent Knight to St Louis. In steam days the Lehigh Valley ran the *Black Diamond Express* between New York, Philadelphia and Buffalo.

The greatest glamour and prestige clung to the expresses that provided the greatest amount of luxury. In 1911 the *Santa Fe De Luxe* was introduced, to convey just 60 people between Los Angeles and Chicago, at a supplement of $25 above the first-class fare. It ran on only one day a week and did not survive World War I.

The less exclusive, though still grand, *California Limited* was more durable, operating until 1954. At its busiest, this train ran in as many as seven separate sections. From the 1880s, when the development of the vestibule meant that passengers could step safely from one car to another, a

Alco DL109 V
Various Railroads: 1940

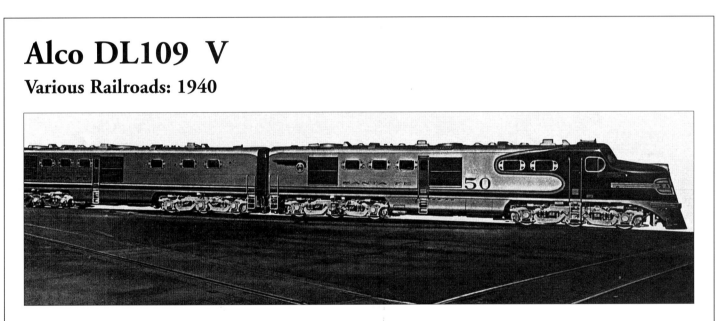

Alco hired Otto Kuhler, one of the best-known industrial designers, to style the streamlined carbody of its first road diesel. These locomotives were known by their specification numbers, DL103b to DL109. Ironically, the paint livery which was applied was actually designed for Santa Fe by the Electro-Motive Corporation.

Type: A1A-A1A, diesel-electric
Power and output: A pair of Alco 6-539T diesels producing 2000hp (1492kW)
Tractive effort: 30,500lbf (136kN) continuous TE at 20mph (32.2 km/h); 56,250lbf (250kN) starting TE
Max. operating speed: 120mph (192km/h) with 58:20 gear ratio
Weight: 337,365lb (153t)
Overall length: 74ft 6in (22.758m)
Gauge: 4ft 8.5in (1435mm)

Steam builder Alco had been building diesels since the 1920s as a sideline to its locomotive business. On the eve of American involvement in World War II, it introduced a high-speed road diesel to compete with the Electro-Motive E. Known by their specification numbers, these locomotives were designated DL103b to DL110, with the most numerous being the DL109 (69 built).

The various DL locomotives had only minor differences between them. They were powered by a pair of turbocharged six-cylinder inline diesels with 12.5 x 13in (317.5 x 330.2mm) bore and stroke operating at 740 rpm.

Otto Kuhler styled the carbodies, giving them a futuristic Art Deco image that contrasted with the cleaner image of Electro-Motive's rather prosaic E-unit.

Alco S-2
Various Railroads: 1940

The Alameda Belt Line was a switching line on the California island of Alameda in San Francisco Bay. The S-2 featured the Blunt truck and a large front-end radiator. American switchers designated the long hood as the front.

Type: Diesel-electric
Power: Alco six-cylinder 539 diesel producing 1000hp (746kW)
Tractive effort: 34,000lbf (151kN) at 8mph (12.9km/h) continuous TE; 69,000lbf (307kN) starting TE
Max. operating speed: n/a
Weight: 230,000lb (104t)
Overall length: 45ft 6in (13.862m)
Gauge: 4ft 8.5in (1435mm)

In the decade between 1940 and 1950, Alco built more than 1500 1000 hp (746kW) model S-2 switching locomotives for service in North America. In 1950 the S-2 was superseded by the S-4 model, while its 600 hp (448kW) S-1 was superseded by the S-3. Alco's S model switchers were a ubiquitous workhorse in yards and on short local freights. They were powered by Alco's successful 539 engine, and many had long careers.

Like all Alco diesels of the period, they employed General Electric electrical components. The generator was a GE GT-533, while traction motors were GE-731-D. Both the S-1 and S-2 models used the unusual Blunt trucks, while S-3, S-4, and later switcher models used variations of the more common Association of American Railroad truck design.

variety of specialized cars began to appear. Sleeping cars, parlor cars, club cars, dining cars, observation cars all featured in the makeup of express trains.

The first observation cars merely had an open platform at the end, and were always attached as the rearmost vehicle. In the 1900s the Canadian Pacific had coaches with raised observation compartments anticipating the vista-domes of

the 1950s. Electricity had replaced gas or kerosene lighting in new cars from around 1896, and the Pullman company began to experiment with all-steel cars from 1907, finally going into line production in 1910. Many other cars retained wooden body construction into the 1920s. The steel Pullman cars could weigh as much as 80 tons (81t) and ten of them made a considerable load for the locomotive. In

1931 the *Trans-Canada Limited*, running on the Montreal-Ottawa-Toronto-Winnipeg-Vancouver service, was equipped with first-class sleeping cars, compartment cars, a dining car, and a "solarium lounge" for its 2886-mile (4645km)journey. In addition, two parlor cars were put on for the Montreal-Ottawa section. Air conditioning, introduced in the 1930s on the *Twentieth Century Limited*, added further to the weight, but on heavy duty rails the massive cars ran with great smoothness. On all special

supplement express trains, attendants were expected to make the passengers feel privileged and cosseted. On the more routine long distance services, it was not always like that:

> *"Syracuse!" the porter cried,*
> *And shook me hard.*
> *"Excuse me, boss—*
> *This is where I'd wake you up,*
> *If you wasn't going to La Crosse."*

Class S1 6-4-4-6
Pennsylvania Railroad (PRR): 1939

Boiler pressure: 300psi (21kg/cm²)		**Cylinders:** 22x26in (558x660mm)	
Driving wheels: 84in (2132mm)		**Grate area:** 132sq ft (12.26m²)	
Heating surface: 5660sq ft (525.2m²)		**Superheater:** 2085sq ft (193.6m²)	
Tractive effort: 71,800lb (35,456kg)		**Total weight:** 1,060,000lb (523.4t)	

Not every design from the heyday of steam (the late 1930s and early 1940s) was a success. Despite a test run at 101mph (162.5km/h) with a 1342 ton (1364t) train, this locomotive was a one-off. A 32 ton (32.5t) maximum axle load limited its use, and its adhesive weight was only 26.5 percent of the total, so both sets of driving wheels tended to slip at the same time on starting. Built at the Pennsylvania Railroad's Juniata shops, it was exhibited

No. 6100 in Chicago on June 24, 1941, at the head of the railroad's luxury train "The General." With six of 10 axles not contributing to adhesive weight, one of the engine's problems can be seen.

at the New York World's Fair in 1939 and 1940, but little used, and was broken up in 1949.

CHAPTER 11

PRODUCTION IN WORLD WAR II

A new world war placed huge responsibility on the railroads, which rose to the challenge, moving record levels of traffic. An extra lease of life was accorded to steam, as the builders raced to provide motive power not only for the civilian war effort, but also for the needs of the US Army in many different war theaters.

Full-scale production of diesel locomotives was delayed by the demands of the war economy, but during those years, the diesel builders laid their future plans carefully. Meanwhile, however, the enormous increase in traffic,

Above: Three Union Pacific trains leave for Colorado, California, and North Pacific Coasts Point from Union Station, Omaha. Left: The illusion of an eye looks forth from the headlight as a polished steam giant stands in the shed. Two proud railroad men give scale to the design: the locomotive is 13 feet (4m) tall.

especially after American entry into the war in December 1941, had to be coped, with very largely by steam power. While Baldwin, Lima, Alco, and the smaller American builders labored to turn out steam locomotives, the development of diesel-powered traction did not come to a halt. General Motors' Electro-Motive Division plant and other diesel builders continued to build both switchers and freight road engines, though building of passenger diesel engines was officially brought to a stop in 1942. Among the new designs was the Alco RS-1, the first diesel locomotive

General Electric 44-Ton
Various Railroads: 1940

The 44-ton was one of several General Electric center-cab switchers built in the 1940s and 1950. This Housatonic Railroad GE center-cab is seen at Canaan, Connecticut.

Alco's Montreal Locomotive Works affiliate produced the RS-18 from 1956 to 1968. In most respects, this model was the same as Alco's RS-11 (specification No. 701), but featured a slightly higher hood style. Rated at 1341kW (1800hp), the RS-18 was comparable to the Electro-Motive Division's GP9 road switcher type and used in a variety of services. Canadian Pacific and Canadian National were the primary users of the RS-18 type and they were common on lines in eastern Canada. Canadian Pacific chopped the nose off most of its RS-18s to improve visibility, and the RS-18 was among the last types of MLW power in service on the railroad, with some locomotives surviving in regular service until the late 1990s.

Type: Bo-Bo, diesel-electric
Power and output: A pair of Caterpillar D17000 eight-cylinder diesels rated between 350hp (207kW) and 410hp (305kW)
Tractive effort: 22,280 lbf (99 kW) starting TE
Max. operating speed: 35mph(56km/h)
Weight: 89,112lb (44t)
Overall length: n/a
Gauge: 4ft 8.5in (1435mm)

designed to work equally well as a switcher and a road engine, and the forerunner of many similar models to come. Acknowledging the emergence of diesel power, Alco and Lima had already set up joint ventures to build diesel-electric locomotives with General Electric and Hamilton respectively; and Baldwin later began collaboration with Westinghouse.

By 1945 and the end of the war, many American railroads were using diesel freight engines. In both the United States and Canada the steam fleets were showing the marks of several years of intensive use, combined with reduced and often less-skilled maintenance. Unlike the position in the previous war, the American government did not take overall control of the railroads. But the strategic planners of the War Production Board directed what equipment the railroads might buy, and promoted a spurt in steam locomotive construction. Steam engines were cheaper to build than diesels, and there was ample construction capacity. The railroads worked together in relative harmony, and in collaboration with the Office of Defense Transportation, to move the traffic. The years between 1939 and 1945 were prosperous for the railroads, with most lines working at near full capacity, and often having to extend it. With many of their colleagues drafted to the US Army Transport Corps, engine crews and maintenance staff earned a great deal of overtime pay. Staff levels generally

Alco RS-1
Rock Island Railroad: 1941

A Green Mountain Railroad RS-1 leads the company's excursion train toward Chester, Vermont, in October 2001.

The basic configuration of Alco's model RS-1 makes it the grand-daddy of all modern American freight diesels. It was one of the most influential designs. First built in 1941 for the Rock Island, the RS-1 was the first road switcher designed to work equally well as a road diesel or yard switcher. Previous diesel models were designed for more specific service. Over a nearly 20-year span, more than 400 RS-1s were built for North American service. More significant than the number of RS-1s built was the effect on future development. Versatility was key to the success of the road switcher type. By 1949 all the major builders were offering road switcher types, and by the 1950s the road switcher had become the dominant type bought by American railroads.

Today nearly all freight diesels are variations on the road switcher. The RS-1 had another significant influence. A variation of the type known as an RSD-1 used a Co-Co arrangement. During World War II, Alco provided a fleet of RSD-1 to the USSR. Soviet diesel development was a direct outgrowth of the RS-1; thousands of Soviet diesels were built based on RS-1 era technology.

Type: Bo-Bo, diesel-electric
Power and output: Alco 6-539 diesel producing 1000hp (746kW)
Tractive effort: 34,000lbf (151kN) continuous TE at 8mph (12.9km/h); 59,500lbf (264kN) starting TE.
Max. operating speed: 60mph (96.6km/h) with 75:16 gear ratio
Weight: 238,000lb (108t)
Overall length: n/a
Gauge: 4ft 8.5in (1435mm)

Green Mountain Railroad Alco RS-1 405 photographed crossing the Connecticut River main line at Bellows Falls, Vermont, in October 2001.

Class 4000 4-8-8-4
Union Pacific Railroad (UP): 1941

Boiler pressure: 275psi (19.3kg/cm²)	**Cylinders:** 22x30in (559x762mm)
Driving wheels: 75in (1905mm)	**Grate area:** 81sq ft (7.5m²)
Heating surface: 3791sq ft (352m²)	**Superheater:** 1542sq ft (143m²)
Tractive effort: 45,300lb (20,548kg)	**Total weight:** 659,000lb (299t)

These were the "Big Boys"—the name was chalked on a smokebox during construction by an unknown employee of Alco, and it stuck. The 25 engines of this class were the largest and most powerful steam locomotives ever built, surpassing the Northern Pacific "Yellowstones" of 1928 in weight and with a length of 132ft 10in (40.49m) compared to 122ft (37.18m); though with a lesser nominal tractive effort. Although the Union Pacific was an early user of diesel locomotives for its passenger express trains, it did not begin to use diesels for freight until 1947. In this department, steam was still unchallenged, but the requirements were severe. The design was worked out by the Research & Standards department of the Union Pacific, in close association with Alco, which built the engines. The moving spirit was Otto Jabelmann, the railroad's head of motive power and machinery since 1936, and Vice-President in charge of research and mechanical standards since 1939. He had also overseen the design of the line's other giant steam locomotives, including the "Challenger" 4-6-6-4s of 1936, which preceded the "Big Boys." The Union Pacific also operated the world's longest rigid-frame locomotives, the 88 three-cylinder 4-12-2s built between 1926 and 1930. However, it was clear that to obtain greater power, an articulated wheelbase would be necessary. The "Challengers" provided the answer. Mallet-type engines, though with simple expansion only, they had front coupled wheels that formed an articulated truck while the rear coupled wheels were set in the frame. On the first engines of the type, the front truck was allowed

The scale of the "Big Boys" can be judged by the size of the engineer of No. 4024. One of the original 1941 locomotives, it is forging its way up-grade with a mixed train of freight cars.

vertical as well as lateral movement. This was one of the few unsatisfactory aspects of the design, giving the front set of coupled wheels a tendency to slip. Until now, articulation had been associated with low-speed slogging, but the "Challengers" could and did run at 80 miles (130km) an hour, riding easily. As the Lima-built "super-power" 2-8-4 of 1925 had done, the great 4-6-6-4 of the Union Pacific and Alco opened a door to further possibilities with steam traction. Other lines soon realized this, and a further eight bought engines of the same type. A total of 254 were built, of which 105 belonged to the Union Pacific.

Wartime traffic gave them much heavier loads, and they often worked double-headed, a thrilling spectacle as they climbed the grade. Their last revenue-earning duties were done in July 1959, and withdrawal began from 1961. Eight of the "Big Boys" are preserved as static museum and display items.

One of the preserved "Big Boys," No. 4012, at the railway museum at Scranton, Pennsylvania, on May 2, 1997.

were down; with many railroad workers in the military, retired operatives often came back to work. Women also came to play a far more important part in the man's world of railroad operation; they had long been present as telegraphers and in railroad catering, but now it was common to find female conductors and signalers.

New Designs

The modern steam locomotives of the 1930s—Northerns, Big Boys, Yellowstones in the United States; Selkirks in Canada, and the others—performed yeoman service. New designs were still appearing, like the giant 2-6-6-6 "Allegheny" type, built by Lima for the Chesapeake & Ohio between 1942 and 1949, and capable of hauling a 5200-ton (5283t) coal train on the hill grade between Hinton, West Virginia and Clifton Forge, Virginia.

The same builders constructed 50 "Mohawk" 4-8-2s of class L4 for the New York Central between 1942 and 1944. Intended for fast freight haulage, these could deputize for

the line's 4-6-4 "Hudsons" on express passenger trains. Comparing 1944 to 1918, the American railroads now had 26,000 locomotives against 40,000, only 75 percent of the number of freight cars, and 70 percent of the passenger cars, but moved almost double the amount of freight and more than double the number of passengers. Certain lines, serving seaports and vast new military depots, saw a much greater increase.

The lean years of the Depression had taught a forcible lesson in efficiency, but technical progress also made a vital contribution. Chemical treatment of the water used in locomotive boilers dramatically reduced the time once taken up by boiler washouts, descaling, and repairs. Locomotives spent less time on the depot and more in

The massive scale of the almost 500 ton (508t) H8 2-6-6-6 can be appreciated in this photogaph, taken at the Baltimore & Ohio Railroad Museum. Its rear truck alone supported more weight than that of a 2-8-0 of the 1890s.

───────────── AN EYEWITNESS ACCOUNT ─────────────

The Home Front

Although the battlefronts were far away, the railroads gave the American people the clearest view of how war affected the whole nation. Stations like Ogden, Utah, and North Platte, Nebraska, ran an endless series of troop trains and hospital trains, their cars marked with red crosses on the sides, bound for military hospitals. The railroads themselves required military protection. In depots, trains loaded with gasoline were patrolled by armed guards to protect the cargo. Much rarer and more exciting, bullion trains could sometimes be seen. The gold bars were transported in special cars with "U.S. Army" signs. The bullion cars were reinforced six-wheelers, only half the length of a regular boxcar, and armed guards traveled with them.

revenue service. In 1918 the average yearly mileage of a freight engine was around 50,000. By 1944 this had almost doubled. Centralized traffic control had trains running to tighter schedules, closely monitored, to anticipate and avoid

A close-up of the six-wheel truck under the firebox of the H8 2-6-6-6, showing its heavy double-frame construction. One of the design problems was to get adequate ashpan capacity between the firebed and the truck.

delays. This method of control had become increasingly common from the 1920s, and many new centralized traffic control systems were installed during the war years. It was of particular value on the lengthy single-track sections, where the old system of train orders, made out by the dispatcher and handed to the engineer and conductor, specifying passing places, had often caused long delays. Now lineside signals, remote-controlled switches,

Class TC S118 "MacArthur" 2-8-2
US Army Transportation Corps (USATC): 1942

Like the other USATC designs built in large numbers, this one not only performed valuable service during World War II, but was a staple engine on many systems for a long time after that. Designed by Alco for the meter (39.4in) or 3ft 6in (1065mm) gauges, 859 were built between 1942 and 1945, with Baldwins, Davenport, Porter, and Vulcan all involved in building. It acquired the unofficial name of "MacArthur," in honor of American General Douglas MacArthur, whose star was high at the time. Maximum route availability was demanded, so the heaviest axle load was 9 tons (9.1t) and it was built to clear even restricted loading gauges, while various different kinds of drawgear and braking equipment could be fitted, and it could easily be switched from coal to oil firing. It was intended to be as economical and simple as possible both in construction and in operation.

Most MacArthurs went to the Indian meter-gauge (39.4in) lines, delivered for assembly on arrival. In the later stages of the war, some went to Burma, Malaya, and Siam (Thailand). Others were in service—in some cases into the 1970s—in Iraq, Algeria, Tunisia, Nigeria, the Gold Coast (Ghana), the East African Railways system, the French Cameroons, the Manila railroad in the Philippines, the Queensland Government Railways in Australia, the United Fruit Company lines in Honduras, and the White Pass & Yukon Railroad in Alaska. After the war, some were built for the Peleponnesus Railway in Greece. One continent was without a "MacArthur": rail-free Antarctica.

A "MacArthur" on the meter gauge (39.4in) of the Southern Railway of India. The robustness and relative simplicity of the design are clearly apparent.

Boiler pressure: 185psi (13kg/cm²)	**Cylinders:** 16x24in (406x609mm)
Driving wheels: 48in (1218mm)	**Grate area:** 27.7sq ft (2.6m²)
Heating surface: 1371sq ft (127.3m²)	**Superheater:** 374sq ft (34.7m²)
Tractive effort: 21,825lb (9900kg)	**Total weight:** 119,000lb (54t)
	(engine only)

An Indian Railways "MacArthur" working hard. The engine is well-kept, and, for an Indian loco, decorated in a restrained style.

TC-S160 class 2-8-0
US Army Transportation Corps (USATC): 1942

Boiler pressure: 225psi (15.75kg/cm²)	**Cylinders:** 19x26in (482x660mm)
Driving wheels: 57in (1447mm)	**Grate area:** 41sq ft (3.8m²)
Heating surface: 1765sq ft (164m²)	**Superheater:** 471sq ft (43.7m²)
Tractive effort: 31,490lb (14,280kg)	**Total weight:** 162,400lb (73.6t) (engine only)

S-160s got as far as China, where they were classed KD6 and worked in mining areas at least into the 1980s. Note the extended upper cab sides.

Commissioned as one of four standard steam types by the USATC, 2120 of the TC S160 class and its variants were built, to standard gauge, at the three major American loco works, Alco, Baldwins, and Lima, between 1942 and 1945. A small engine by American standards, built to fit within the relatively tight British loading gauge, it was a typically American design, with bar frames; two outside simple-expansion cylinders operated by piston valves and actuated by Walschaerts gear; a high-set boiler; and a wide, round-topped steel firebox.

Driving position was on the right; on the fireman's side a tiny door opened frontward onto the running plate. The engines had steam brakes plus a Westinghouse air brake pump, with air cylinders placed under the running plate on each side. The compressor pump was fitted to the left of a narrowed smokebox door. On the engines used in Britain, dual air/vacuum brake equipment was fitted. Fireboxes were fitted with rocking grates and hopper ashpans. On the boiler top, dome and sandbox were in a single housing. The standard American three-point suspension system gave them a stable ride even over ill-maintained and bomb-blasted tracks. Despite a number of American "convenience" fittings, which made the locomotives popular with British and European crews, there was no power reverser. The great majority were coal-burners, though some oil-burners were built or converted, including 106 for the south-west region of France, which had oil-fueling facilities. Two types of standard eight-wheel tender carried 8 tons or 10 tons (8.1 or 10.1t) of coal and 6480gals (24,529l) of water. The design was a very sound one, with only one significant defect that emerged with time, a weakness in the screw fixing of the firebox roof stays, which caused a number of firebox collapses.

The first overseas destination for the S160s was Britain, partly to provide extra motive power under the Lend-Lease scheme, partly as a holding base for the invasion of Europe. In September 1943, the Great Western Railway's repair shops at Ebbw Junction, Newport, in South Wales, became the HQ of No. 756 Railway Shop Battalion, US Army, and engines were readied here for use or storage. As back-up in the North African campaign, 139 were shipped to Oran by mid-July 1943. By late 1944 they were being shipped to the continent in large numbers, to operate in liberated and Allied territory. Two Military Railway Services control departments kept track of their locations and allocated their functions, together with those of other military locomotives like the British WD types. Apart from military use in troop, munitions, and general supply trains, and ambulance trains, they were loaned to supplement deficiencies in available power on civilian services. Usage peaked in 1945; then, as hostilities ceased in Europe, many were gathered in a huge "dump" at Louvain in Belgium and also at other depots.

The S160s had been built as wartime engines, with no expectation of a long life, but in Poland and Hungary large numbers were still in regular service in the early 1970s. In these two countries particularly, the S160s were invaluable freight engines during the hard years of the later 1940s, running in service with their wartime rivals, the German class 50 and 52 2-10-0s.

Class L4-a 4-8-2

New York Central Railroad (NYC): 1943

Boiler pressure: 250psi (17.5kg/cm²)	**Cylinders:** 26x30in (660x761.4mm)
Driving wheels: 72in (1827mm)	**Grate area:** 75sq ft (6.9m²)
Heating surface: 4675sq ft (434.2m²)	**Superheater:** 2103sq ft (195.3m²)
Tractive effort: 59,900lb (27,165kg)	**Total weight:** 401,100lb (181.9t)
	(engine only)

This was a mixed-traffic locomotive, known by the New York Central as the "Mohawk" type: "Mountain" was not deemed appropriate by the managers of the "Water Level Route." With the first in 1916, the railroad had over 350 in service. The 50 of class L4-a were built between 1942 and 1944 by Lima, then a division of Lima-Hamilton (the steam firm of Lima had merged with the diesel engine Hamilton company); 25 of class L4-a and 25 of the almost

Class L-4a, No. 3113 gets a heavy westbound freight on the move past Dunkirk, New York, on a winter morning in 1952. By this time the class was mostly employed on freight traffic, with very little passenger work, due to the advent of more powerful engines.

identical L4-b. Capable of running at 80mph (130km/h), they were able to deputize for "Hudsons" in express service.

additional crossing loops, and telephone links increased the capacity of such lines by up to 75 percent.

By 1944 the total railroad traffic volume in the United States amounted to 783 billion ton-miles (1252.8 t-km) of freight. Passenger travel saw a similar increase, with 95 billion passenger-miles (152 billion km) recorded in 1944. During the war, American railroads carried 43 million members of the armed forces in 114,000 special troop trains.

With operations on such a huge scale, there were also

difficulties and problems. Despite an unshakable national commitment to victory, labor troubles were not unknown, spurred by the knowledge that the companies were making profits undreamed of in the lean 1930s. Even passenger operations, whose losses had been subsidized by freight, were turning in a profit between 1942 and 1945.

Gas rationing, restricting automobile use, helped pack the trains. (There would be a price to pay after the war, however. Travelers who resented over-filled trains and service delays often vowed never to use a train again if they could help it). In the spring of 1943, miners' "cost of living" strikes over pay briefly threatened a fuel crisis, and in the following winter, when strikes threatened to paralyze some lines, the federal government used its wartime powers to take charge of the railroads during December and January in order to maintain services. The War Labor Relations Board, set up in 1941 to help in labor disputes, had a busy time.

Class Q2 4-4-6-4
Pennsylvania Railroad (PRR): 1944

On the PRR test plant, the Q2 developed around 8000bhp at 83km/h (57 mph), with steam cut-off at 40 percent—believed to be a record output for a steam locomotive with reciprocating motion.

The Pennsy did not give up easily in the campaign to perfect the "duplex drive" which had already produced the T1 4-4-4-4.

In 1942 a 4-6-4-4, class Q1, was built, but found unsatisfactory. The prototype Q2 followed, and trials were successful enough for the War Production Board to allow a production run of 25, built in 1944 and 1945. A booster engine was fitted to the rear bogie.

Although the least problematic of the duplex drivers, these engines had surprisingly short careers, most being put into store in 1949; by this time the railroad's diesel fleet was growing rapidly, and all the Class Q2s were scrapped between 1953 and 1956.

The shark-nose design was dropped, though the Q2 had a skyline casing along the boiler-top, partially enclosing the chimney.

The maximum axle load was 35.5 tons (36t), among the heaviest of any locomotive of the period, which restricted its route availability and caused some worries in locomotive yards.

Boiler pressure: 300psi (21kg/cm²)
Cylinders: front 19.75x28in (502x711mm); rear 23.75x29in (603x737mm)
Driving wheels: 69in (1751mm)
Grate area: 1216.6sq ft (113m²)
Heating surface: 6169.25sq ft (573m²)
Superheater: 3628.3sq ft (337m²)
Tractive effort: 100,800lb (45,722kg)
Total weight: 619,000lb (280.7t)

Class 2900 4-8-4

Atchison, Topeka & Santa Fe Railroad (ATSF): 1944

Boiler pressure: (cm²)	**Cylinders:** 28x32in (710x812mm)
Driving wheels: 80in (2030mm)	**Grate area:** 32.8sq ft (10m²)
Heating surface: 1617sq ft (493m²)	**Superheater:** 718sq ft (219m²)
Tractive effort: 66,000lb (29,932kg)	**Total weight:** 510,150lb (231.4t)

Thirty of this class were built by Baldwins, the Santa Fe's last fling with express steam. They were fitted with roller bearings throughout, and like some other 4-8-4s they were reputed to have operated at 100mph (161km/h) and more. One of their racing grounds was between Los Angeles and San Diego, though they also ran the long haul between Los Angeles and Kansas City without change of engine. They later went on to run freight trains in Texas and Oklahoma, but

Santa Fe No. 2928 pilots a triple-unit diesel-electric on the "Super Chief," eastbound from San Bernardino, up the 2.2 percent Cajon Pass grade in California. The smoke-stack is fully extended.

were all taken off between 1959 and 1960. Some of them had the curious Santa Fe special feature of an extensible chimney that could be raised to improve drafting. Several are preserved.

Peak Period

Every railroad town in the United States and Canada operated at peak activity throughout the war period. Schenectady's Alco Works, which had built only 42 locomotives in 1934, hit a production peak of 1414 in 1944. At the same time, the shops were building M-7 anti-tank guns and M-3 medium Grant tanks. The staff at North Platte Station, Nebraska, on the Union Pacific, were dealing with up to 10,000 military personnel passing through every day. In this war, with heavy action taking place in the Pacific

as well as in Europe, east-west traffic was just as important as the west-east flow. The Ogden Union Station also serviced a tremendous amount of both freight and passenger traffic.

During the war years, as many as 120 passenger trains a day moved through Ogden. There were 17 tracks for passenger service, and all were needed. The underground passageway from the station to the platforms was almost permanently crowded with people. Ogden, as well as its locomotive depot, had car and wagon repair shops, and

S1 "Niagara" class 4-8-4
New York Central Railroad (NYC): 1945

Boiler pressure: 275psi (19.3kg/cm²)	**Cylinders:** 25.5x32in (648x813mm)
Driving wheels: 79in (2007m)	**Grate area:** 100sq ft (9.3m²)
Heating surface: 48.27sq ft (4.48m²)	**Superheater:** 2060sq ft (191m²)
Tractive effort: 61,570lb (27,936kg)	**Total weight:** 891,000lb (405t)

In theory designed for passenger and freight work, but in practice purely passenger engines, the S1s, far better known as "Niagaras," were designed at a time when air competition scarcely existed, and the fast way from New York to Chicago was by express train.

Ten years later, things looked very different. But these engines showed that the railroad's era of monopoly had not led to complacency. Massive as they were, they were built for consistent high speed and performance, to a degree that was probably never equalled with steam.

Twenty-five were built between 1945 and 1946 by Alco, to the specifications of Paul Kiefer, the New York Central's head of motive power. The 928 mile (1493km) New York–Chicago run, once requiring up to four locomotive changes, was to be run by the same engine, with a pause for a rapid top-up of the tender coal. Water could be picked up from pans laid between the tracks.

A classic 1947 image of American passenger railroading with steam, Class S1 No. 6016 fronts a passenger train formed from nine cars and a matching baggage car, at Oscawanna, New York.

An annual distance run in excess of 275,000 miles (442,000km) could be expected. And average speeds were high. The prime train was the *Twentieth Century Limited* with a timing of 16 hours, requiring an average of 58mph (93km/h) including stops. By this time steam engines were not permitted within New York City limits, so electric locos hauled the fliers out to Harmon, where the "Niagaras" took over. Mile after mile at a speed exceeding 80mph (128km/h) was required to maintain the schedule. Sophisticated and swift work in the depots at each end was needed to keep the engines serviced to a peak of efficiency. For consistent heavy-duty performance, this class was unrivaled anywhere in the world.

intensive usage of the rolling stock also meant a constant high level of activity in these shops.

The war record of the railroads was an overwhelmingly good one and their contribution immense. Unlike the railroads of war zones, they did not suffer from the destruction of stations, installations, and rolling stock, though intensive use and often-makeshift repair meant that

much of the rolling stock and many installations were in a dilapidated state by 1945. But, as commercial concerns, they benefited from the extraordinary levels of traffic. The Illinois Central was typical in its economic success. By 1944, its operating ratio had fallen to less than 65 percent of revenue, and it had succeeded in reducing its funded debt by $100 million.

"Centipede" Model DR-12-8-1500/2
Pennsylvania Railroad (PRR): 1945

Intended for high-speed passenger work, Pennsylvania Railroad's Baldwins "Centipedes" worked their last days as freight helpers, such as these two seen shoving a freight around the Horseshoe Curve near Altoona, Pennsylvania.

Type: 2-Do+Do-2, diesel-electric
Power and output: A pair of Baldwin eight-cylinder 608SC engines producing 3000hp (2235kW)
Tractive effort: 52,800lbf (235kN) continuous TE at 17.8mph (28.7km/h); 102,205lbf (454kN) starting TE
Max. operating speed: 93.5mph (150km/h) with 21:58 gear ratio
Weight: 593,700lb (269t)
Overall length: 91ft 6in (27.889m)
Gauge: 4ft 8.5in (1435mm)

During World War II, Baldwins of Pennsylvania Railroad set out to build a multi-engine high-speed diesel based largely on electric locomotive practice. This 6000hp (4470kW) machine was intended for speeds up to 117mph (187km/h). However, it never entered production.

Baldwins did build a scaled-back diesel with two engines that produced 3000hp (2235kW) per unit using an articulated frame with a 2-Do+Do-2 wheel arrangement.

It was known as a "Centipede" because of its many wheels and baby-faced cab. Seaboard Air Line was the first to order the type; Pennsylvania Railroad and National Railways of Mexico also bought them. The Pennsylvania Railroad had the largest fleet, used initially in passenger service.

CHAPTER 12

RAILROADS IN THE POSTWAR ERA

Massive changes in social habits swept across North America, with the rise of the automobile and the long-distance airplane. The railroad corporations, so long accustomed to dominating surface transport, were faced with a grave challenge. Modernization on a huge scale was launched by the big companies.

In many ways, the victory year of 1945 saw the railroads in good shape. The war years had left them prosperous, though there was heavy demand for capital expenditure on neglected and dilapidated buildings and installations. There

Above: By the late 1940s, all locomotives were built in a streamlined style that dominated for the remainder of the century. Left: The Santa Fe's striking colors and design, inspired by Native American models, have crossed the deserts and mountains for more than 60 years, on a wide variety of locomotive types.

were other calls for modernization, on communications, signaling, the laying of heavier track for more powerful locomotives; and, not least, for the resumption of large-scale construction of diesel-electric locomotives. The railroads invested heavily in a massive program of modernization and renewal.

For most companies, an explicit part of this program was the phasing out of steam traction. From 1945, only a very small number ordered new steam locomotives, and these tended to be lines with a strong involvement in coal

Alco FA/FB

Various Railroads: 1946

A double-unit FA1, photographed in September 1946 during road tests in Eastern Pennsylvania. The Santa Fe was among the railroads which bought it, for use on long-haul expresses like the "Super Chief."

Type: Bo-Bo, diesel-electric
Power and output: Alco 12-cylinder 244 diesel producing 1500–1600hp (1119–1194kW)
Tractive effort: 37,500lbf (167kN) continuous TE at 12.5 mph (20.1km/h); 57,500lbf (256kN) starting TE (depending on weight)
Max. operating speed: 65mph (105km/h) with 74:18 gear ratio
Weight: 230,000lb (104t)
Overall length: 51ft 6in (15.697m)
Gauge: 4ft 8.5in (1435mm)

The FA/FB, intended for heavy road freight service, had an Alco/GE standard cab unit and the same basic configuration as the more common EMD F-unit. It had similar streamlining to the PA passenger diesel, but was shorter and featured a Bo-Bo wheel arrangement. The FA was intended to operate in sets of three or four, and was often run in multiple with other Alco types, especially RS-2 and RS-3 road switchers. The FA/FB type was produced between 1946 and 1956.

haulage, like the Chesapeake & Ohio and the Norfolk & Western. The latter, like the Pennsylvania Railroad, was unusual in building most of its own locomotives; for it, the investment in the workshops and workforce were another strong argument for retention of steam power. For most companies, however, the issue was already cut and dried. They needed new locomotives, and the diesel offered low

maintenance, intensive use, and, not least, the need for fewer staff. With money in the bank, and post-war traffic levels remaining high, the elevated capital cost of new diesel units did not seem to be a serious problem. Railroad staff in general was enthusiastic about the change.

The labor unions, seeing a massive fall in their membership about to happen, struggled to maintain a role

EMD F-Units, Model F7
Various Railroads: 1946

The success of the FT during World War II set up EMD as the leading builder of road diesel-electric locomotives. After the war ended and the restrictions on implementing new designs were lifted, EMD improved its F-unit line and introduced the F3 (an interim model, designated F2, was built for a short period). The F3 was

Burlington Northern displays its "Executive F-units" at Galesburg, Illinois, in June 1996. Burlington Northern used these two F-units on its deluxe business train.

slightly more powerful than the FT, with each of its units rated at 1500hp (1119kW), instead of 1350hp (1007kW).

Other mechanical improvements enhanced the F3's performance and reliability. In 1949 the F7 superseded the F3, although output remained the same. Then, in 1954, the F9 superseded the F7. The F9 was rated at 1750hp (1306kW). EMD's streamlined F-units were a ubiquitous symbol of American dieselization and used by nearly all of the railroads.

Type: Bo-Bo, diesel-electric
Power and output: EMD 16-567B producing 1500hp (1119kW)
Tractive effort: Various
Max. operating speed: Various
Weight: Various
Overall length: 50ft 8in (15.44m) (A-unit)
Gauge: 4ft 8.5in (1435m)

Alco RS-2/RS-3

Various Railroads: 1946

RS-3 engine No. 8223 in Dewitt, New York, awaits servicing and repairs while working on a shortline route.

After World War II, American railroads set out to transfer to diesel as quickly as possible. Alco introduced several new models that proved popular with railroads. In the late 1940s, its 1500hp (1119kW) semistreamlined RS-2 road switcher was one of its better selling designs. The versatility offered by the road-switcher type allowed railroads to assign them to a variety of different services. New York Central, for example, used RS-2s in suburban and local passenger service, on local freights that needed to switch en route, on branch-line freights, and in multiple on heavy road freights. In 1950 Alco boosted the output of its 12-244 engine to 1600hp (1194kW). Some RS-2s were built with the higher rating, but, by mid-1950, the RS-3 superseded the RS-2. With more than 1350 RS-3s built for North American service, it became one of the most common Alco designs.

In 1956 Alco's RS-11, powered by the newer 251 diesel, superseded the RS-3. Despite greater reliability, fewer RS-11s were sold, as by that time most railroads had largely finished their transfer to diesel. The RS-11 had a taller hood and more boxy appearance than the RS-2/RS-3 models. A few RS-3s had very long service lives; some survived on shortlines past the year 2000.

Type: Bo-Bo, diesel-electric
Power and output: 12-cylinder Alco 244 producing 1500hp (1119kW)
Tractive effort: 61,000lbf (271kN) starting TE
Max. operating speed: 65mph (105km/h) with 74:18 gear ratio
Weight: 244,000lb (111t)
Overall length: 55ft 6in (16.91m)
Gauge: 4ft 8.5in (1435mm)

An Alco RS-3 parked in the sidings at Eagle Bridge, New York. The RS-3 was built with a larger engine capacity than the RS-2, and some RS-3s were still in service 40 years later.

for a second man in the locomotive cab. To the companies, a large part of the diesels' charm was that a single man could operate several big locomotives, linked up as a multiple unit. In fact, a combination of state laws and union pressure made single-manning a rarity for about twenty years.

The constant labor troubles in the American coal industry also helped the demise of steam power. Strikes and lockouts interrupted fuel supplies and caused cancellations of service. The price of coal rose sharply. Although lines like the New York Central and the Norfolk & Western had brought steam design, maintenance, and reliability to a point where it was claimed to match the efficiency and operating costs of diesels, they were pushing against the flow. Other companies, like the Union Pacific and Santa Fe, had for some years a dual-type policy, with diesel hauled passenger trains and steam hauled freight. But the last steam locomotive for domestic use was built by Lima in 1949.

Market Leader

Among locomotive builders, the Electro-Motive Division emerged as the market leader, profiting both from its high profile publicity of the later 1930s and from the wartime work of its locomotives, especially the FT four-unit set introduced in 1939, familiar from many Santa Fe desert scenes. Alco and Baldwin, joined in partnership with General Electric and Westinghouse respectively, while Lima merged with Hamilton. The manufacturers fought for a share of the hungry market, and were joined in the struggle by the Fairbanks-Morse Company. But they were essentially geared to steam construction—and still busy building steam locomotives for export—and steadily lost ground. Lima-Hamilton merged with Baldwin, who had built more locomotives than any company before or since, but production stopped after 1951.

Alco's partnership with General Electric came to an end in 1953 and GE forged ahead in building their own locomotive range while Alco remained a distant third among suppliers. In 1963 Fairbanks-Morse dropped out. By the end of the 1960s, Alco gave up locomotive building, and the two giants, General Motors and General Electric, were left to compete with each other. Though GM's market domination in the 1950s was strong enough to provoke a Congressional anti-monopoly investigation, GE eventually pulled ahead as the bigger supplier.

A pair of Nickel Plate Road Alco PA diesels is seen leading a Buffalo-bound passenger train at Dunkirk, New York, in March 1952.

With the new motive power also came serious attempts to improve services. The traditional, serviceable, straight-sided passenger car, painted a dull green or brown, was replaced by brightly painted or metallic finish cars in aluminum and stainless steel. The transcontinental lines introduced the dome car, an idea taken up by others that traversed picturesque country and had a suitable loading gauge. The scene seemed set for a new era of success. Postwar America was richer than it had ever been; the mass of the population had never had so much disposable income and leisure time. The railroads used intensive publicity to promote their new, improved services.

To their surprise and dismay, passenger numbers, instead of going up, fell steadily. It was not that Americans were less mobile than before. Business, vacation, and leisure travel were all increasing steadily. But the alternatives to railroads

TRAVELERS' TALES
A Lucky Change of Train

In September 1950, Clark Johnson Jr was a young railroad enthusiast heading from his home in the Twin Cities (Minneapolis/St Paul, Minnesota) to the National Model Railroad Association convention in Milwaukee, Wisconsin. He and about 20 other conventioneers were riding overnight on Chicago & North Western's North Western Limited, and hoped to get to Milwaukee by morning in order to catch a special excursion on the Milwaukee Electric Rapid Transit & Speed Rail—a suburban electric interurban line. Johnson recalls: "A lot of my friends were planning to ride. It would have been a lot of fun."

In the early morning hours, the North Western Limited paused at Merrillan, Wisconsin, a five-way junction in the northern part of the state.

"When our train pulled in, I saw a short local passenger train at the station. I thought it was the local run to Manitowoc. It had a little old Ten Wheeler [4-6-0], a couple of baggage cars, a mail car, and a lone coach. A friend and I made a quick decision to get off the through train to Milwaukee, and jump on this cross-country local instead. It didn't go where we were headed and it would not travel very fast, but it was a lot more interesting!"

The chance to ride such a classic train seemed more important than the model railroad convention and the special excursion. Here was a small piece of history. At one time, local passenger trains such as this one connected almost every town in the United States, but by 1949 they were a dying breed. Within a couple of years, the train would be canceled, the rails pulled up, and North Western's little Alco-built R-1 4-6-0, now sitting there at the Merrillan depot happily steaming away, would be cut up for scrap.

As it turned out, Johnson's choice to climb onboard was a good one that may have saved his life. Soon, he and his friend were riding through the Wisconsin scenery, listening to the music generated by the small locomotive pulling the train. As the local made its way east it paused at small, out-of-the-way stations, picking up mail and passengers, just as it had for decades.

"After we got on, we found that this train was only going as far as Kaukauna, and not making it all the way to Manitowoc. It didn't matter—we enjoyed the ride, not caring that we would miss the interurban special. When would we ever get back to ride a steam train like this? As it turned out, we never made it to Milwaukee, and it was lucky too! The excursion we had hoped to ride was involved in a terrible fatal accident when it collided head-on with another car at Hales Corners near Milwaukee. Ten or 11 people died in the crash, including a couple of my friends. If I had gone to Milwaukee I would have been on that excursion, and I might have been killed too."

Sometimes it pays to follow your intuition!

EMD E-Units; Model E7
Various Railroads: 1946

Wisconsin & Southern E8A 801 at Horicon, Wisconsin, in 1995.

> **Type:** A1A-A1A, passenger diesel-electric
> **Power and output:** A pair of EMD 12-567-A diesel producing 2000hp (2681kW)
> **Tractive effort:** 18,800lbf (84kN) continuous TE at 33 mph (53.1km/h); 53,075lbf (236kN) starting TE
> **Max. operating speed:** 98mph (157.7km/h) with 55:22 gear ratio
> **Weight:** 315,000lb (143t)
> **Overall length:** 71ft 1in (21.673m)
> **Gauge:** 4ft 8.5in (1435mm)

The Electro-Motive E-units were the answer to railroad requests for a practical streamline diesel-electric locomotive with conventional couplers that was not integrated in a fixed train set.

Baltimore & Ohio and Santa Fe were the first railroads to use the Es. All E-units used a pair of high-output two-cycle diesel-engines in a streamlined body riding on A1A trucks. The earliest Es (models EA & EB, E1 and E2) were powered by Winton 201 diesels. However, from mid-1938 onward, the Es were powered by the Electro-Motive 567 diesel in 12-cylinder configurations. The "E-unit" designation reportedly stems from the locomotive's initial output of "eighteen-hundred" (1800hp/1343kW) per unit. With the introduction of the 12-567 engine, the per unit output was boosted to 2000hp (1492kW), but the "E" designation continued.

The earliest Es, built for Baltimore & Ohio, Santa Fe, and Union with each railroad's locomotives being treated differently. With the E3, the styling became more standardized. Models E3 to E6, built from 1938 until 1942, featured a steeper sloping nose than the postwar E7, E8, and E9s, which used the standard "Bulldog" nose that debuted on the FT freight diesel in 1939. The E5 was a model built only for Burlington, and featured stainless-steel styling to match its Zephyr consists. The A1A truck was a three-axle design, with the two outside axles powered and the center axle used to help distribute the locomotive weight.

The two most numerous E-unit models were the E7 and E8, which were built from 1946 to 1949, and 1949 to 1953, respectively. The last E-unit type was the 2400hp (1790kW) E9, which remained in production until 1963. By then American passenger operations were in serious decline; there was almost no market for new passenger locomotives. E-units were built in both "A" and "B" configurations, the later type being a cabless "booster" type. Most railroads ran E-units in multiples to haul long-distance passenger trains, including New York Central's *Twentieth Century Limited*, Pennsylvania's *Broadway Limited*; Southern Railway's *Crescent;* and Illinois Central's *City of New Orleans.* (Amtrak inherited a sizeable fleet of E-units, operating some until the mid-1980s.) As passenger services declined in the 1960s, a few lines, such as Erie-Lackawanna, assigned Es to freight services, often using them on priority intermodal trains. The last large fleet of E-units in regular service was Burlington Northern's used to haul its "Dinkys"—Chicago area suburban trains.

In the livery of the Gulf, Mobile & Ohio Railroad, a pair of EMD E7s leaves Chicago with a southbound train in 1952.

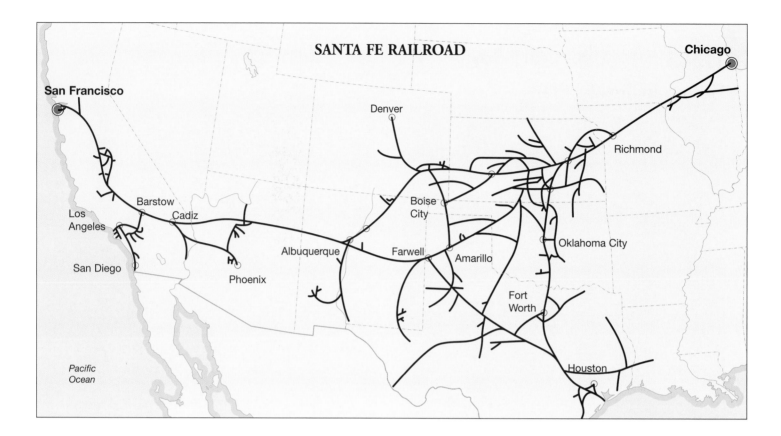

SANTA FE RAILROAD

Above: The Santa Fe was one of the best-known lines in the West, connecting Chicago with Texas and California. Today, it is a component of the Burlington Northern Santa Fe Railway.

Below: The Union station at El Paso, Texas, had an ecclesiastical air with its spired tower. The absence of a clock is unusual. Passengers remained in the concourse until the arrival of the train.

UNION STATION, EL PASO TEXAS

Baldwin "Shark Nose"
Various Railroads: 1947

The Pennsylvania Railroad was the only railroad to order passenger locomotives with the "shark nose" body style. A pair of DR-6-4-20s is seen in 1963, toward the end of their active service.

In the postwar race to dieselize American railroads, Baldwins looked to distinguish its road diesels from those of the Electro-Motive Division. Its early road units had a carbody style that looked remarkably similar to the Electro-Motive's, so it hired a industrial design firm to give its locomotives a distinctive look. The result was the so-called "shark nose" body style. This name was not formally used by Baldwins.

Several different locomotives used this style, including DR-6-4-20 A1A-A1A high-speed passenger diesels built for the Pennsylvania Railroad. Other DR-6-4-20s did not use the shark nose body, but instead had a "Babyface" body style. Likewise, only some Baldwins DR-4-4-15s, a Bo-Bo freight diesel, used shark nose bodies, while others used a "Babyface" design. These locomotives were built

Type: Bo-Bo, diesel-electric
Power: Baldwins eight-cylinder 608A producing 1600hp (1194kW)
Tractive effort: 73,750lbf (328kN)
Max. operating Speed: 70mph (112km/h)
Weight: 248,000lb (113t)
Overall length: 54ft 11in (16.73m)
Gauge: 4ft 8.5in (1435mm)

between 1947 and 1950. The most numerous type of "Sharks" were 1600hp (1192kW) RF-16s built in the early 1950s. These were bought by the Pennsylvania Railroad, New York Central, and Baltimore & Ohio. The RF-16 was essentially an upgraded DR-4-4-15. The Baldwins engine was good for low-speed heavy freight service, and many "Sharks" worked in coal and iron ore service. The last "Sharks" in service were a pair of former New York Central RF-16s that worked for Monongahela, then Delaware & Hudson, and later shortlines in Michigan.

had become far more accessible. Mass production of automobiles, and the building of thousands of miles of inter-city and inter-state freeways, diverted a huge number of journeys onto the roads. Cars, trucks, and buses accounted for most of the huge increase in journeys. And airlines began to claim the long haul business traffic. Their marketing was as slick as that of the railroads, and their message of convenience was more convincing. By the middle 1950s, most railroad passenger services were in a state of crisis.

Great urban terminals, built fifty or sixty years before in opulent style, began to acquire a forlorn appearance. Their architecture recalled a bygone age, their wide spaces were too great for a reduced number of users, and their great spreads of track were largely redundant. A process of retrenchment set in. Services were cut, rails were lifted, and in a self-accelerating process, the cutbacks made railroad travel even less inviting and reduced passenger numbers further. For the companies, it was a novel, even baffling experience. In a struggle to retain or retrieve their passengers, some introduced new styles of trains. The diesel railcar, introduced by the Budd Company of Philadelphia in 1949, was widely used as an alternative to locomotive-hauled trains on local and medium distance trains. But its limited capacity was a sign of the times. On the still busy New Haven-New York lines, the New Haven Railroad

Alco PA/PB
Various Railroads: 1947

The Budd Rail Diesel Car was well suited to secondary passenger services. In 1983 Metro-North assigned RDCs to its Waterbury branch in Connecticut. A single car is pictured near Derby.

Edward Budd, the founder of the Budd company, had previously worked for the McKeen Company, which produced self-propelled gasoline-engine railcars in the early 1900s. The Philadelphia-based Budd Company, however, was to enter the limelight with the introduction of Burlington's famous *Zephyr*, which used Budd's lightweight, stylish streamlined stainless steel cars.

By the late 1930s, Budd was producing streamlined passenger cars for many of the American railroads. The company's fluted stainless steel cars were assigned to some of America's best known trains, including Santa Fe's famous "Super Chief."

Although Edward Budd died in 1946, his company went on to design a successful diesel-powered railcar. The first Budd Rail Diesel Car (commonly known as an RDC) was built in 1949. Like Budd's passenger cars, the RDC used lightweight stainless-steel construction and featured fluted sides. RDCs were designed to operate singly or in multiples.

In the 1950s, hundreds of Budd Cars were ordered by North American railroads for use on secondary passenger services. While some RDCs were relegated to branch-line or suburban services, others were equipped for long-distance runs. There were several standard types of cars. The RDC-1 was a basic coach, while the RDC-2 had a baggage compartment, and the RDC-3 had baggage and Railway Post Office sections, in addition to its coach seats.

Type: Self-propelled diesel-hyraulic passenger rail car
Power and output: A pair of GM 6-110 diesel engines producing 275hp (205kW) to 300hp (224kW)
Tractive effort: n/a
Max. operating speed: 85mph (136km/h)
Weight: 126,730lb (58t)
Overall length: 85ft (25.9m)
Gauge: 4ft 8.5in (1435mm)

GE "Little Joe"
Various Railroads: 1949

Above: Interurban electric railroad Chicago, South Shore & South Bend operated three Little Joes in freight service until the early 1980s. Its freights are now diesel powered.

Below: Milwaukee Road received 12 of the 20 Little Joe electrics built for the USSR. These were used on Milwaukee's Rocky Mountain electrification. Some remained in service until 1974.

Type: 2-Do-Do-2, electric
Power: 3000V DC on Milwaukee/1500V DC on South Shore
Tractive effort: 110,750lbf (492kN)
Max. operating speed: 70mph (112km/h)
Weight: 535,572lb (243t)
Overall length: 88ft 10in (27.08m)
Max. axle load: 55,100lb (25t)
Gauge: 4ft 8.5in (1435mm)—originally built for 5ft (1524mm)

In 1948 General Electric constructed 20 very powerful modern streamlined electrics for the Soviets. Cold War hostilities between the United States and the Soviet Union, however, prevented the locomotives from reaching their intended buyer, and General Electric sought other customers for the machines which became known as "Little Joes" in reference to the then Soviet leader, "Big Joe" Stalin.

Milwaukee Road took 12 of the "Little Joes" for use on the eastern electrified segment of its Pacific Extension between Harlowton, Montana, and Avery, Idaho (Milwaukee Road operated two disconnected segments of electrification, and the western segment was in Washington State). Chicago-area interurban electric

line Chicago, South Shore & South Bend took three "Little Joes", while Brazil's Paulista Railway was to buy the remaining five. As the Russian standard gauge is 5ft (1524mm), the locomotives needed new wheel sets to accommodate the American 4ft 8.5in (1435mm) gauge.

EMD SD7/SD9

Southern Pacific Railroad: 1949

An SD9 engine, No. 4372, waits in the sidings for repairs and servicing. Units were often stored if business was slack.

Type: Co-Co, diesel-electric
Power: EMD 15-567C (on SD9) producing 1750hp (1303kW)
Tractive effort: continuous TE 67, 500lbf (300kN) at 8mph (12.8km/h)
Max. operating speed: 65mph (105km/h)
Weight: 324,000lb (147t)
Overall length: 60ft 8in (18.49m)
Gauge: 4ft 8.5in (1435mm)

In Electro-Motive parlance, SD stood for "Special Duty." When the Division brought out its first six-motor road switcher, the SD7, in 1952, there was only minimal demand for such a locomotive. Greater tractive effort with lower axle-loading was the primary attraction of the SD7 type, which was basically a six-motor variation of the GP7 "General Purpose" diesel. In 1954, the Electro-Motive Division increased the power output of its 16-567 engine, resulting in new model types. At this time the SD9 replaced SD7.

With its heavily graded profile, Southern Pacific was the largest user of these early SDs. Southern Pacific operated many of its SD7s and SD9s for more than 40 years, extending their lives by rebuilding them at its Sacramento, California, shops. On Southern Pacific, they were known as "Cadillacs."

This SD7 was used by Southern Pacific for more than 30 years throughout California.

introduced a dual-power locomotive in 1956, the FL9. Built by Electro-Motive Division, it had both diesel power and a third-rail electric pick-up for city tunnels where diesel smoke was no more welcome than coal smoke had been. New style trains were introduced, like the New Haven lightweight "Talgo" train based on Spanish technology (the name is a Spanish acronym for "lightweight articulated train"). But nothing stemmed the decline.

Decline of Passenger Services

In 1950 the United States had 147,511 miles (237,389km) of passenger railroad; by 1970, this was reduced to around 42,000 miles (67,590km). Famous trains were dropped from the schedules. The Lehigh Valley's *Black Diamond Express*, its name sadly out of date, perished in 1961. In 1967 the most iconic of all express trains, the *Twentieth Century*

Limited, made its last run. A significant sign of the railroads' fall in public esteem was the demolition of the world's largest passenger station, Pennsylvania Station in New York City, in 1964. This vast classic style building, with its train shed behind, had been opened with pomp and ceremony in 1911. Fifty-three years later it had vanished, and the rails ran underground in a confined concrete structure.

Its fate was to be typical of many great and small station buildings across the country, from Chicago's Grand Central and Chattanooga's historic Union Station, both demolished in 1971, to the attractive wayside depot of Palestine, Texas, razed with hundreds of others in the early 1970s.

Virginian No. 130 is lead unit of a pair of General Electric EL/C locomotives as a coal train is prepared for departure. The high-clearance power wire required very tall pantographs.

The railroads might have survived the loss of their passenger services without suffering serious harm. Freight had always been their bread and butter. James J. Hill, builder of the Great Northern, had once said of the passenger train that it is "like the male teat—neither useful nor ornamental." Freight services held out much better— here the railroads retained their advantage in long distance haulage at competitive rates. Demand for new and more powerful freight locomotives remained steady. But the pattern of freight transportation was changing. Coal traffic,

once the backbone of great railroads, was diminishing rapidly as alternative energy sources were brought into use. Trucks were rapidly taking away the railroads' market in short haul mixed freight, and the rural way freight, picking up boxcars here and there in a leisurely progress, was becoming an anachronism. Such lines were also feeders into the main system, and their traffic was gradually lost.

Manufacturing and distribution companies, which once considered it essential to have a rail spur directly into the factory or warehouse, were beginning to invest in their own

H-24-66 "Train Master"
Various Railroads: 1953

In 1953 Fairbanks-Morse brought out the most powerful of its road switcher types, the 2400hp (1790kW) six-axle, six-motor model H-24-66, advertised as the "Train Master." These were powered by a 12-cylinder Fairbanks-Morse opposed piston engine. In its time, the "Train Master" was the most powerful single engine road switcher on the market, and it proved versatile.

The Virginian used its H-24-66 in heavy coal service, while Southern Pacific used it on its weekday San Francisco–San Jose suburban services and on weekends for heavy freight work. Despite its versatility, "Train Master" production totaled just 127 locomotives; tiny compared to the number of Electro-Motive road switchers built in the same period.

Against the backdrop of the Manhattan skyline, Central Railroad of New Jersey F-M Train Master 2413 leads a five-car suburban train west from the railroad's Jersey City terminal in May 1964.

Type: Co-Co, diesel-electric
Power and output: 12-cylinder Fairbanks-Morse opposed piston diesel producing 2400hp (1790kW)
Tractive effort: 112,500lbf (500kN)
Max. operating speed: Various depending on gear ratio
Weight: 375,850lb (170t)
Overall length: 66ft (20.11m)
Gauge: 4ft 8.5in (1435mm)

EP-5

New Haven Railroad: 1955

A New Haven EP-5 leads a Boston-bound passenger train near Woodlawn in the Bronx in the summer of 1961.

New Haven Railroad's last new straight electrics were 10 double-ended streamlined EP-5s built by General Electric in 1955 and 1956. These used then state-of-the-art ignitron rectifier technology to convert 11,000V AC from New Haven's overhead catenary to low-voltage DC traction motors. Ignitron rectifier tubes were a variation of mercury arc technology. The EP-5s featured a cab style very similar to those used by Alco-GE built FA diesel-electrics.

Type: Co-Co, passenger electric
Power: 11kV AC at 25Hz from overhead
Output: 4000hp (2980kW) at 44mph (70km/h)
Tractive effort: 87,000lbf (387kN) starting TE; 34,000lbf (151kN) continuous TE
Max. operating speed: n/a
Weight: 348,000lb (157t)
Overall length: n/a
Max. axle load: 65,000lbs (30t)
Gauge: 4ft 8.5in (1435mm)

road fleets, and the rail links rusted or were torn up. As with passenger service, the railroad companies devised new ways of attracting traffic, including inter-modal or "piggy-back" trains, in which road trailers were carried cross-country. But they remained supreme only in bulk haulage, where single load trains of vast tonnage could be run at rates which road haulage could not hope to compete with.

The Poor Relations

Railroads, which in the nineteenth century had been the economic engine of the country, able to dictate to state governments, and often arrogant in their ability to outsmart whatever attempts the federal government made to control them, were reduced to poor relation status in the America of the 1950s and 1960s. A multiplicity of state laws, dating back to their time of monopoly, now impeded their struggles to compete.

Many of their services were regulated by state law and their efforts to cut or terminate these were fiercely resisted by state legislatures. Other regulations resulted in expensive overmanning of trains: in an age when engineers and conductors were in radio contact with each other and with control towers, and trains had automatic braking systems, crews of up to six men were not required, but the unions,

Alco RS-11
Various Railroads: 1956

Type: Bo-Bo, diesel-electric	

Type: Bo-Bo, diesel-electric

Power and output: Alco 12-cylinder 251B engine producing 1800hp (1341kW)

Tractive effort: n/a

Max. operating speed: n/a

Weight: n/a

Overall length: n/a

Gauge: 4ft 8.5in (1435mm)

A former Central Vermont Railway RS-11, lettered for Genesee Valley (a locomotive leasing company), is seen here on the Rochester & Southern at Brooks Avenue Yard in Rochester, New York.

Alco's post–World War II road locomotives were powered by its 244-series diesel engine. Flaws in this design unfortunately resulted in greater maintenance costs and poorer than hoped for sales by Alco. To rectify this situation, Alco developed a better engine design, its 251-series, which was first used in six-cylinder configuration on the S-5 and S-6 switcher models built in 1954 and 1955.

In 1956 Alco introduced the 1800 hp (1341kW) RS-11 road switcher powered by a 12-cylinder 251B engine. This locomotive featured a taller hood and a more boxy appearance than Alco's earlier RS-2/RS-3 road switcher types. More than 425 RS-11s were built over the next five years for North American service. The RS-11s were to be brought into service by many lines, including the Central Vermont, the Delaware & Hudson, the Lehigh Valley, and the Pennsylvania Railroad.

and many state authorities, fought hard against any change. The railroads' old reputation for great wealth, and for unscrupulous management, now counted against them. It was hard for outsiders to believe that these mighty corporations could not fulfil their obligations. The railroads received no subsidies and in many areas were subject to special taxes. The Interstate Commerce Commission still controlled rates and, perhaps also influenced by the bad old days of rebates and pooled rates, often refused railroads permission to reduce their charges in order to compete. Inevitably, there was an implosion.

Bankruptcies

Large-scale railroad bankruptcies began in 1957, with the New York, Ontario & Western Railway, a line which had depended on coal traffic. Old rivals discussed merger plans and formed new joint companies, like the Virginian and the Norfolk & Western in 1959. By 1960 all main line railroads

had sent their last steam locomotives to museums, or to stand as monuments on cut off track, or to the breakers' yards; only a few industrial concerns still ran steam on private lines. American railroads were the first in the world to complete the elimination of steam haulage. But modernization did not save them. Their traffic and fortunes continued to decline through the 1960s. In 1962 the Baltimore & Ohio and Chesapeake & Ohio Railroads merged (taking the name Chessie System in 1972).

Though they shook the railroading world, these were merely steps on the downhill path: the amalgamated Penn Central itself went bankrupt in 1970, pulled down by a massive deficit on its passenger business. In that year, the Burlington Northern was formed out of the Chicago, Burlington & Quincy, the Northern Pacific, the Great Northern, and the Spokane, Portland & Seattle railroads. The series of bankruptcies and mergers went on remorselessly, and gloomier observers from the railroad scene joined with the more sanguine advocates of road transportation to prophesy that by the end of the century the United States would have no railroads at all.

The crisis in passenger transportation finally prompted action from Congress. On May 1, 1971, the National Railroad Passenger Corporation was established. This government-owned corporation, better known as Amtrak, took over responsibility for almost all inter-city passenger services. Simultaneously, the services themselves were drastically reduced, with half the already much depleted route mileage taken out, leaving a 21,000- mile (33,795km) system. The government had to step in again in 1976, to

EMD FL9

New Haven Railroad: 1956

Amtrak regularly assigned its small fleet of former New Haven FL9s to Empire Corridor trains between Albany–Rensselaer and New York City; FL9 484 is seen at the former station in October 1993.

The EMD FL9 was a specialized hybrid locomotive developed especially for the New Haven Railroad. An unusual adaptation of the diesel-electric locomotive, it was equipped with third-rail shoes that allowed it to run as an electric locomotive in electrified territory. This allowed New Haven to run the FL9s directly into New York's Grand Central Terminal and Penn Station, both of which required long journeys through tunnels where diesel engine

emissions were prohibited. By using these dual-mode locomotives, the New Haven Railroad was able to run through passenger trains from Boston to New York without changing locomotives.

Type: B-A1A diesel-electric/electric
Power and output: EMD 16-567C producing 1750hp (1305kW) and powered by a 660 volt DC third rail.
Tractive effort: 58,000lbf (258kN)
Max. operating speed: 90mph (145km/h)
Weight: 286,614 lb (130t)
Overall length: 58 ft 8in (17.88m)
Gauge: 4ft 8.5in (1435mm)

form Conrail (the Consolidated Railroad Corporation) out of the ruins of Penn Central and such other proud names as the Central of New Jersey, the Lehigh Valley, and the Reading Railroad. Under the Carter presidency, the Staggers Act of 1980 allowed for a substantial degree of deregulation, and the tax regime on railroads was favorably

revised during the following Reagan administration. The old Interstate Commerce Commission was wound up and replaced by the Surface Transportation Board.

The war was hardly over when passenger revenues had begun to plummet. The losses sustained by American railroads providing passenger services, increased five-fold

EMD SD24
Various Railroads: 1958

A brand-new SD 24, readied for the Burlington Route as No. 505, stands outside the Electro-Motive plant at La Grange, Illinois, in 1958. The extension of the hood side, needed to house the turbocharger, can clearly be seen.

The SD24 was Electro-Motive's first turbocharged high-horsepower six-motor diesel. Introduced in 1958, and built until 1963, this 2400 hp (1788kW) machine was a preview of the type of motive power that would become the standard on most American freight railroads. Externally the SD24 was similar to EMD's SD9, although the SD24 could easily be identified by the circular bulge located behind the cab on the long hood that housed the turbocharger. Santa Fe and Union Pacific both ordered SD24s with the low nose

option that was just becoming popular and, by the late 1960s, would be a standard option, while Burlington and Southern had high-hood SD24s. Santa Fe rebuilt its SD24 fleet with EMD 16-645 engines to boost output and improve reliability; these were re-designated as SD26s.

Type: Co-Co, diesel-electric
Power: EMD 16-567D3 producing 2400hp (1788kW)
Tractive effort: 95,700lbf (425kN)
Max. operating speed: n/a
Weight: 382,800lb (174t)
Overall length: n/a
Gauge: 4ft 8.5in (1435mm)

EMD GP20

Various Railroads: 1959

Several railroads, including Santa Fe, originally assigned GP20s to fast freight service. Later they were often used on local freights.

One of the strengths of Electro-Motive early diesel locomotives was the powerful, compact, and extraordinarily reliable 567 engine. Thousands of Fs, GPs, Es, and switcher types were powered by variations of the 567 diesel. The 567 was traditionally supercharged using a Roots scavenger blower. In the late 1950s, Union Pacific modified some of its Electro-Motive GP9s with turbochargers to obtain greater output. The Division followed suit by introducing its own turbocharged 567 diesel, the 2000hp (1492kW) GP20. This model was also one of the first that was offered with either a traditional high short-hood (nose section) or a low short-hood for better visibility. The GP20 was well suited to fast services, and the model set an important technological precedent; however, it was relatively short lived and was in production only until 1962.

Type: Bo-Bo, diesel-electric
Power and output: EMD 16-567D2 producing 2000hp (1492kW)
Tractive effort: 45,000 lbf (200kN) at 14 mph (22.4 km/h)
Max. operating speed: 65mph (104 km/h)
Weight: 256,000 lb (116t)
Overall length: 56ft 2in (17.12m)
Gauge: 4ft 8.5in (1435m)

between 1946 and 1953. Almost one-third of passenger trackage was abandoned between 1947 and 1957. By 1973 passenger miles would be less than a tenth of the 1944 figure. While passengers had traditionally been subsidized by freight, losses now added up to almost half of the railroads' net freight revenue, clearly an unsustainable level.

Buffalo was typical of medium-size cities in seeing usage of passenger services fall, and its passenger services steadily trimmed away until the proud Central Terminal, a city landmark built earlier in the century by the New York Central was like a ghost station. Passenger train movements in the Buffalo area went from 172 in 1943 to 124 in 1954,

GE U25B
Various Railroads: 1960

In the early 1980s, Maine Central acquired a small fleet of General Electric U25Bs from the defunct Rock Island.

General Electric had long been a producer of straight electric locomotives, a supplier of electrical components for diesel-electric locomotives, and a builder of small diesel locomotives for switching and industrial service. Until 1960, however, when it debuted its U25B road switcher, it had not directly competed in the American market for heavy freight locomotives. General Electric's Universal line began with the U25B, a four-motor heavy freight locomotive. It was powered by 7FDL-16 diesel engine, a design GE licensed from Cooper-Bessemer. With the U25B, GE established its place in the

American market and in 1963 it introduced a six-motor road diesel, the U25C. One of the largest proponents of the GE's U25B was Southern Pacific, which had been looking for more powerful diesel locomotives.

Type: Bo-Bo, diesel-electric
Power and output: General Electric 7FDL-16 producing 2500hp (1863kW)
Tractive effort: Various
Max. operating speed: Various
Weight: 260,000lb (118t)
Overall length: 60ft 2in (18.33m)
Gauge: 4ft 8.5in (1435mm)

Southern Pacific's first six Krauss-Maffei locomotives were traditional carbody units, such as No. 9000 pictured here. Later hydraulics were built as road switchers.

a 28 percent decrease. Central Terminal was quickly becoming a huge liability to the New York Central. In 1957 the railroad paid over $370,000 in taxes on the station. Between 1947 and 1957, ticket revenue at the terminal declined by almost $850,000, about 25 percent. Local passenger train services became ever fewer and ever less patronized. In 1957 the Central lost over $110,000 on the five daily round trips between Buffalo and Niagara Falls. The Public Service Commission finally allowed the New York Central to abandon the local Buffalo-Niagara Falls service in 1959, leaving only one through train between New York City and Niagara Falls, which ran until 1961. Buffalo's experience was being repeated all across the country.

Who was to Blame?

How far were the railroads to blame for their own disastrous history between 1946 and the end of the seventies? There is a "They should have seen it coming" school of thought among historians, as well as an "It was inevitable" viewpoint. Those who believe the railroad managers failed to understand the new world in which they found themselves can point to some significant evidence. They accuse the railroads of trying to discourage passenger travel, with increases in fares and reductions in services and standards. The railroads did not do enough to promote their own routes and advantages. Advertising by the railroads was significantly less than that of airlines. During the first seven years of the 1950s, airline advertising doubled, while railroad advertising fell by twenty-five per cent. It has also been suggested that the railroad companies should have collaborated on route and service planning in order to cut out unnecessary duplication of passenger services.

No doubt the railroad managers were often complacent, at least in 1945 and 1946, and often might have been smarter, more competitive against other forms of transport, and more cooperative within their own industry. But most of the criticisms are leveled with hindsight. In the later 1940s, anyone giving an accurate picture of the North American scene in the late 1970s would have been accused

GE U50C

Union Pacific: 1963

As No. 41 of the Union Pacific's diesel-electric fleet, a 280-ton, 5000hp (6702 kW) GE U50D unit stands at the manufacturers' works, ready for hand-over, in 1964. Ten were built in this form.

Union Pacific, well known for its extraordinarily large and powerful locomotives, experimented with very large double-diesels in the 1960s. General Electric supplied two varieties.

The first were U50s (sometimes described as U50Ds), which rode on four sets of Bo trucks in a Bo-Bo+Bo-Bo arrangement like that of Union Pacific's early gas-electric turbines. These were built between 1963 and 1965. The later locomotives used a more common Co-Co wheel arrangement and were built between 1969 and 1971.

Both the U50 and the U50C delivered 5000hp (3730kW);

however, while the earlier locomotives used a pair of 7FDL-16 diesels, the U50Cs used smaller 7FDL-12 engines.

All of these big General Electrics possessed unusually tall cabs with almost no nose section, marking them as especially odd in the annals of American dieseldom.

Type: Co-Co, diesel-electric
Power and output: A pair of 7FDL-12 diesel engines producing 5000hp (3730kW)
Tractive effort: n/a
Max. operating speed: n/a
Weight: n/a
Overall length: 79 ft (24.07m)
Gauge: 4ft 8.5in (1435mm)

of writing science fiction: social changes might happen quickly, but not all at once. And the sorely tried railroad bosses had much to contend with that was not of their own making. Government subsidization of highways and airports greatly aided those transportation developments and kept their costs low.

Railroads did not receive government assistance or subsidy until long after the war, when their decline was fully apparent. In fact, a wartime 15 percent excise tax on tickets,

meant to discourage wartime civilian train travel, remained in effect, keeping fares higher than necessary. This tax was reduced slightly in 1954, but was not completely removed until 1962.

Collaboration

Government regulations, allowing for increase of municipal property taxes, and towns using these property taxes to help subsidize roads and airports, added to the expenses of railroads while eating into their passenger travel market. Collaboration between railroad companies, easy to suggest after the event, was difficult to achieve, especially in a declining market, when every business was looking to protect itself.

Where pooled or shared services were possible, every company wanted to be the one which ran the service, thereby maintaining its staff, stock, and financial well-being at a better level than the others'. The services themselves were controlled by external agencies, whose permission for change had to be granted, and which did not always understand the situation.

It was not so much complacency as their own past successes that were the undoing of the railroads. Their critics also underestimate the sheer volume of investment, corporate planning, and management time that went into

EMD SD45
Various Railroads: 1965

With 3600hp (2686kW) produced by a single turbocharged 20-cylinder engine, the SD45 quickly became the shining star of many American railroads. By the 1960s fast freight was the story of the day, and the SD45 locomotive the one to move it. Western railroads, such as the Southern Pacific and Santa Fe, were especially keen on the SD45 and subsequent 20-cylinder types, and they ordered hundreds of them. Although enthusiasm for the 20-cylinder engine faded because of its higher maintenance costs and greater fuel consumption when compared with the 16-cylinder 645E, some railroads continued to operate SD45s down to 2002. From the mid-1980s, the type was popular among regional railroads looking for second-hand "bargain" power.

New York, Susquehanna & Western acquired a fleet of second-hand SD45s in the 1980s. NYSW SD45 3620 leads an eastbound Delaware & Hudson freight at Dixons east of Attica, New York, in March 1989.

Type: Co-Co, diesel-electric
Power: EMD 20-645E producing 3600hp (2686kW)
Tractive effort: 74,200 lbf (330kN) at 9 mph (14.4km/h) continuous TE
Max. operating speed: 77mph (125km/h)
Weight: 407,000 lb (185t)
Overall length: 65ft 9.5in (20.05m) or 65ft 8in (20.01m)
Gauge: 4ft 8.5in (1435m)

the changeover from steam to diesel power. Resulting in the replacement of over 50,000 locomotives by a little over half that number, all of which could be operated by one man rather than two, it was not the action of complacent, idle or —whatever the steam aficionados might say—stupid managers. One could make a better case for the railroad companies struggling to renovate their industry, but being hamstrung by a combination of factors: ties to past practices, a huge and expensive infrastructure inherited from the past, and a raft of government and local regulations which prevented swift and sensible, if painful, decision-making.

The Threat from the Skies

By 1970 airlines carried 73 percent of long-distance passenger travel. Railroads carried only 7.2 percent, but it is very hard to see how the railroads could have maintained their old supremacy. Even if they had been competing on a

Baltimore & Ohio GP40, No. 3684 has been preserved and is displayed at the Baltimore & Ohio Railroad Museum in Baltimore, Maryland.

level field with airlines and coach lines, they lacked the speed of the airplane and the convenience of the coach. As it was, they were compelled to charge prices which road transport was free to undercut. As its wealth increased, the traveling public placed an increasingly high value on time and convenience.

The story of technical advance, on other fronts apart from that of locomotive design, in the years after 1946, is another account which hardly squares with the picture of inert or incapable management. In 1945, year of the first vista-dome cars, the Federal Communications Commission first allocated exclusive radio channels for railroad use. In 1948 America's first experimental gas-turbine locomotive was introduced—too late, as the diesel-electric revolution was well under way, though some gas-turbine locomotives went into production.

By the end of 1949, the first long-distance microwave communications system was installed on a railroad. Computers went into use in 1955, in a small way at first, as with the rest of industry, but by the mid-1980s, before the microprocessor revolution, there were already over 700 computers in use by 60 railroad companies. The use of these

Alco C-630
Various Railroads: 1965

Alco C-630 locomotive No. 2032 moves some trucks in the McMillan freight depot in Toronto, in July 1981. Most C-630s ended working on Canadian lines.

Type: Co-Co, diesel-electric
Power: Alco 16-cylinder 251E diesel producing 3000hp (2238kW)
Tractive effort: 103,000lbf (458 kN) starting TE
Max. operating speed: 65mph (105km/h)
Weight: n/a
Overall length: 69ft 6in (21.18m)
Gauge: 4ft 8.5in (1435mm)

Alco's Century-630, or C-630, was its six-motor, 3000hp (2238kW) diesel, built to compete with the Electro-Motive SD40 and General Electric's U30C. While by far the most stylish of these three models, it had the worst reputation in service. Fewer than 100 were built for American railroads, although slightly more than 50 were constructed in Canada by the Montreal Locomotive Works for Canadian lines.

American C-630s were built for just two years, starting in 1965, and are noted as the first North American locomotives to employ an AC-DC transmission system, a type soon adopted by the Electro-Motive Division and General Electric as well.

extended to the TRAIN (TeleRail Automated Information Network), which came into use in 1970 in order to keep track of the entire American stock of freight cars.

From 1962 satellite communications were in use. From 1965 Centralized Traffic Control was used over more and more sections of track, and its use in turn enabled engineers to reduce the amount of multiple track; in many congested areas, two tracks could now carry the traffic previously carried on four. The tracks themselves were of heavy, high-grade steel, welded into long sections to eliminate the wear and tear on wheels caused by the rail-joints of older trackage, and with built-in circuitry for train control.

Nowadays, train-to-tower radio communication and on-board computer systems are the norm. Helper engines in the middle of a lengthy train can be unmanned, controlled wholly by radio signals from the sole driver up front.

EMD GP38
Various Railroads: 1966

A single New England Central GP38 is seen here leading the "Great Train Escapes" fall tour train across a wooden trestle at New London, Connecticut, in September 1998.

Type: Bo-Bo, diesel-electric
Power: EMD 16-645E producing 2000hp (1492kW)
Tractive effort: 55,000lbf (245kW) at 10.7 mph (17.2 km/h)
Max. operating speed: 65mph (104 km/h)
Weight: 262,000lb (119t)
Overall length: 59ft 2in (18.03m)
Gauge: 4ft 8.5in (1435mm)

The American locomotive market in the 1960s was dominated by new turbocharged high-horsepower models such as the SD45. But there was still a large demand for more moderately powered machines. The GP38 was among the new 645 diesel models that the Electro-Motive Division introduced in the mid-1960s and was effectively an improved version of the popular "General Purpose" models that had dominated Electro-Motive's locomotive production through the 1950s. It used a normally aspirated 16-cylinder 645 diesel to produce 2000hp (1492kW). The GP38 and its successor GP38-2 were standard workhorse locomotives that handled a variety of freight services from local switching work to heavy unit coal trains. They were ordered by most American railroads and were a typical example of new freight power in the 1970s.

A trio of New England Central GP38s leads southbound freight 608 through Stafford Springs, Connecticut. New England Central operates the former Central Vermont main line.

In the 1960s and after, commercial magnates were traveling by private jet, and the wonderful private railroad cars of an earlier generation were demolished or became museum pieces. Car-building generally was going through a lean time, as the drastic slump in the number of passenger trains had resulted in a huge number of redundant, though also out-dated passenger cars, partly because many new cars, based on prewar designs had been ordered in 1945 and 1946. Apart from some prestige services, especially those which could fit vista-dome cars into the loading gauge, there

was not a strong demand for new passenger rolling stock after 1950, and well into the 1950s it was quite common to see the massive cars of prewar days still in use. There was demand, however, for the Budd Company's railcar: locomotive and car all in one. Like so many "new" items on the railroads, it was not at all a new concept. The gas-electric "Doodlebug" railcars went as far back as 1906.

But the stainless steel Budd cars were wholly modern in terms of construction, fittings, power, and acceleration. Among other features they had disc brakes, introduced to

EMD GP40
Various Railroads: 1966

A Guilford Rail System GP40 leads a consist of four Electro-Motives hauling a freight bound for Portland, Maine, at Dover, New Hampshire, in March 2002.

The Electro-Motive Division's GP40 was introduced along with other new models that shared the 645 engine in 1965. This engine was basically an expansion of the successful 567 design. The new 645-powered locomotives also featured improved electrical components and an AC/DC transmission system (yet still used conventional direct current traction motors). The GP40 was a high-output four-motor locomotive designed for fast freight service. Its 16-645 engine delivered 3000hp (2235kW). New York Central was first to order GP40s, and the type became popular with other

railroads that had ordered Electro-Motive's earlier high-output four-motor types. Variations of the GP40, such as the GP40P, were designed for passenger service. In 1972 the model was succeeded by the GP40-2, which had most of the same characteristics and looked basically the same.

Type: Bo-Bo, diesel-electric
Power: EMD 16-645E3 producing 3000hp (2235kW)
Tractive effort: 48,000lbf (213kN) at 13mph (21km/h)
Max. operating speed: 65mph (104km/h) to 77mph (123km/h)
Weight: 277,500 lb (126t) (based on CSX units)
Overall length: 59ft 2in (18.03m)
Gauge: 4ft 8.5in (1435mm)

EMD SD40

Various Railroads: 1966

Union Pacific assembled one of the largest fleets of SD40 and SD40-2 locomotives, altogether consisting of more than 800 units. Here five Union Pacific SD40-2s lead an eastbound freight at Echo, Utah.

Type: Co-Co, diesel-electric
Power: 16-cylinder 645 producing 3000hp (2235kW)
Tractive effort: Depends on gear ratio
Max. operating speed: 65–88 mph (104–141km/h) depending on gear ratio
Weight: 382,000 lb (173 tonnes)
Overall Length: 65ft 8in (20.01m)—based on earlier models
Gauge: 4ft 8.5in (1435mm)

Introduced in 1966, the SD40 quickly became a standard model on many American railroads for heavy freight services. The winning combination of high horsepower, reliability and versatility made the SD40 the first choice for many main-line services. The locomotive used a 16-cylinder version of the new 645E3 engine. With a 60:17 gear ratio, the SD40 could operate at a maximum speed of 70mph (113km/h), which was the absolute maximum allowable speed for freight operations by most American railroads. The SD40 used a AR10 main generator and D77 traction motors. In 1972 the type was improved with the introduction of the Electro-Motive Division's Dash-2 line; the subsequent SD40-2 became one of the bestselling American diesel-electric models, with more than 4000 built for North American service.

the railroads by Budd in 1938, but not widely used until the 1950s. For the time being, Budd survived, as did Pullman, but the American Car & Foundry Corporation gave up its railroad car business in 1960. In 1968 the Pullman sleeping car finally came to the end of the road, though from 1947 the ever-reducing number had been operated by a railroad combine and not by the Pullman Company. In the 1960s no American railroad was likely to buy in new passenger cars, except for urban rapid transit; for long-haul, the problem was not lack of cars, but lack of passengers. However, when Amtrak was established in 1971 its executives were painfully aware of the antiquity and sheer tonnage of the cars at its disposition. Their program for purchase of new cars had two

In the 1960s, the Government of Ontario's GO Transit ordered GP40TCs from General Motor's Canadian locomotive subsidiary, General Motors Diesel.

fundamentals: they should be modern, and they should be lightweight. Modernity, to Amtrak managers in the 1970s, meant like airplanes and road coaches, and so the stainless steel "Metroliner" cars appeared on the electrified north-east corridor lines.

Diner and sleeper variants followed. These cars stood the test of heavy usage and time, unlike some lightweight cars produced for rapid transit systems. For high-speed, heavy-duty, rail work, there was a limit to which plastics and light aluminum could be employed, without sacrificing safety as well as durability.

Dominant Diesel

On the locomotive front, progress continued with development of diesel technology. The dominance of the diesel was such that it not only eclipsed steam, but also displaced such long-established electric routes as the Milwaukee Road's Cascades line, which had been electrified since 1919, but went over to diesel haulage in the 1950s. In 1949 General Motors' Electro-Motive Division brought out its GP ("General Purpose") road switcher. This was by no means the first of its kind, but the GP series came to dominate the market, and the road switcher, with its single cab set behind a "nose" and the hood unit with its side walk-ways stretching behind, became the standard freight locomotive of North America.

During their years of virtual monopoly, the Electro-Motive Division maintained the policy of standardization, offering a set range of models. Experience was proving that the combination of the diesel engine with electrical transmission produced a machine that had adequate power and flexibility for virtually all uses. The GPs were somewhat low-powered at 1750hp (1305kW), but they were relatively cheap and adaptable; if more power was needed, another

GE U30B
Various Railroads: 1966

Type: Bo-Bo, diesel-electric
Power: GE 7FDL-16 producing 3000hp (2235kW)
Tractive effort: 51,500lbf (229kN) continuous TE at 13mph (20.8km/h)
Max. operating speed: 79mph (127km/h)
Weight: 272,000 lb (123.5t)
Overall length: 60ft 2in (18.33m)
Gauge: 4ft 8.5in (1435mm)

A Pennsylvania short-line freight hauler, these Blue Mountain & Northern former Conrail U30Bs lead a freight at Solomon Gap in October 1997.

Keeping pace with new models introduced by its rivals in the mid-1960s, General Electric boosted the output of its Bo-Bo Universal Line road switcher models. In 1966 it introduced the U28B, which was more powerful than the company's pioneering U25B. In late 1966 it introduced the U30B, which remained in production for most of the next decade. Intended to compete with Electro-Motive's GP40/GP40-2, General Electric's U30B did not enjoy the same robust sales. Both high-nose and low-nose U30Bs were built to customer specifications. Burlington, New York Central, and Western Pacific were among the lines to order new U30Bs.

locomotive could always be added. Customization for individual railroads was restricted to minor details, and the purely cosmetic aspect of paintwork and logos.

In 1956 the great names of Baldwin and Lima disappeared from the locomotive scene. Latterly, as Baldwin-Lima-

Hamilton, they had been fighting to build up a diesel locomotive business, but the power of General Motors marketing and sales techniques, plus their long experience and commitment to internal combustion, was very hard to combat. Baldwin-Lima-Hamilton's attempt to maintain

GE U30C
Various Railroads: 1967

Type: Co-Co, diesel-electric
Power: GE 7FDL-16 producing 2235kW (3000hp)
Tractive effort: 74,000lbf (329kN) at 11.4mph (18.3km/h) (varied—these figures based on some Burlington Northern U30Cs)
Max. operating speed: 70mph (113km/h)
Weight: 388,000 lb (176t)
Overall length: 67ft 3in (20.49m)
Gauge: 4ft 8.5in (1435mm)

Above: A GE U30C, No. 1582 of Family Lines, at Dalton, Illinois, on February 26, 1983. Lines in the CSX system were among the main users of the "U-boats."

Below: The U33C, seen here near Charlemont, Massachusetts, on January 2, 1986, extracted a further 300hp (224kW) from the FDL-16 power unit. In total 375 were built in the same time span as the U30C.

In the 1960s General Electric developed its Universal line, taking it to second place in American diesel-electric manufacturers, pushing one-time partner Alco into a distant third. By the end of the decade, Alco exited the market. The biggest seller of General Electric's "U-boats," as these locomotives came to be known, was its six-motor U30C, which competed directly with Electro-Motive's SD40/SD40-2 as a heavy freight locomotive. In a 10-year span starting in 1967, Electro-Motive sold nearly 600 U30Cs in the United States, and also offered the more powerful U33C and the U36-C. All three locomotives used the same 7FDL-16 diesel-engine. In 1977 General Electric's improved DASH-7 line superseded the Universal line, and the C30-7 replaced the U30C, proving more successful.

EMD FP45
Santa Fe Railroad: 1968

Santa Fe–painted F45 5972 leads a freight on the Wisconsin Central near Fond du Lac, Wisconsin, in March 1995.

In 1967 Santa Fe needed new passenger locomotives for its highly acclaimed streamlined stainless steel passenger trains, including the "Super Chief." The company ordered semistreamlined diesels from both the Electro-Motive Division and General Electric. Unlike early streamlined diesels such as the Electro-Motive F-units where the outer carbody was integral to the locomotive structure, these second-generation passenger locomotives used road-switcher platforms with a non-structural metal "cowl" covering. Initially, Santa Fe ordered nine FP45s which used the 20-645E3 engine.

These contained a large steam generator to provide steam heat for passenger cars. Later it ordered a freight-only version which was designated F45. These were similar to the FP45, but did not feature the large steam generator and were several feet shorter.

Type: Co-Co, diesel-electric
Power and output: Not known
Tractive effort: 171,000lbf (316kN) at 13.2mph (21km/h)
Max. operating speed: 77mph (123km/h)
Weight: 386,000 lb (175t)
Overall length: 67ft 5.5in (20.56m)
Gauge: 4ft 8.5in (1435mm)

their market share by greater willingness to customize designs merely pushed up their costs and made the Electro-Motive Division alternative seem even more attractive.

New Technology

Just before the end of World War II, the Fairbanks Morse company, from their marine engine experience, developed an opposed-piston diesel engine which worked effectively in locomotives. For fourteen years, up to 1958, it offered a range of switching and road engines which were used by

several railroads, but which never achieved a substantial share of the market. General Electric, which had built small diesels on its own since the end of its agreement with Alco in 1952, moved into the field of large locomotives in 1960 with the introduction of the U25B. Its 2500hp (1864kW) power unit established a new standard.

A significant step forward was taken in the mid-1960s with the introduction of silicon rectifiers, enabling three-phase alternators to be installed in engines, allowing for the replacement of the direct-current generator, which had a

This picture of an SD 39 at the Electro-Motive Division's La Grange factory makes an interesting comparison with that of the SD 24 of just over 10 years before, particularly in cab design. It is also lighter and more compact.

maximum power limit of around 2800hp (2088kW). The high costs of research and development, and of retooling, were among the reasons for the reduction in builders, around this time, to the two giants, the Electro-Motive Division and General Electric. The latter's U for "Universal" (though better known to railroad men as "U-Boats") vied with the Electro-Motive Division's GP. The alternator-fitted U28B of 1966, rated at 3000hp (2237kW), was the most powerful all-purpose locomotive of its day, and was followed in 1967 by the U30C. For ten years this range dominated the high-power end of the market.

General Motors showed its own capacity for heavy haulage with the DDA40X, a double unit with a combined horsepower of 6600. Built between 1969 and 1971 for the Union Pacific, weighing 247 tons (251t), and riding on two four-axle trucks, they maintained the United States

railroads' reputation for producing the "world's biggest," in the centennial year of the first transcontinental line.

The Electro-Motive Division had made an innovation in 1967 with the so-called "cowl unit" introduced first on the FP45 locomotive produced for the Santa Fe. In passing, it may be noticed that the "take it or leave it" policy of earlier days was no longer operative; it was accepted that big customers and special conditions might require and receive special adaptations. But the cowl unit still employed the basic frame as used on the road switcher and its car-body was not integral. The FP45 was interesting for another reason. Bucking the trend of declining passenger traffic, the Santa Fe was enjoying success with its streamlined, stainless steel "Super Chief" train, and wanted locomotives to haul it that did not look like freight engines. In a small way, it was a reversion to the grand manner of the 1930s, and the cowl unit, in Santa Fe livery, looked the part.

The DASH

The next step forward was the introduction of the Electro-Motive Division's DASH 2 range in 1972. Reliability in performance and ease of maintenance were the criteria behind the design, rather than any major technical innovation. But many small improvements were made, with modular electric controls, and few parts of the design were left unchanged from previous models. The new range, combined with a major refit and enlargement of the La Grange plant, now more than thirty years old, was based on

a close but upbeat assessment of American locomotive needs after twenty years of the diesel era: "Of the present 30,000 diesel locomotives in service on American railroads, almost half—or 12,600—are over 15 years of age, economically obsolete, and prime candidates for replacement … Obviously, the rate of locomotive purchases has not been sufficient to keep the fleet modern. Even if the

EMD DDA40X
Union Pacific (UP): 1969

Union Pacific retains one DDA40X in its historic fleet, and this locomotive is variously used on passenger excursions and occasionally in freight service.

The largest and last of Union Pacific's "double-diesels" were the 47 DDA40Xs built by the Electro-Motive Division. These locomotives were effectively two GP40s on one frame. Interestingly, the DDA40X used a "wide nose" cowl-style cab, as first introduced on Santa Fe's FP45 in 1967. This cab style predated the now common North American Safety Cab by more than two decades. Each DDA40X was powered by a pair of turbocharged 16-645E engines. The DDA40Xs are the world's largest diesel locomotives—known as "Centennials"

and numbered in the 6900 series because they were introduced in 1969 (the 100th anniversary of the completion of the American transcontinental railroad). By 1985 most were out of service, but one locomotive, No. 6936, remains in Union Pacific's heritage fleet.

Type: Do-Do, diesel-electric
Power: Two 16-645E3 diesel engines producing 6600hp (4923kW)
Tractive effort: 133,766 lbf (596kN) starting TE
Max. operating speed: n/a
Weight: 545,400lb (247t)
Overall length: 98ft 5in (30m)
Gauge: 4ft 8.5in (1435m)

railroads were caught up on locomotive obsolescence, they would require some 1500 to 1600 new units each year to replace the number of units that annually become economically obsolescent." The comments are those of B.B. Brownell, the Electro-Motive Division's General Manager. No doubt the railroad engineers took them with a pinch of salt. "Economic obsolescence" was not a concept that the

diesel manufacturers had made much of when first introducing their products, and fifteen years, even at high intensity of usage, did not seem a very long life for a locomotive. Many diesel units were kept going for twice this period and longer, through rebuilds and refits.

Brownell's comments were also based on a positive assessment of the rail freight market. In 1960 American

CF7

Santa Fe Railroad: 1970

Louisiana & Delta, one of the Genesee & Wyoming family of short lines, operates former Southern Pacific branch lines with a fleet of former Santa Fe CF7s. The railroad's CF7 1503 is seen at the the railroad's shops in New Iberia, Louisiana.

Throughout the 1960s and 1970s, many American railroads traded in their 1940s and early 1950s era Electro-Motive F-units for new locomotives. The Santa Fe railroad took a different approach and, between 1970 and 1978, converted more than 230 of its F7s into home-built road switchers, which were designated CF7. As the F-unit used a supporting carbody, Santa Fe needed to manufacture a frame, hood, and cab for the CF7. The main mechanical/electrical components from the F7 were retained and incorporated in the

"new" CF7. Early CF7s featured a contoured cab that matched the profile of the F7 carbody, while the later CF7s were to feature a taller cab. In the early 1980s, Santa Fe began selling off its CF7 fleet, and many were bought by short lines. Amtrak acquired a few in exchange for its SDP40Fs and assigned them to maintenance trains.

Type: Re-manufactured Bo-Bo diesel-electric
Power: EMD 16-567BC producing 1500hp (1119kW)
Tractive effort: n/a
Max. operating speed: n/a
Weight: n/a
Overall length: 55ft 11in (17.04m)
Gauge: 4ft 8.5in (1435mm)

GE E60

Amtrak: 1974

Although largely supplanted by AEM-7s after 1981, a few of Amtrak's General Electric-built E60 electrics remain in passenger service on the Northeast Corridor.

In 1972 Amtrak ordered the first of 26 new electrics from General Electric, which were intended replacements for Amtrak's inherited GG1 fleet. The new locomotives were designed for high-speed passenger service and planned for 120mph (192km/h) operation. Two varieties were delivered between 1974 and 1975: seven E60CPs that featured a steam generator to provide heat for older passenger stock and 19 E60CHs that used headend power for modern passenger stock such as Amtrak's Budd-built Amfleet cars. Problems with the E60's ability to track at high speeds limited the locomotives

Type: Co-Co passenger electric
Power: Alternating current: 12.5 at 25Hz; and 25kV at 60Hz
Tractive effort: 75,000lbf (334kN) to 82,000lbf (364.4kN)
Max. operating speed: 85mph (137km/h)
Weight: 387,900lb (176t)
Overall length: 71ft 3in (21.71m)
Max. axle load: 64,650lbs (29t)
Gauge: 4ft 8in (1435mm)

to just 85mph (137km/h), forcing Amtrak to look overseas for a practical high-speed electric. In the 1980s Amtrak sold many of its E60s, yet some have remained on its roster and, as of 2002, were still being used on heavy long-distance trains.

inter-city railroads moved 579 billion ton-miles (926.4 ton-km) of freight. In 1970 this had risen to 765 billion (1224 billion ton-km). Rather unfortunately, it suffered a downturn in the early 1970s. By the later 1970s, however, railroad freight was once again rising, helped by the fuel crisis of 1979. But the increase in traffic masked an overall decline in market share. In 1950, the railroads had moved over 55 percent of freight, but by 1977 this had fallen to 35 percent. From that year a gradual recovery began, with rail holding steadily around 40 percent of total freight business.

Heavy Loads

At this time, traffic managers were contemplating trainloads far greater than ever before. The average freight train in

EMD F40PH

Amtrak: 1976

A pair of Amtrak F40PHs leads Amtrak's Vermonter at CP83 in Palmer, Massachusetts, in October 2000. To the right, a pair of new CSX AC6000s wait to head west with a long freight bound for Selkirk, New York.

The F40PH was introduced in 1976 and quickly became the standard Amercian passenger locomotive. It is essentially a "cowl" version of the GP40 road-switcher type. Amtrak, the nationally run passenger operator which had assumed most intercity passenger operations from the private railroads in 1971, was the largest operator of the F40PH. Amtrak assigned F40PHs to passenger services networkwide. On the unelectrified section of the Northeast Corridor between Boston, Massachusetts, and New Haven,

Connecticut, F40PHs were permitted to operate at their highest speeds. By 2002, Amtrak had retired most of its F40PHs, largely replacing them with General Electric GENESIS types. F40PHs are still operated by commuter agencies and Canada's VIA Rail, while a few have been modified for freight service.

Type: Diesel-electric
Power: 16-cylinder 645 engine producing 3000hp (2235kW).
Tractive effort: 68,440lbf (304kN)
Max. operating speed: 64mph (103km/h)
Weight: 257,985 lb (117t)
Overall length: 56ft 2in (17.12m)
Gauge: 4ft 8.5in (1435mm)

1944 had weighed around 1100 tons (1118t). Now twice that was normal. Locomotive departments were looking for something more than multiple working, and extra power and greater tractive effort became strong sales points for the manufacturers.

In a pattern familiar from the steam era, however, the improvements on the locomotive side were swallowed up

promptly by the traffic managers. On trains loading to over 2500 tons (2540t), even a 3000hp (2237kw) locomotive might not suffice, and so multiple use continued, though at ever-more cost-efficient levels.

For the same reason, the design of freight cars underwent change, as operators demanded the optimum balance of strength, durability, lightness, and load-bearing capacity.

The length of flat cars went up to 89ft (27.1m) in the 1950s, and that of boxcars to 86ft (26m), and welded steel construction became universal. Tank cars were enlarged to a capacity of 12,000 gallons (45425l).

Automated freight handling had always been a feature of the North American railroad, and with the development of the intermodal container, this took on a new importance. Container traffic, interchangeable between water, road, and rail-borne transport, became a major aspect of railroad operations. It was ideally suited to long-haul by rail.

The Southern Pacific led the way in developing the double-stacked container train. Many detail modifications in car design and construction were needed in order to allow for trains of unprecedented length and tonnage. Bogie trucks and braking systems were improved.

The strength and resilience of draft gear was vital. In the old days, steam locomotives were helped to get the "drag" on their trains by relatively loose couplings, so that the earlier part of the train was already on the move while the wagons further back were still stationary. With closer, tighter coupling, often with whole sets of cars semi-permanently close-coupled, this procedure was no longer possible. The low gearing of diesel-electrics enabled them to get larger tonnages on the move. Their capacity for dynamic braking was also valuable as massive trains negotiated downhill grades.

GE B23-7
Various Railroads: 1977

Conrail B23-7 1933 was semi-permanently assigned to haul the company's track geometry train. It is seen here climbing around the Horseshoe Curve, west of Altoona, Pennsylvania, in August 1987.

General Electric's U23B moderate horsepower Bo-Bo road-switcher was replaced with the B23-7 when the Dash-7 line supplanted the company's older Universal line in 1977. Using a 12-cylinder 7FDL diesel engine operating at 1050rpm to produce 2250hp (1676kW), the B23-7 was well suited for moderately heavy freight service, and switching and branch-line work, making it comparable to Electro-Motive's GP38-2. Conrail, CSX, NS, Santa Fe, and Union Pacific were among large railroads that employed fleets of B23-7s. Conrail was the first line to order B23-7s, and it used them in a variety of secondary freight services. On its New England Division, it used them to switch yards and work local freights, as well as running them in sets of five or more to haul heavy ballast trains.

Type: Bo-Bo, diesel-electric
Power and output: GE FDL-12 producing 2250hp (1676kW)
Tractive effort: 61,000lbf (271kN) at 10mph (6km/h) with 83:20 gear ratio
Max. operating speed: 70mph (112km/h)
Weight: 280,000lb (127t)
Overall Length: 62ft 2in (18.94m)
Gauge: 4ft 8.5in (1435mm)

GE C36-7
Various Railroads: 1978

Conrail's twenty-five C36-7s were built in 1985. In 1997 a Conrail C36-7 leads a westbound freight at Tyrone, Pennsylvania.

General Electric's high-horsepower C36-7 was introduced in 1978 and succeeded its earlier 3600hp six-motor U36-C. As with other DASH-7 models, the C36-7 featured a number of small improvements over earlier designs, which were aimed at improving locomotive reliability. Early C36-7s were nearly identical to General Electric's 3000hp(2237kW) C30-7, the primary difference between being a change in the output of the 7FDL-16 diesel-engine.

From 1983 the company supplied an improved C36-7 that incorporated some of the microprocessor controls featured on the DASH-8 types and also a new adhesion system. The last of the type featured a slightly higher output and had a pronounced hump behind the cab that housed dynamic brake grids. In 2002 a fleet of former Union Pacific C36-7s were rebuilt by General Electric and shipped to the Estonian Railways.

Type: Co-Co, diesel-electric
Power and output: GE 7FDL-16 producing 3600hp (2686kW)
Tractive effort: 96,900lbf (431kN) at 11mph (17.6km/h) with 83:20 gear ratio
Max. operating speed: 70mph (112km/h)
Weight: 420,000lb (189t)
Overall length: 67ft 3in (20.5m)
Gauge: 4ft 8.5in (1435mm)

The traction motors become generators, taking power from the wheels and thus slowing the train. But whereas an electric locomotive can feed the resultant power back into the catenary, in the case of the diesels it has to be fed through resistance banks and dissipated as heat. Freight speeds were still relatively low, with an average of only around 20mph (32km/h) in the 1970s, though the averages were reduced by waiting time when one train crossed another on single-track lines.

End of Passenger Services

From May 1971, the railroad managers had no longer had to worry about passengers. Jim Hill's wish was fulfilled, and they were free of them, though still responsible for the rail infrastructure which Amtrak shared with the freight trains. The passenger business was a semiprivate corporation: all its preferred stock was held by the US Department of Transportation, but the common stock was open to general purchase, and four railroads became stockholders.

A former Norfolk & Western C30-7 and an EMD, both wearing the colors of Norfolk Southern, lead a double-stack container train.

The new brand name replaced the original, less euphonious "Railpax." In its first two years, Amtrak was almost wholly reliant on the locomotives and rolling stock of the railroad companies, using them on a leasing basis. Only three Class 1 railroads chose to operate their own

passenger services, the Rock Island (to 1979), the Southern (also to 1979), and the Denver & Rio Grande Western (to 1983). After two difficult initial years, subject to a constant barrage of criticism from the road lobby, Amtrak gradually established itself. Its original brief had been to cover at least half of its operating costs from its own revenues, and this was achieved within its first ten years.

The Amtrak logo and livery became familiar across the nation, and though the range of services was even more curtailed than that offered by the independent companies prior to 1971, the improvements to the rolling stock, and the purchase of new locomotives, began to show the traveling public a new and more attractive view of long-distance rail travel.

AEM-7
Amtrak: 1979

Type: Bo-Bo, high-speed electric locomotive
Power: AC—12.5V at 25Hz; 25kV at 60Hz
Tractive effort: 53,300lbf (237kW)
Max. operating speed: 125mph (200km/h)
Weight: 199,500lb (90.47t)
Overall length: 51ft 2in (15.58m)
Max. axle load: 49,875lb (22.6t)
Gauge: 4ft 8.5in (1435mm)

Seen at Washington Union Station in October 2001, Amtrak 918 wears a Spartan livery that reflects the change to the Acela name for North East Corridor services.

By the late 1970s, Amtrak's venerable former Pennsylvania Railroad GG1 electrics were nearly worn out, and the General Electric E60s built to replace them had been deemed unsuitable for high-speed service. Amtrak needed a new electric for its New Haven–New York–Washington, DC, route and turned to European designs for a practical solution. It tested French and Swedish electrics and decided upon a variation of the Swedish Rc-4 built by ASEA. Amtrak's

AEM-7s were built, starting in 1979, by General Motor's Electro-Motive Division under license from ASEA. The AEM-7 closely resembles its Swedish antecedent, but is a heavier locomotive and designed to operate much faster than the Rc-4. Top speed on the North East Corridor was 125mph (200km/h).

CHAPTER 13

INTO THE NEW CENTURY

After a time when the future seemed bleak, for passenger services at
least, the railroads began to find a viable role in modern transit,
both inter-city and in urban rapid mass transit. Electric power, new
diesel-electric technology, and computers all helped to sustain this
new role, and a new perception of railroads was born.

Following these measures there were at last signs of recovery.
Conrail turned in a profit in 1981. In 1987 the business was
floated as a public corporation by the Department of
Transportation, at a valuation of $1.8 billion. Mergers and

**Above: Although anticipated as the power of the future, EMD's
1990s era SD90MAC-H faded into obscurity as smaller locos do
most of the heavy work.**
**Left: Amidst Chicago skyscrapers a Metra-liveried Electro-
Motive Division F40 PHM-2 runs a two-deck cross-city service.**

consolidations were resulting in a small number of strong
regional networks. By the end of the 1990s these comprised
the Burlington Northern, the Santa Fe, the Union Pacific,
the Norfolk Southern, and CSX (formed in 1980 from the
Chessie System). In 1998 Conrail was jointly acquired by
the Norfolk Southern and CSX. Focus on key traffic routes
and the development of container and intermodal traffic on
a large scale helped bring the railroads back into
profitability. After a shaky beginning and much derided
attempts to operate railroads as if they were airlines, Amtrak

gradually developed a core of passenger services. On its prime route, the Washington–New York–Boston corridor, new 150mph (241km/h) Acela trains provide a service which, center-to-center, rivals that of the airlines. Amtrak's national map of passenger routes retains a skeletal appearance, but it still offers four transcontinental lines and links between most major cities, as well as some regional routes. An updated version of the Talgo design was used in

the Seattle-Portland-Eugene Cascades service from the late 1990s. However, the great resurgence in this field has been in metropolitan rapid transit. In 2002, Metro-North—its backbone the old New York and Harlem line which Vanderbilt had transformed—carried over 72,000,000 passengers between New York City and the region to the north. The other great success is the revival of rail borne freight. Intermodal traffic tripled between 1980 and 2000.

GE B36-7
Various Railroads: 1980

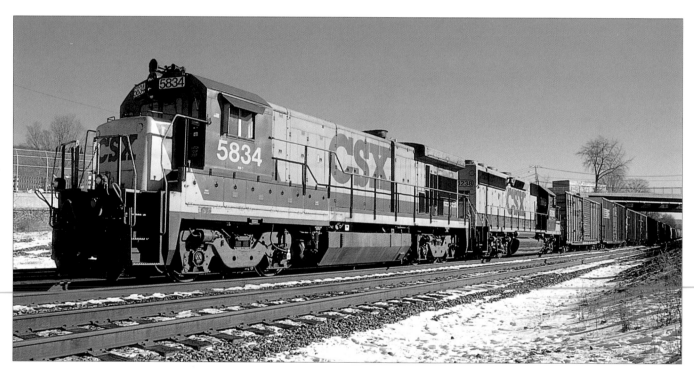

Demoted from priority intermodel service, CSX B36-7 5834 and an Electro-Motive GP40-2 lead a westbound local freight on the old Boston & Albany at CP 83 in Palmer, Massachusetts, in December 2000.

General Electric's B36-7 was a high-horsepower four-motor (Bo-Bo wheel arrangement) locomotive intended for fast freight service and typically used in multiples on priority intermodal trains. Externally, the B36-7 closely resembled lower output Dash-7 four-motor General Electric diesel electrics. The B36-7s were normally equipped with the company's FB-style bogie, a type often known as the floating bolster truck. Santa Fe, Seaboard System (a component of CSX), Southern Pacific, and Conrail were primary

Type: Bo-Bo, diesel-electric
Power: GE FDL-12 producing 3600hp (2686kW)
Tractive effort: 64,600lbf (287kN) with 83:20 gear ratio
Max. operating speed: 70mph (113km/h)
Weight: 280,000lb (127t)
Overall length: 62ft 2in (18.94m)
Gauge: 4ft 8.5in (1435mm)

users of the B36-7 type. Conrail typically used B36-7s in sets of three (or mixed with GP40-2s) on its fast "Trail-Van" intermodal trains which regularly operated at speeds up to 70mph (113km/h). Likewise, Southern Pacific often assigned its B30-7s and B36-7s to intermodal trains operating on its Sunset Route.

GE B39-8 'DASH 8'

Various Railroads: 1984

A trio of General Electric LMX leasing B39-8s leads a long freight on the former Burlington (later Burlington Northern, now BNSF) Chicago to Aurora, Illinois, triple-track main line.

General Electric pioneered microprocessor control systems designed to improve the performance and efficiency of diesel-electric locomotives. Its microprocessor controlled locomotives appeared in the early 1980s as its DASH 8 line. Prior to regular production of DASH 8 locomotives, General Electric built several fleets of "pre-production" DASH 8s for service on North American railroads. Santa Fe operated three B39-8s, numbered 7400 to 7402. These locomotives produced 3900hp (2909kW) and, like other high-horsepower Bo-Bo types, were primarily used on fast intermodal

Type: Bo-Bo, diesel-electric
Power: GE 7FDL-16 producing 3900hp (2909kW)
Tractive effort: 68,100lbf (303kN) continuous TE at 18.3mph (29.3km/h) with the 70mph (112km/h) gear option
Max. operating speed: 70mph (112km/h); 75mph (120km/h) using optional gearing
Weight: 280,000 lbs (127t)
Overall Length: 66ft 4in (20.21m)
Gauge: 4ft 8.5in (1435mm)

trains. Later, the company built production B39-8s (designated B39-8E by some sources) for Southern Pacific and LMX, the latter being a lease fleet originally assigned to Burlington Northern. The B39-8 was superseded by the DASH 8-40B in the late 1980s.

At the present time, over 130,000 miles (209,209km) of track are in use, with around 20,000 diesel locomotives at work, and a total of 1,400,000 freight cars.

The Survivors

Only two major American locomotive builders remain, both with their roots in modern technology: General Motors' Electro-Motive Division, and General Electric. The most important technical innovation of recent years was the introduction of an alternating current traction system for diesel-electric locomotives, first used commercially in Electro-Motive Division's SD70MAC on the Burlington Northern in 1993. Since 1989 all new freight diesels have used the "North American Safety Cab" design first used in Canada, its wide nose occupying the full body width of the locomotive. Passenger locomotives, following the European

TRAVELERS' TALES

A Day Late and on Schedule

The days of precision timekeeping on American railroads have long since passed. Since the majority of the United States railroad network is designed for heavy freight operations that do not require strict timetables, it is now very difficult to maintain long-distance passenger schedules. Long-distance trains often run an hour or two late, despite padded schedules that help trains make up lost time. Nowhere is this more acute than in the west, where some Amtrak passenger trains have to cover more than 2,000 miles (3,218km) between terminals. In the winter, storms and heavy freight traffic frequently conspire to delay Amtrak, and efforts to maintain tight schedules can prove frustrating. Since Amtrak rarely owns or operates the tracks it runs on, its trains are subject to the will and priorities of its host railroads—priorities that don't always hold Amtrak in the highest regard.

In the winter of 1994, Amtrak was having a particularly difficult time with its *California Zephyr*, which operates between Chicago, Denver, and Oakland, California, crossing several mountain ranges and long stretches of lonely desert. Heavy freight traffic on the Southern Pacific's former Rio Grande lines west of Denver, combined with extremely bad weather, ruined Amtrak's best efforts at keeping the *Zephyr* to schedule. For several weeks the train would routinely arrive at Oakland many hours behind time. By February it seemed that every day the train was running a little later. One clear morning, after racing across the Nevada desert, Amtrak No. 5, the *California Zephyr*, pulled into Sparks yard, near Reno, Nevada, exactly at its posted time. This was an unusual event indeed, given the train's recent performance. The yardmaster, from his perch in the Sparks tower, radioed the engineer of the train with enthusiasm:

"Number five, you're right on schedule today!"
The engineer replied somewhat gloomily:
"Yeah, it's a pity we're 24 hours late!"

---

pattern, were normally of boxcab design, sometimes, as with the General Electric Genesis models of 1993 and later, having a monocoque body whose shell is not mounted on a frame but is integral to the whole structure. The latest in electric technology is incorporated in the Acela trains and locomotives built in Montreal by the Alsthom-Bombardier combine. The HHL electric locomotive, introduced in 1998 and intended for hauling heavy passenger trains, develops 8000hp (5968kW) and maintains 125mph (201km/h).

Locomotives and power cars, equipped with microprocessors, are designed to reach new standards of efficiency and minimal maintenance, and to reduce fuel and power consumption. The newest, like the Electro-Motive Division's latest SD70Ace diesel-electric locomotive, anticipate legislation and regulations concerning emissions of gases—in some cases by several years. At the same time, the Association of American Railroads estimated that a gallon of diesel moved one ton of freight for 406 miles (650km) in 2003, compared with 235 miles (376km) in 1980.

The Last 20 Years

It had been an astonishing 20-plus years. In 1980 the United States had 20 large railroad companies, and 82 smaller companies. These latter ranged from the Fort Worth & Denver, with 1343 route miles (2161km) and 20 locomotives, and the 494 mile (795km) Bangor & Aroostook, with 45 locomotives, to the one mile (1.6km) route of the Virginia Central (a feeder to the Richmond, Fredericksburg & Potomac Railroad) and its two locomotives. Amtrak was 10 years old and in the middle of its experimental phase, with 15 lightweight Swedish-designed locomotives on order, and a large order of 125 stainless steel passenger cards and 25 food service cars beginning to come through from the Budd company. In the aftermath of the Staggers Act, most companies were positive, even bullish.

Some appeared to be making substantial profits, and some were investing heavily in track and infrastructure improvement. All were benefiting from the Railroad Revitalization and Regulatory Reform Act of 1976. The

Atchison, Topeka & Santa Fe Railroad had experienced an almost 12 percent uplift in freight traffic, attributed to more unit—single commodity—trains, and to its increased freedom in negotiating rates, which had enabled it to improve car loadings by 30 percent, and piggy-back shipments by 26 percent, in the last seven months of 1979.

The Santa Fe had laid 1.7 million new sleepers that year, and 425 miles (684km) of continuous welded rails. Norfolk & Western had just reported the best financial

GE DASH 8-40C
Various Railroads: 1987

A quartet of GE DASH 8-40Cs leads a westbound autorack train down Archer Hill near Burns, Wyoming, in September 1989. Each locomotive develops 4000hp (2984kW), giving this consist has a combined output of 16,000hp (11,931kW), more than five Electro-Motive Division SD40-2s.

Type: Co-Co, diesel-electric	
Power: GE 7FDL-16 producing 4000hp (2984kW)	
Tractive effort: n/a	
Max. operating speed: n/a	
Weight: 389,500lb (176.6t)	
Overall length: 70ft 8in (21.53m)	
Gauge: 4ft 8.5in (1435mm)	

General Electric's DASH-8 line introduced microprocessor controls to obtain greater locomotive performance and reliability. The DASH 8-40C was a six-motor model introduced in 1987. This was among GE's most successful products and helped the company to become America's foremost locomotive builder. With 4000hp (2984kW), the DASH 8-40C is a powerful machine designed for heavy freight service, with the "40" in the designation indicating horsepower and the "C" six-motors. The production DASH-8s such as the DASH 8-

40C featured more boxy cabs than those used by early pre-production models such as the C32-8. Union Pacific was the first to order the DASH 8-40C and amassed a roster of 256 numbered in the 9100-9300 series. It acquired more DASH 8-40Cs (which Union Pacific designates C40-8) with the purchase of Chicago & North Western in 1995.

EMD SD60M

Various Railroads: 1989

The Electro-Motive Division's SD60M was the first American type to use the modern North American Safety Cab, a style that has become predominant with new freight locomotives. In this photograph a former Conrail SD60M leads a westbound at Mexico, Pennsylvania, in November 2001.

Type: Diesel-electric	
Power: 16-cylinder 710G producing 3800hp (2831kW)	
Tractive effort: 100,000lbf (445kN) continuous TE; 149,500lbf (664kN) starting TE with 70:17 gear ratio and 25 percent adhesion	
Max. operating speed: n/a	
Weight: n/a	
Overall length: 71ft 7in (21.81m)	
Gauge: 4ft 8.5in (1435mm)	

In 1984 Electro-Motive introduced the SD60 model which used its new 710G engine, a power plant that replaced the troubled 645F engine in the Division's domestic locomotive line.

Rated at 3800hp (2831kW), the SD60 was nominally more powerful than the SD50 model, yet it was substantially more reliable. In 1989 the Union Pacific railroad received the first SD60Ms, which were significant because of their first use of the North American Safety Cab, the so-called "wide-nose" cab. This particular cab has since become the predominant crew accommodation on new American locomotives. The "M" prefix used in Electro-Motive's designation indicates the Safety Cab option.

Some later locomotives were equipped with an "Isolated Cab" (with considerably better sound proofing); these locomotives are designated SD60I. Union Pacific, Conrail, Burlington Northern, and Soo Line were among SD60M operators.

performance in the company's history. It was engaged in building numerous new lines to access new coal mines and power facilities.

The Burlington Northern was less bullish, noting that its rail activities produced 81 percent of corporate revenue but only 23 percent of corporate pre-tax income. In November 1980, the Chessie System and Seaboard Coast Line Industries merged to form CSX. Chessie's own revenues

went up by 16 percent between 1978 and 1979. The Seaboard Line, presumably typically, recorded that its fuel costs had risen by 47 percent in 1979. By February 1980, fuel costs on the Denver & Rio Grande Western were running at 17 percent of revenue.

On the huge, unwieldy, and ailing Conrail the losses, though still gigantic, were decreasing steadily; but the company was requesting a further loan from the government, of $900 million, in addition to loans of $3.3 billion already received. In June 1980, the Illinois Central Gulf entered into a 20-year agreement with Hoosier Energy and Freeman United Coal Company for the transportation of 26 million tons of Illinois coal to generating plants in Colorado and Texas.

The Milwaukee Road, which had been managed under trusteeship since filing for bankruptcy in December 1977, made a drastic reduction in its route mileage during 1980, from 9500 (15,288km) to 3500 miles (5632km). The Southern Railroad System increased its revenues in 1979 by $217 million, but of that $174 million was consumed in increased costs. It proudly showed off a solar-paneled caboose, the sunlight providing power to operate the rear marker light, but cabooses did not have much longer to run. The Southern had also bought 81 new diesel locomotives and 3753 freight cars in 1979, with a further 76 locomotives and 2944 freight wagons in 1980.

The Union Pacific's automated westward classification yard at North Platte, Nebraska, had just come into full service, able to dispatch 150-car trains, and the combined

The former Pennsylvania Railroad main line is one of the busiest freight corridors in North America, as shown here with three freight trains on the move simultaneously. Leading a RoadRailer on the center track is a General Electric DASH 8-40CW.

eastward and westward yards here were the largest in the world, capable of handling 500,000 tons (508023t) of freight in 100 trains each day. A Union Pacific merger with the Missouri Pacific was announced in January 1980, adding the MoPac's 12,000 route miles (19,312km) to the Union Pacific's 9500 (15,288km). The St Louis-San Francisco Railroad Company had 36 percent of its 4608 route miles (7415km) under Centralized Traffic Control, and was also extending its microwave communication system. One of the very few lines dependent on passenger traffic, the Long Island Railroad—essentially a commuter line—doubled its revenue, earning $301 million in 1979 against $140 million in the previous year. Yet its operating costs were $338 million. It was a wholly owned subsidiary of the New York Metropolitan Transportation Authority. Great changes lay ahead for all these railroad concerns, large and small. But on the whole, the next twenty years would be kinder to them than the previous two decades had been.

EMD GP60M
Santa Fe Railroad: 1990

In the early 1990s, Santa Fe's GP60Ms were among the line's star performers in transcontinental intermodal service. Several lines, including Santa Fe, ordered GP60s with conventional cabs.

It was the Santa Fe railroad that led the development of the North American Safety Cab in the late 1980s, in order to provide its crews with a better and safer working environment. Based in part on the Cowl locomotives of the 1960s, and on the Canadian Cab used since the early 1970s, the North American Safety Cab was designed to provide a better forward view and greater crew protection in a collision. The first Santa Fe locomotives to use the new cab were its Electro-Motive GP60Ms delivered in 1990. These were also the first

Type: Diesel-electric
Power and output: EMD 16-710G producing 3800hp (2835kW)
Tractive effort: n/a
Max. operating speed: n/a
Weight: 260,000lb (118t)
Overall length: 59ft 9in (18.21m)
Gauge: 4ft 8.5in (1435mm)

new locomotives since the 1960s to be delivered in the railroad's famous "Warbonnet" livery. Designated as Super Series machines, the GP60Ms were primarily assigned to priority intermodal freight. Santa Fe was the only line to order them.

EMD F40PHM-2
METRA: 1991

Type: Bo-Bo passenger diesel-electric
Power: EMD 16-645E producing 3200hp (2384kW)
Tractive effort: n/a
Max. operating speed: n/a
Weight: n/a
Overall length: 56ft 2in (17.2m)
Gauge: 4ft 8.5in (1435mm)

The F40PHM-2 was a type peculiar to Chicago's Metra commuter rail operator. They are known as "Winnebagos" because their appearance resembles the popular highway camper.

The F40PHM-2 is a model produced by the Electro-Motive Division between 1991 and 1992 for Chicago's METRA suburban passenger railroad. In most respects, the F40PHM-2 is the same as late model Electro-Motive F40PH-2s—the primary difference is a modified cab style. The roof line of the F40PHM was extended forward and, instead of a traditional nose, the windshield dropped down at an angle to join the front of the locomotive. This cab style was first used on Electro-Motive's experimental F69PH-AC—a model which was used in the late 1990s to forward AC traction technology and assigned to Amtrak.

As with METRA F40PH models, the F40PHM-2 has two sets of headlights, the top headlights being of the oscillating variety. The F40PHM-2s were largely used to replace aging Burlington Northern E9s on the Chicago Union Station to Aurora route.

At the close of the twentieth century, rail remained by far the largest freight carrier in both the United States and Canada. In America, the rail freight traffic amounted to 1.47 trillion ton-miles(2.5 trillion ton-kilometers) in 1999, more than 25 percent more than road freight. Its proportion of the overall market was holding steady at around 40 percent. Progress had been consistent since the deregulation process begun by the Staggers Act of 1980 (the name commemorating Congressman Harley Staggers,

Shortly before Conrail was divided by CSX and Norfolk Southern, it received 15 SD70MACs from the Electro-Motive Division built to CSX specifications. A pair of SD70MACs is seen at Lock 10, near Hoffmanns, New York.

GE DASH-9-44CW

Various Railroads: 1993

Type: Co-Co, diesel-electric
Power: GE 7FDL-16 producing 4400hp (3278kW)
Tractive effort: Varies with options
Max. operating speed: Not known
Weight: Varies with options; 400,000lb (181.6t)
Overall length: 73ft 6in (22.4m)
Gauge: 4ft 8.5in (1435mm)

Above: Burlington Northern Santa Fe has settled on General Electric's DASH 9-44CW as its standard locomotive for intermodal and general freight work. These DASH 9-44CW's wear the BNSF "Heritage II: livery.

One of the features of the DASH 9-44CW is the Hi-AD truck. This style of truck, or bogie, was also utilized on some AC4400CWs, a model built concurrently with the DASH 9.

In 1993 General Electric was to introduce its "DASH 9" line to reflect important technological modifications in its domestic locomotive line—improvements that resulted in better fuel efficiency, tighter emission control, and better adhesion. Externally one of the most obvious differences between the DASH 9 line and DASH 8 models is the use of a new bogie design known as General Electric's "Hi-AD" truck. The DASH 9 line became the company's standard direct current traction model line. The DASH 9-44CW should not be confused with the outwardly similar AC traction AC4400CW.

Initially the DASH 9 line consisted of just the DASH 9-44CW, which was ordered by Chicago & North Western, Southern Pacific, and Santa Fe among other carriers. Later other models were ordered, such as the DASH 9-40C which was taken up by Norfolk Southern.

chairman of the House Commerce Committee at that time). Railroads were able to offer volume discounts, and to negotiate special contracts with major customers. If a carriage rate fell below 160 percent of out-of-pocket costs, the railroad was free to raise it, without application to the Interstate Commerce Commission.

One of the side-effects of deregulation was to make life possible for regional and local freight lines, operating on tracks with relatively modest but adequate freight potential, in some cases acting as feeders to the five major systems. The prime traffics of the railroads in 1997, in order of value, were transportation equipment, chemical, pulp and paper, petroleum, clay and concrete, primary metals, non-metallic minerals, lumber and wood, metallic ores, food,

A pair of Southern Pacific AC4400CWs works as a radio-controlled remote helper on the back of an empty coal train ascending the Colorado Front Range in March 1997.

farm produce, and coal. Half a century earlier, coal would have topped the list. Transportation equipment, the new leader, refers to intermodal trains, carrying either trucks or containers. These twelve categories accounted for 86 percent of all ton-miles, most of which was hauled on a medium or long-term contract basis. Rail freight tariffs, which had historically been the highest in surface transport, were now the lowest. Since deregulation they had dropped gradually, and fell below road and water transport in 1990.

Technological Efficiency

Greater efficiency in all operating departments, and a constant emphasis on mechanization, automation, and electronic technology, including robotics, helped to maintain profitability as the railroads competed for business. Self-propelled, automated track inspection vehicles can be sent along the rails to report back automatically on the condition of the track and pinpoint

the location of problems. The wagon-recording systems of only ten years before were made obsolete by the introduction of cell phones, personal computers, and web-related technology. Smart cars now identified themselves to checkpoints as they rolled by. Not only railroad personnel, but also the shippers of goods, could follow the progress of freight cars and of individual shipments across the country. Speech recognition technology, with advanced telecommunication systems, can allow customers to call up empty railcars for loading. Railroad company operations control rooms use computer networks and outsize display screens to help in the co-ordination of rolling stock movements, train paths, and disposability of locomotives and crews. That once-familiar item on the end of every freight train, the brakeman's caboose, had vanished from the rails by the end of the 1980s, being replaced by a high-tech end-of-train device, or ETD, containing a flashing red light, a motion detector, and an air-brake line monitor.

In 1920 American railroads had employed over two million personnel, and in 1954 the number was still around

GE GENESIS, Model DASH-8-40BP
Amtrak: 1993

A pair of GENESIS and a pair of Electro-Motive Division F40PHs lead Amtrak's *Southwest Chief* over the former Santa Fe. Today the GENESIS type is the most common long-distance passenger locomotive used by Amtrak.

By the early 1990s, Amtrak's fleet of Electro-Motive F40PHs, the mainstay of its long-distance passenger fleet for almost two decades, was showing its age. Amtrak worked with General Electric to design an all-new locomotive specifically for passenger service. Specification for the new locomotive was AMD-103 (which is what the locomotives were often called in their early years), but they are also known as model DASH 8-40BP, called P40s by Amtrak and the GENESIS type by General Electric. The locomotive used a newly

Type: Bo-Bo, passenger diesel-electric
Power: GE 7FDL-16 producing 4000hp (2984kW)
Tractive effort: 38,500lbf (171kN) at 33mph (53km/h) with 74:20 gear ratio
Max. operating speed: 103mph (165km/h)
Weight: 268,240lb (121.8t)
Overall length: 69 ft (21.03m)
Gauge: 4ft 8.5in (1435mm)

designed monocoque body, where the shell is integral to the structure of the locomotive. The first GENESIS locomotives were built in 1993 and numbered in the 800 series. There are now three types of GENESIS, including a dual-mode AC traction model.

EMD F59PHI
Various Railroads: 1994

An Amtrak F59PHI leads a Sacramento to San Jose Capitols across the Yolo Bypass near Davis, California.

In 1994 the Electro-Motive Division brought out its new passenger locomotive. Designated as F59PHI, it featured a streamlined design with a distinctive rounded cab. Electro-Motive promotional literature described the new image as "Swoopy," but the similarity between the F59PHIs and the popular General Motors Chevy minivan resulted in many railroaders nicknaming them "Luminas." Amtrak was the first customer and assigns its F59PHIs for medium-distance trains on the West Coast. Some suburban passenger operators, such as Los Angeles' Metrolink, also acquired small fleets

Type: Bo-Bo, passenger diesel-electric
Power: EMD 12-710G producing 3200hp (2387kW)
Tractive effort: n/a
Max. operating speed: 110mph (176km/h)
Weight: 254,900lb (115.6t)
Overall length: 58ft 7in (17.856m)
Gauge: 4ft 8.5in (1435mm)

of F59PHIs. Perhaps the most unusual owner of the type was cigarette manufacturer Marlboro, which acquired two for use on a deluxe passenger train as part of a promotional scheme; however, the scheme was scrapped before the locomotives were used.

a million and a half. By 1998 the Class One roads employed just around 200,000 people. Productivity per employee, indexed at 100 in 1982, stood at 420 by the end of the century. It was a dramatic and significant change. A further change that would have astonished the hoggers of 1945 was that some of the vastly powerful new locomotives were being driven by women. In the new world of the railroads, there were none of the old employment barriers, whether visible or invisible. On another vitally important measure, safety in operations hit new heights. The Federal Railroad

Administration noted that the years 1993-99 were "the safest years in rail history, for every category that we measure." In the last two decades of the twentieth century, the railroads' accident rates fell by 66 percent, with employees' injury rate falling by 70 percent. The main source of accidents remains unguarded level crossings, where, despite warning systems, collisions still ocurr.

Safety Today

The Association of American Railroads maintains the Transportation Technology Center, at Pueblo, Colorado, whose wide brief is defined as: "accelerating the rate at which beneficial new technologies are safely and efficiently used by railways." With 48 miles (77km) of track apart from its laboratories and engineering shops, the Center is probably the world's largest and most advanced facility of its kind. It has links with the Massachusetts Institute of Technology, the University of Texas, and, with historical appropriateness, the University of Illinois, which was one of the earliest institutions in the country to set up a locomotive testing workshop. An important aspect of the Center's work is in training employees for work with hazardous materials. Railroads are the safest and most

reliable way of transporting potentially hazardous substances, but staff have to be aware of the dangers and methods of dealing with spillages and accidents.

In the new century, freight transport by rail seems assured of a secure future—but what of its poor relation, inter-city passenger transport? Here many factors come into play, apart from the sort of straightforward profit-and-loss accounting that can be read in company ledgers. As urban regions grow more densely populated and reach out toward each other, the problems of congestion and pollution become more pressing.

The experience of Amtrak's first thirty years showed how rail services could help toward resolving these problems in the most densely populated region of the United States. Building on the foundations laid by the Pennsylvania Railroad, the New York, New Haven & Hartford, and others, which had already electrified long sections of track, Amtrak completed electrification to Boston. It gradually put together a service which rivaled the prime European inter-city lines in its density and speed of service, with a maximum of 150mph (240km/h). The economics of Amtrak remain controversial, even though it had received just $10 billion in federal aid compared to $750 billion shared between highway and aviation industries. At that time, problems in servicing its debt threatened to swamp the Amtrak business, although its ratio of revenue to cost compares favorably with similar systems in other countries.

A Canadian National EMD SD70I no. 5690 takes a line of tank wagons off the sidings at Lee, Illinois. Canadian Railways were the pioneers of the now widely-used "safety cabs."

EMD SD80MAC
Conrail: 1995

A pair of Electro-Motive SD80MAC grinds upgrade at the "Twin Ledges" west of Middlefield, Massachusetts, with a heavily laden train of ballast in tow.

One of the more unusual modern American AC traction diesel-electrics were Conrail's 30 Electro-Motive SD80MACs built in 1995. Externally these locomotives were very similar to the SD90MAC, but used a 20-cylinder 710G engine to develop 5000hp (3730kW) for traction. This made the SD80MAC the most powerful single-engine diesel-electric until the first 6000hp (4476kW) locomotives were ready for service in the late 1990s. Initially Conrail bought 28, numbering them in the 4100 series. It later bought two SD80MAC demonstrators. All the SD80MACs were painted in an attractive blue and white livery to distinguish them from Conrail's DC fleet. In 1999, the SD80MAC was split

Type: Co-Co, AC traction diesel-electric	
Power: EMD 20-710G3B producing 5000hp (3730kW)	
Tractive effort: 147,000lbf (653kN) continuous TE ; 185,000lbf (822kN) starting TE with 83:16 gear ratio and 35 percent adhesion	
Max. operating speed: 75mph (120km/h)	
Weight: 425,000lb (192.7t)	
Overall length: 80ft 2in (24.43m)	
Gauge: 4ft 8.5in (1435mm)	

between Norfolk Southern and CSX when the two railroads divided Conrail operations between them. These locomotives were provided with a new design of power bogie, the HTCR-11, which acted to steer the long frame into curves and also minimized adverse impact on the rails. They were also operated by Canadian Pacific. Their rugged looks make the SD80 MACs popular with locomotive modelers.

GE AC6000CW

Union Pacific Railroad (UP): 1995

In May 2002, a pair of CSX AC6000CWs leads an eastbound intermodal train east of Palmer, Massachusetts, at CP79. They reamin standard power on the old Boston & Albany route.

A single 6000hp (4476kW) locomotive was appealing because it would allow for a two-for-one replacement of older 3000hp (2238kW) locomotives. A single-engine Co-Co delivering 6000hp (4476kW) for traction was made practical with the development of three-phase AC traction and the development of new diesel engines. Instead of the standard Cooper-Bessemer–inspired 7FDL diesel, the AC6000CW uses the new 7HDL engine. As the new engine was not ready at the time that Union Pacific (one of two American AC6000CW users) needed them, some locomotives were delivered

Type: Co-Co, diesel-electric, AC traction
Power: GE 7HDL-16 producing 6000hp (4476kW)
Tractive effort: 166,000lbf (738kN) at 11.6mph (18.8km/h)
Max. operating speed: 75mph (120km/h)
Weight: 425,000lb (192.7t)
Overall length: 76ft (23.16m)
Gauge: 4ft 8.5in (1435mm)

with 7FDL engines and temporarily rated at 4400hp (3282kW). General Electric's AC6000CW is almost 3ft (9ocm) longer than conventional AC4400CWs and has a large radiator section at the rear of the locomotive. AC6000CW uses General Electric 5GEB13 AC traction motors.

High-speed Development

At the same time, further "corridor" zones for high-speed rail development were being identified. These high-speed rail corridors are the Pacific Northwest, from Vancouver through Seattle to Eugene; the California Corridor, linking San Francisco, Sacramento, Los Angeles, and San Diego; the South Central Corridor linking Tulsa, Little Rock, and San Antonio; the Florida Corridor linking Tampa, Orlando, and Miami; the Gulf Coast Corridor, from Houston through New Orleans to Atlanta, which joins the South-East Corridor linking Atlanta to Jacksonville and Washington, DC. This in turn would join the North-East Corridor. Then there is the Keystone Corridor, linking New York City with Albany and Buffalo; the Empire Corridor between Boston and Montreal, and the North New England Corridor between Boston and Portland. Apart

HHL Electric
Amtrak: 1998

Amtrak's HHLs are used on heavy Northeast Corridor trains. Although they share styling with the Acela Express trains, these locomotives are double-ended, not permanently coupled to tilting train sets.

In conjunction with Amtrak's long-awaited electrification of its Boston, Massachusetts, to New Haven, Connecticut, segment of the Northeast Corridor route, Amtrak ordered additional electric locomotives. The HHL (sometimes listed as HHP-8) is a double-ended, streamlined machine with the cab and nose sections using the same style as the high-profile Acela Express six-car 150mph (240km/h) train sets.

"HH" in the designation signifies "high-horsepower." At the time of writing, 15 locomotives, Nos. 650–664, had been built by a

Type: Bo-Bo high-speed electric locomotive
Power: 12kV AC at 25Hz, 12kV AC at 60Hz, 25kV AC at 60Hz
Output: 8000hp (5968kW)
Tractive effort: n/a
Max. operating speed: 125mph (200km/h)
Weight: 220,500lb (100t)
Max axle load: Not known
Overall length: n/a
Gauge: 4ft 8.5in (1435mm)

consortium of Alsthom and Bombardier, which also built the Acela Express trains. The HHLs are rated at 8000hp (5968kW), allowing them to handle longer consists than the AEM-7 electrics. The first HHLs were built in 1998.

Acela Express
Amtrak: 1999

America's fastest train is Amtrak's Acela Express, which reaches a top speed of 150mph (240km/h). One of these streamlined trains is seen at Washington Union Station.

In the late 1990s, after years of discussion and planning, Amtrak finally electrified all the way to Boston, Massachusetts, and ordered all-new high-speed train sets to operate on the Boston–New York–Philadelphia–Washington, DC, Northeast Corridor route. For years, Amtrak trains would change from diesel to electric locomotives at New Haven, Connecticut. New Haven Railroad had overcome the need to change engines by using the dual-mode FL9, but the advantage of using this type was greatly diminished when Amtrak took over and began running most Boston to New York trains through to Washington, DC.

In December 2000, Amtrak introduced its Acela Express service, using high-powered six-car tilting train sets that can operate at speeds up to 150mph (240km/h). These use Bombardier's tilting system (originally devised for the Canadian LRC trains) and an Alsthom electrical propulsion system similar to that employed on the French TGV.

Although the Boston–Washington route is now entirely electrified, there are still several different electrification systems in place on various sections of the line as a result of complex history of the route. Because of this, the Acela Express needs to adjust to different voltages and frequencies as it travels along the Northeast Corridor. Each train has a semi-permanently streamlined locomotive power car at each end.

Type: Eight-piece/six-car high-speed electric train
Power: 12kV AC at 25Hz, 12kV AC at 60Hz, 25kV AC at 60Hz
Output: 12,337hp (9200kW)
Tractive effort: 50,000lbf (222kN) starting TE
Max. operating speed: 150mph (240km/h)
Weight: 1,248,000lb (566t) for whole train set
Train length: 663ft (202.08m) for whole train set
Power car length: 69ft 7in (21.209m)
Max. axle load: n/a
Gauge: 4ft 8.5in (1435mm)

Acela Express trains can operate up to 150mph (240km/h) on certain portions of the Northeast Corridor between New London, Connecticut, and Boston, but are restricted to slower speeds leaving Washington Union Station.

from all these corridors, there is also the Chicago Hub, with lines radiating out from Chicago to Kansas City, Minneapolis-St Paul, Louisville, and Cleveland. The experience of setting up and running the high-speed passenger service in the Northeast Corridor means that Amtrak now possesses the experience and know-how to embark on these projects.

However, the cost of developing high-speed rail transport in all these areas runs into billions of dollars, and which ones, if any, will be developed is not yet clear. There is no doubt that on all these routes, modern passenger trains could provide a valuable service which combines all the desirable aspects of traveler convenience, center-to-center travel, reduction of road congestion, fuel economy, low emissions, safety, and reliability. But they could only be run as subsidized services, and so a political will is needed to make it happen.

In 2003 the Association of American Railroads, the industry's representative and lobbying body, had ten full members, including the four giants and Amtrak, as well as Rail America, with its 47 short line roads in the United States and Canada, ranging from the Mackenzie Northern to the Dallas Garland & North Eastern in Texas, Chicago's

Metra urban transit system, the Kansas City Southern group, Vermont Railroad Systems, and the Wheeling & Lake Erie, a name once blazoned on the mighty tenders of 2-6-6-2 articulated steam giants, and resuscitated by private investors from the Norfolk & Western-Norfolk Southern merger of 1990. But in the continuing saga of North American railroading, nothing can be relied on to remain stable. As a government-owned and subsidized body, Amtrak has no shortage of hostile critics. In 2003, the Association was going into battle to oppose new proposals for imposing regulation on the railroad companies, brought on by concern among midwestern customers about the semimonopolistic position of the Big Four.

We can be sure only of one thing—the one thing that has remained a constant through North America's tumultuous railroad history—the trains will roll on, and controversy will go with them.

In 2003, Electro-Motive's new SD70ACe GM73 was introduced. Surpassing the Environmental Protection Agency's emission standards for 2005, this engine has advanced self-diagnostics to facilitate maintenance and repair. The power plant is a powerful 2-stroke V16710 G3C-ES T2.

INDEX